The Road Back

The Road Back

BY A LIBERAL IN OPPOSITION

J.W. PICKERSGILL

UNIVERSITY OF TORONTO PRESS

Toronto Buffalo London

© University of Toronto Press 1986
Toronto Buffalo London
Printed in Canada
ISBN 0-8020-2598-6

Printed on acid-free paper

Canadian Cataloguing in Publication Data

Pickersgill, J.W., 1905-
The road back

Includes index.
ISBN 0-8020-2598-6

1. Canada–Politics and government–1957-1963.* 2. Pickersgill, J.W., 1905-
3. Liberal Party of Canada–Biography. 4. Legislators–Canada–
Biography. 5. Canada. Parliament. House of Commons –
Biography. I. Title.

FC615.P53 1986   328.71'092'4   C86-094564-2   F1034.2.P53 1986

Preface

My most recent book about politics, *My Years with Louis St Laurent*, published in 1975, required more than two years of hard labour. I resolved not to undertake another for at least a year. In fact, ten years passed before *The Road Back* was undertaken seriously. Throughout those ten years I thought I might one day try to account for my part in public life while L.B. Pearson was leader of the Liberal party. With this in mind I went systematically through *Hansard* and my personal papers as an MP and a minister from 1957 to 1967 when I left Parliament. Although I had copious notes I was a long way from starting another book.

The Liberal defeat in 1984 was as crushing as had been our defeat in 1957. The apparent parallel focused my attention on the Liberal years in Opposition a generation earlier. An account of the politics of Liberal Opposition in those years might, I thought, be interesting to compare with the political scene as it unfolds in parliament after 1984. Early in 1985 I started to work in earnest on a project called *The Road Back, by a Liberal in Opposition*. I decided to include the period after the Liberals regained office in 1963 when I was House leader for the Pearson government, for I saw those months as the final stage in *The Road Back*. It is essentially a book about the practice of politics by one member of a small band of Liberals who survived the Tory flood of 1958, with enough background to make the narrative intelligible.

When the Liberal party went into Opposition in 1957, I had been a close observer of government and Parliament during fifteen years in the Prime Minister's Office and one year as secretary to the cabinet and clerk of the Privy Council. Then I had a four-year apprenticeship as a cabinet minister. This background of experience helped me to take a leading part in the turbulent years of Opposition.

Douglas Fisher, a CCF MP through the years in Opposition, published a profile of me in the Toronto *Telegram* of 11 May 1963, in which he exaggerated by saying 'Pickersgill was the top Liberal in Opposition by quite a margin.' Himself a star performer in debate, he credited me with 'creating the necessary myths that the Diefenbaker ministers were dawdling, procrastinating bunglers; that they made a hopeless show of running an efficient Commons; that they were led by a super-egotistical prima donna.' He added that 'insofar as Diefenbaker fell through the spread of this interpretation ... Pickersgill rates the top acknowledgment.'

I was flattered by Fisher's opinion and immodest enough to believe I was one of the more effective debaters on the Pearson team. I was not, however, flattered by Fisher's doubt that I would be a successful House leader. He asked what it would mean in terms of the mood and performance of the new Parliament with me as House leader. He answered: 'It hardly seems a guarantee for either cooperation or long life.' Similar scepticism was expressed in other commentaries in the press and by cries of outrage by one or two Tory MPs.

I felt confident I could do the job if anyone could and I believed we Liberals would not be at the end of *The Road Back* until we had demonstrated that we could survive in office without a majority. That is why I have included the period of my House leadership within the scope of this book.

The narrative owes most to *Hansard*. In those years the press and the public still paid serious attention to the debates in Parliament. It was quite literally by parliamentary debate that the Diefenbaker government was defeated. I have tried hard to be factually accurate. Former colleagues and other friends to whom I am grateful have been helpful about verifying questions of fact. The opinions expressed are inevitably not free from bias.

The main assistance in shaping the book has come from my wife, Margaret. She edited the text meticulously. No phrase and no word escaped her scrutiny. For that reason and because she lived those years, the text is much more readable. I owe as well a debt to Shirley Tink who was my secretary for the whole period in Opposition, and who devoted much of her leisure to transcribing the manuscript. Without their help there would have been no book.

I am grateful to the University of Toronto Press for the judgement that *The Road Back* deserves to be published and for editorial advice and assistance. Convention dictates that I accept the blame for any and all imperfections.

J.W.P.

Contents

June 1957: Shock!

10 June 1957 was a day of deception for me – and for the majority of Canadians. When the federal election had been called that spring, the Liberal government under Louis St Laurent's leadership was thought to be unbeatable. The Liberals entered the campaign with over 170 members in a Parliament of 265; the Conservatives had 51. We anticipated our huge majority would be reduced but had no doubt we would win.

I had no fear of the outcome on election day. My wife, Margaret, and I voted in Ottawa on that beautiful June morning. We left shortly after to drive to Quebec City to attend the victory celebration at the home of the prime minister. On arrival we checked in at the Chateau Frontenac. By then the polls were already closed in Newfoundland and the Maritimes, but the results could not be published in Quebec before the polls closed there. I lost no time in telephoning my executive assistant, Charles Granger, who was in St John's. He told me I had won my seat by an overwhelming majority (87 per cent) but that, as expected, the Liberals had lost the two seats in St John's. While we were talking, I could hear the first results from Halifax on the radio in Granger's hotel room: the Conservatives were leading by substantial margins. I was shocked! If we were losing in Halifax – a Liberal stronghold for most of half a century – I realized Liberal prospects were grim.

When I returned to the sitting room, Margaret exclaimed that I looked as though my best friend had just died. I replied that we were losing the election. By the time we had had some sandwiches and gone to the prime minister's house, I was over the first shock. The Liberals had held most of Quebec, but Ontario was a shambles. When the disastrous Manitoba returns came in, our slight lead began to disappear.

It was then that Mr St Laurent said to me: 'I hope they get a few more seats than we do, so we can get out of this mess.' I agreed completely and went off into a quiet corner to start drafting a statement for use when all the returns were in. St Laurent, meanwhile, went to the telephone and began calling ministers who had been defeated: Robert Winters in Nova Scotia, Milton Gregg in New Brunswick, Hugues Lapointe in Quebec, C.D. Howe, Walter Harris, Paul Hellyer, and James McCann in Ontario, and, later on, Stuart Garson in Manitoba, and Ralph Campney in British Columbia.

When all the returns were in, at the end of a long, long night, the Conservatives had elected five or six more members than we had, but were far short of a majority. Constitutionally, the St Laurent government could have stayed in office until Parliament met and sought a vote of confidence. That had been done by Mackenzie King after the 1925 election, when Liberals had won only 101 seats to the Conservatives' 116, and the prime minister himself had been defeated in his own riding. But there were two basic differences. In 1925 Mackenzie King was fifty years old; in 1957 St Laurent was seventy-five. In 1925 the Liberal government had been in office less than four years, in 1957 almost twenty-two years. The Liberals had much less prospect of securing the support of the 25 CCF and 19 Social Credit members in 1957 than Mackenzie King had of securing the support of the Progressives in 1925.

That evening, St Laurent had no doubt that the government should resign and give John Diefenbaker, the Conservative leader, the chance to form a government. Senator Chubby Power, who was with us, agreed with him and so did I. St Laurent's statement to the press clearly indicated that view, though he undertook to consult the cabinet before making a final decision. That night, I had no doubt what the decision would be.

Defeat was less of a shock for me because, when I accepted office in the St Laurent government on 12 June 1953, I knew that a cabinet post was not a job for the rest of my working life. The Liberal government was bound to be defeated before I was old enough to retire.

The next morning I realized my annual income would be reduced from $27,000. to $10,000. On a parliamentary indemnity as a private member, our family would face an intolerable reduction in our standard of living. We had a mortgage-free house but no savings. With four children aged 16 to 7 we faced years of providing for their education. Even with additional income, we would have to live frugally. As survivors of the pre-war depression and wartime wage and salary control, frugal living had fortunately become a habit for Margaret and me. There was a theoretical choice between supplementing my income as a MP or leaving Parliament and seeking more lucrative employment elsewhere. But I did not for one moment consider leaving Parliament.

The first thing I did that morning was to decide what to do with the schooner we had bought in 1955. Many of our friends had regarded this as a wild extravagance. The *Millie Ford*, a two-masted schooner, was 101 feet long, 126 tons, had two diesel engines, and required a crew of six. She was a very beautiful old vessel, built in New England, moved to Nova Scotia and ultimately to Newfoundland – a not uncommon history. We bought the vessel for $7,500, after it had been inspected and passed as seaworthy by our friend, Captain Max Burry of Glovertown, a shipbuilder. He agreed to maintain the vessel, improvise living quarters for our family, and, when we did not need her, employ the schooner in carrying freight on his own account.

Owning this schooner was not a wild extravagance. More than half the settlements in my riding of Bonavista-Twillingate could not be reached by road, so we needed some means of visiting them by sea. This we did during the summer of 1956 when the whole family made a voyage on the *Millie Ford* from end to end of the riding. This adventure attracted the attention of *Weekend* magazine which sent a reporter and photographer to accompany us for part of the voyage. The publicity we received was priceless. It was a red-letter day at Valleyfield on the north side of Bonavista Bay when my old friend and colleague, Jimmy Sinclair, flew out from St John's with the Soviet minister of fisheries who was visiting Newfoundland fishing operations, to inspect the fish plant and visit our schooner which was tied up at the wharf. The Soviet minister was clearly puzzled by the almost primitive fashion in which a Canadian minister travelled.

The whole family loved the schooner. We had a grandiose plan for 1957 to sail around the island of Newfoundland, through the Strait of Belle Isle, and along the north shore of the St Lawrence to Montreal. But we realized at once it would be impossible to operate the schooner on the pay of a private MP. Quite early the morning after the election I telephoned Charlie Granger in St John's and asked him to call Max Burry and tell him to look for freight.

The only specific reduction in our standard of living we made at home was to begin using margarine which was much cheaper than butter. I remember this economy because, for me, it was a sentimental blow to give up butter. On the farm in Manitoba, I had won first prize for butter-making at the boys and girls fair each fall. There were a few small embarrassments: Margaret was shocked when one of the local shopkeepers asked whether we would be able to pay our monthly account!

Luckily I quickly found a temporary solution to our income problem. There was no way of knowing how long Mr St Laurent would remain leader of the Liberal party in Opposition, but I knew he would need help, beyond his office staff, as long as he did. I offered to act unofficially as his special assistant, if he wanted me. He did. He arranged to have the National Liberal Federation pay me an allowance at the rate of $5,000 a year. This was an adequate stop-gap which made it possible for me to give my full attention to political activity.

A new prime minister

John Diefenbaker did not win the election of 1957; the Liberal party lost it. I was reminded years later by an old friend who followed elections closely that he had met me about half-way through the 1957 campaign and had asked me how the election was going. He said my answer was that we would win, but our campaign was so bad we did not deserve to. I had forgotten this exchange, but my opinion was obviously based mainly on my assessment of Diefenbaker as a leader and a potential prime minister.

He was in his sixty-second year and his thirty-two years in political life had been far from spectacular. He had tried unsuccessfully to be elected to Parliament in 1925 and 1926, and later to be elected to the Saskatchewan Legislature, repeatedly without success. In 1938 the Conservatives did not win a single seat in the Legislature when he was provincial party leader. Diefenbaker was one of two Conservatives elected to Parliament from Saskatchewan in 1940 and the only Conservative elected from that province in 1945, 1949, and 1953.

He had failed to be chosen leader of the Progressive Conservative party at national conventions in 1942 and 1948. On both occasions, the party selected a provincial premier who had never sat in Parliament. Even in 1956 when he replaced George Drew as leader, the party was sharply divided over his leadership. It was not surprising that few observers expected him to win the election in 1957. Though he did not win a majority, there was considerable evidence that, in the last ten days of the campaign, he had lit a spark which, I believed, would become a flame if a second election was held at an early date.

I had observed his performance in Parliament over his seventeen years in Opposition. He was a formidable debater, but a lone wolf, not a team player. For example, he took almost no part in the pipeline debate. He scarcely tried to conceal his lack of loyalty to his party leader. In the House he was always seeking personal publicity and the acclaim of the press gallery. Under his leadership in Opposition the party had no policies and no discernible goals except getting into office. I believed that, given enough time, he would expose his incapacity to lead a government. But I felt that it would be three or four years before the public would realize that Diefenbaker was not fit to be prime minister. Meanwhile, the Liberal Opposition should do whatever it could to keep the Tories in office. Diefenbaker had only a short time to form his cabinet before going to London for a meeting of Commonwealth prime ministers. He did not appoint ministers for all the departments, but gave several of the new ministers a second portfolio in an acting capacity. The original cabinet as sworn in on 21 June 1957 had only sixteen members, though the outgoing Liberal cabinet had twenty.

Not a single newly elected member was chosen; all the new ministers had been in Parliament for at least four years, and some much longer: two since 1935. The ministers did not lack parliamentary experience, but the cabinet was regionally unbalanced. The Tories had nine seats in Quebec, seven held by French Canadians. But the original cabinet contained only two ministers from Quebec, one whose mother tongue was English. This was a foretaste of Diefenbaker's attitude to French Canada. There were five ministers from Ontario, none from west of Hamilton or east of Oshawa and none from the north. All the other provinces except British Columbia had one minister each, though Diefenbaker was the only one from Saskatchewan. British Columbia had three. In view of the predominance of Toronto I once described it as a nation-wide government stretching from the Humber to the Don.

Diefenbaker kept External Affairs for himself. Howard Green who had been a candidate for the party leadership in 1942 was number 2 in the cabinet. The only French Canadian minister was sixth in seniority. Green was minister of public works and acting minister of defence production. He was acting prime minister when Diefenbaker was absent and, when Parliament met, became government House leader. Despite his partisanship in Opposition and his unique capacity to arouse St Laurent's indignation, Howard was well liked in Parliament and proved a wise and reasonable manager in the House. His integrity and his loyalty to his leader were beyond question. As a colleague, he was an asset Diefenbaker never really appreciated.

Next in seniority to Howard Green was Donald Fleming who had already contested the party leadership twice although he had been elected only in 1945 and was still relatively young. He had earned his place by hard and effective work and by his vigour and pugnacity in debate. He had two flaws: too long-winded, a fault he might have corrected, and a total lack of a sense of humour which was innate. Fleming was also colour-blind; everything was black or white; as his memoirs (*So Very Near*, Toronto 1985) show, he himself was always clothed in spotless white. In these memoirs he accuses me of having a special animus against him which I exhibited frequently. No judgement could have been faultier. I was grateful for his presence in Parliament. From my earliest days in the House, his pomposity and infallibility made him an irresistible target for me. I missed Fleming when he left public life in 1963. He was a loss to his party and to Parliament. Except for his attitude in the Coyne affair, Fleming had the good sense to trust the staff in the Department of Finance and the Bank of Canada, and that trust was reciprocated. He was obviously a competent administrator.

Next to Fleming in seniority was Alfred Brooks, elected first in 1935. He had seniority in New Brunswick, and became minister of veterans affairs and acting minister of health and welfare. Brooks was colourless and undistinguished.

George Hees became minister of transport. George was regarded by everyone, including himself, as a light-weight. Lionel Chevrier and I met him casually just after the election and stopped to congratulate him. We asked how he felt. He replied: 'completely exhausted – just a voice in a suit.' It was not a bad caricature. Despite a lack of substance, Hees was often effective and, more often, outrageous in debate in Opposition. In office, he was moderate and conciliatory. By trusting his officials he avoided mistakes and put on a good show as minister. This was especially true after he was moved in 1960 to trade and commerce where he assumed the role of a super-salesman.

The only French Canadian in the cabinet was Leon Balcer. He represented Trois-Rivières, which Premier Duplessis represented in the Quebec Legislature, and he was believed to be close to the premier. He was certainly not close to Diefenbaker. Not only had he supported Fleming for the leadership, but he had led a number of the Quebec delegates out of the national convention as a protest against Diefenbaker's failure to have his nomination either moved or seconded by a French Canadian.

Because of his seniority in Parliament where he was the only Tory MP from Quebec elected in 1949 still in Parliament, Balcer could hardly be passed over, but his position was depreciated by giving him the post of solicitor general, then virtually without functions. Considering the unconcealed antipathy of the prime minister, Balcer performed surprisingly well, when he was later made minister of transport.

Next in seniority in the cabinet was General George Pearkes, VC. Pearkes had had a long and distinguished military career. A greater claim to office, in the prime minister's eyes, was probably his conspicuous admiration and support, reflected in his nomination of Diefenbaker for the party leadership in 1956. Pearkes had the bearing of a lifetime soldier, but he proved to be moderate in his outlook and modest in his manner. I had hardly known Pearkes while he was in Opposition and thought he had no sense of humour until one day in 1958 I was surprised to see him walking across the street carrying a pair of shoes in his hand. Later that day, in the House, I sent him a note asking him if he had been carrying his shoes when I spied him from my car and, if so, whose tracks he was trying to hide. A note came right back saying they were the shoes he had worn to follow John and they needed new soles. A pair of foot-prints and the appeal to 'Follow John' had been the most effective poster used by the Tories in the election. I decided he was no Colonel Blimp after all.

Pearkes was in defence during a quiet period and he took little part in debates beyond the scope of his department. He persuaded the government that Canada should participate in NORAD – which it later seemed was a decision taken without appreciation of its probable consequences.

Gordon Churchill, the minister from Manitoba, despite his name was not a traditional Tory. He had flirted with the CCF before becoming a Tory candidate in a by-election. He was colourless in Opposition, a boring speaker in the House, and proved to be an indifferent administrator, in part because of his unfounded suspicion that the bureaucrats could not be trusted. He was a conscientious worker and a loyal colleague on whom Diefenbaker could depend at critical moments. Churchill started in trade and commerce but was later demoted to veterans affairs to make room for George Hees.

In seniority, Davie Fulton was the third and most junior minister from British Columbia. From his first session in Parliament, he was a fluent and effective debater. Mackenzie King had once predicted he might be a future prime minister. He was far and away the most effective Tory during the notorious pipeline debate. After contesting the leadership with Diefenbaker he could scarcely be passed over, though rumour had it that Dief had tried to persuade him to become Speaker of the House. As a minister, he continued to perform well in the House and was one of the few ministers who realized at once that he was no longer in Opposition. He became minister of justice and acting minister of citizenship and immigration. He established a reputation in Justice as a competent administrator with an imaginative outlook. He was soon regarded as one of Diefenbaker's probable successors. Diefenbaker was jealous of the publicity Fulton received and soon began to resent him personally.

George Nowlan was far and away the outstanding Tory MP from Nova Scotia and there was no way he could be left out of the cabinet. Diefenbaker had bitterly resented Nowlan's repeated and unconcealed efforts to prevent him from becoming leader. He never ceased to detest him, but he could hardly fail to realize that Nowlan's popularity in the House, his breezy and conciliatory manner, and his ability to get business through the House were assets for a government which did not possess them in super-abundance. He was given the minor portfolio of national revenue.

Douglas Harkness was the obvious choice as minister from Alberta. He had a distinguished career in the war and he remained, in spirit, a soldier with a substantial following among veterans. In Opposition he had been a mediocre debater, but he performed better in the House when he was in office. He was given the relatively minor portfolio of northern affairs and was also made acting minister of agriculture (and later in the year was promoted to minister). He was considered a competent administrator, but his relations with the farmers were not good. He was probably as relieved as the farmers were when he became minister of defence in 1960. In Defence he was completely at home and in due course became a prominent and controversial minister.

Ellen Fairclough was the first woman to become a cabinet minister. That fact alone gave her a high profile. Her performance both in the House and in her successive departments was above average, though she did encounter some pitfalls in Immigration which displeased the prime minister. I had occasional encounters with her in the House in my capacity as critic of her department, but our personal relations were always friendly.

Angus MacLean, the minister from Prince Edward Island, had a distinguished record in the Royal Canadian Air Force. He was a farmer whom I once described as the finest farmer who had ever been minister of fisheries. MacLean was not a great parliamentarian, but he handled himself quietly and competently in the House and rarely aroused partisan feelings. I was shocked one day when he made an attack on me which was so bitter in tone that I felt it was entirely out of character and did not resent it. I had occasionally been critical of his administration of Fisheries but never in a provocative way. I ignored the attack and our personal relations remained friendly as they had always been before his outburst. MacLean proved durable as a minister and continued in the cabinet with the same portfolio until the Diefenbaker cabinet resigned in April 1963.

Michael Starr became minister of labour and, like MacLean, retained the same portfolio throughout the life of the Diefenbaker government. Starr had an attractive personality. I first met him early in 1949 when I accompanied St Laurent on an official visit to Oshawa. Starr was mayor of the city. He received the prime minister with grace and dignity. When we returned to Ottawa, I suggested to the Liberal organization that we make a serious effort to recruit Starr as the Liberal candidate for the federal riding. From my conversation with him, I formed the impression that he had a taste, as well as an aptitude, for public life but no partisan affiliation. My advice was not taken. Not long afterwards, Premier Leslie Frost recruited Starr as a provincial Conservative candidate. He did not win, but he became identified as a Conservative and won a federal by-election in 1952. Starr was the first Ukrainian Canadian to become a cabinet minister. That recognition had a profound influence on the Ukrainian Canadian community, most of whom had up till then been Liberal. Starr was effective in the House and respected in the trade union movement. He was one of Diefenbaker's greater assets as a minister.

William Hamilton, the postmaster general, was one of the two ministers from Quebec. He had become one of the most effective performers in Opposition, and one of the most irreverent. Shortly after he became a minister I congratulated him. He replied that the hardest part of being a minister was having to try to behave like a gentleman! He was, in fact, a first-class minister and a real loss to public life when he was defeated in 1962.

In my opinion, the finest human being in the Diefenbaker cabinet was J.M. Macdonnell. He suffered in Diefenbaker's eyes because of his loyalty to George Drew and, I always believed, because of his utter integrity. Macdonnell had been the financial critic of the Opposition and might have expected to be made minister of finance, though he did not resent the preference given to Donald Fleming whom he admired and had supported for the leadership. But it was a little short of an insult to him to be made a minister without portfolio. In August 1959, he was dropped from the Cabinet. Jim

Macdonnell and I gradually became close friends and the better I knew him the more I admired his sterling character and utter devotion to his country.

William Browne, the minister from Newfoundland, was given no portfolio, though he was the only member of the Diefenbaker government who had been in a cabinet before 1957. Browne had, as a young man, served briefly in the last cabinet in Newfoundland before responsible government was ended in 1934. He had been an anti-Confederate and had made little impression in Parliament between 1949 and 1953, when he had lost his seat. After serving for a time in the Newfoundland House of Assembly, he was re-elected to Parliament in 1957 as one of the two Conservatives from Newfoundland. I could never understand why Diefenbaker did not give Browne a portfolio. The insult to the province was all the greater as several ministers had been entrusted with two. Failure to give Browne a portfolio was one of the first of Diefenbaker's many mistakes which ended by alienating Newfoundland.

Before Parliament met in October four more ministers were added – two of them new members. On 7 August Paul Comtois was given the minor post of Mines and Technical Surveys for which Balcer had been acting. Comtois was an old Tory war-horse in his constituency. It is no exaggeration to say that he added neither influence nor prestige to the government, though he doubled the French Canadian representation. He was made lieutenant-governor of Quebec in 1961. He died tragically in the fire which destroyed government house in Quebec some years later.

On 22 August, Waldo Montieth became minister of national health and welfare. Montieth had been elected in 1953. A rumour reached the editor of the local Stratford newspaper that Montieth was likely to be appointed; he was advised to delay publication that day until the rumour could be confirmed. He was reported to have refused, saying that no one would appoint Waldo to a cabinet. He was wrong, and Montieth soldiered away without distinction but with modest competence until the defeat of the government in 1963.

The other minister appointed on 22 August was Alvin Hamilton, from whom little was expected. He had served as unsuccessfully as Diefenbaker had before him as leader of the provincial Tory party in Saskatchewan. Neither won a seat in the Legislature for himself or any other Tory. Hamilton was given northern affairs which Harkness had held originally. No one guessed that, of all the ministers, he would become Diefenbaker's greatest electoral asset. Alvin had a soaring imagination and an unequalled capacity to get publicity. He was the main author of the Diefenbaker 'vision' which appealed so powerfully in the 1958 election. More durable politically than the 'vision' was his success in portraying the Tory party as the friend of the farmers, especially in the West. This process began in 1960 when Hamilton succeeded

Harkness as minister of agriculture. He won the hearts of the farmers. I encountered Alvin a day or two after his appointment to Agriculture and asked him whether I should offer congratulations or condolences. With incredible candour, Alvin told me that when the 'Chief' had offered him the portfolio he had said he knew nothing about agriculture, but if it was a salesman Dief wanted, 'I am your man.' And how right he proved to be! Many of Alvin's visions were too grandiose: when I expressed scepticism about one of them to Howard Green, he replied, 'Alvin can't add.' I am sure many of his colleagues agreed, but as a votegetter he was unrivalled in rural Canada.

Finally, on 13 September 1957, Diefenbaker went outside the House for a minister for external affairs. He persuaded the president of the University of Toronto, Sidney Smith, to accept the portfolio. Smith entered Parliament in a by-election in November. Although he had never been elected to Parliament, Sidney Smith had been sought twice as a candidate for the party leadership. The appointment added to the prestige of the government.

Diefenbaker inflicted public indignities on Smith on more than one occasion. Sid Smith had been a colleague and friend of Lester Pearson years before at the University of Toronto; he had taught Chevrier and Martin at the Law School; and he was president of the University of Manitoba during the years I was a member of the faculty. No doubt his friendly relations with all of us aroused Diefenbaker's distrust. Sidney Smith was too gentle for the rough and tumble of public life. He doubtless found the contempt of his leader hard to bear. His experience of political life may well have contributed to his early death in March 1959.

Apart from Diefenbaker, the only ministers known at all outside their own regions were Howard Green, Donald Fleming, and Davie Fulton – Green because he had been prominent in Opposition for over twenty years and once a candidate for the party leadership; Fleming and Fulton for their leading part in the pipeline debate of 1956. None was yet a national figure. Even Diefenbaker had become well-known only after his selection as leader of his party in 1956.

The switch to opposition

Two days after Diefenbaker became prime minister he had to leave for London to attend a meeting of heads of government of the nations of the Commonwealth. St Laurent, who was very tired, left Ottawa for his summer home at St Patrick near Rivière-du-Loup on the lower St Lawrence. No one had thought of providing the retiring prime minister with a private railway car, in which he had become accustomed to travel. I never ceased to be grateful, as St Laurent was, to N.R. Crump, the chairman and president of Canadian Pacific, for sending his own private car to carry the former prime minister into retirement.

Neither Diefenbaker nor St Laurent had any inclination to concern himself with the various housekeeping arrangements involved in a change of parties in office. St Laurent told Diefenbaker he had given me *carte blanche* to deal with these problems on his behalf. Diefenbaker designated Derek Bedson, who had been his private secretary as leader of the Opposition, to work the arrangements out with me. I knew Bedson well and we worked in harmony. There were really only two housekeeping problems on the Liberal side: one, to provide us with suitable accommodation as the Opposition; the other, to look after the staffs of former ministers.

In the past, members of Parliament, except for ministers and the leader of the Opposition, had usually been placed two in a room and got secretarial help from a stenographic pool. I persuaded Bedson this arrangement would be hard on former ministers and that each of them should have a room to himself and a room for a secretary next door. He agreed that it was not likely to be twenty-two years before parties changed sides again, and we should try to create useful precedents for both government and opposition. Better accommodation for ex-ministers did not require much extra space as the former ministers were not numerous! J.G. Gardiner, Lionel Chevrier, Paul Martin, L.B. Pearson, James Sinclair, Jean Lesage, George Marler, and I were the lone survivors. My own rooms were immediately adjacent to those of the leader of the Opposition. Once Parliament met, this arrangement made it easy for me to assist Mr St Laurent unobtrusively so long as he continued to lead the Opposition.

The leader of the Opposition had adequate quarters in the Parliament building and a small staff. Pierre Asselin had been private secretary to the prime minister and agreed to occupy the same post with the leader of the Opposition.

I was entitled only to a secretary of junior status. Shirley Tink, who had worked with my executive assistant, Charles Granger, mainly on Newfoundland business, agreed to become my secretary. Shirley Tink worked closely with Audrey McQuarrie, who was too senior to be on my staff but was given a post on the staff of the leader of the Opposition. She remained there until she became my private secretary when the Pearson government took office in 1963.

Under the law in those days the staffs of all ministers lost their jobs on the day a minister left office for any reason. After a certain number of years of service, some members of the staffs of ministers were entitled to appointment to the civil service. These former ministerial secretaries were often resented by permanent public servants and frequently failed to get posts commensurate with their abilities. Bedson and I worked closely with the Civil Service Commission and got the problem cases dealt with promptly. My own executive assistant, Charles Granger, did not want to stay in Ottawa as a civil servant. Instead Premier Smallwood had him appointed deputy minister of highways in Newfoundland, a post in which he was very helpful to me during the short period he occupied it.

Once these parliamentary housekeeping arrangements were settled and the schools had closed at the end of June, there was no reason for our family to stay in Ottawa. Charlie Granger had a car which he had left in Ottawa and wanted brought to St John's. He asked us to drive it to Newfoundland. We left at once. At North Sydney the car was put on a later ferry than the one we travelled on. We had to wait several uncomfortable hours at Port aux Basques in the pouring rain until the car arrived. It was late afternoon when we left Port aux Basques and dusk by the time we had driven about fifty miles. I failed to see a rock in the middle of the road and drove over it, ripping several vital parts from the bottom of the car. We managed, after some time, to find someone to tow us to the nearest garage – they were few and far between and not well equipped – and learned it would take days or even weeks to get the necessary parts to repair the car.

There was no place to stay nearer than Stephenville Crossing, about another fifty miles away, and no means of getting there. It would have been very difficult to hitch-hike with a wife and four children and all our luggage! Fortunately the garage had a telephone. I called Albert Martin, the general manager of Bowater's paper mill at Corner Brook, whom I knew only slightly. I explained our plight and Martin at once sent a car for us and offered to put the whole family up at Bowater's guesthouse, Strawberry Hill, near Corner Brook. It was the most luxurious accommodation in all Newfoundland. After a very long, slow drive, we were finally installed at Strawberry Hill about one o'clock in the morning. We stayed on for two or three days, hoping to get favourable news of the car. When we learned it would take at least another week to repair it we decided we must move on.

Albert Martin meanwhile had reported our plight to the manager of the paper mill in Grand Falls who invited us to spend a night at their guesthouse which was almost as grand as Strawberry Hill. After a night in Grand Falls, we were driven to Gander and from then on made various gypsy-like arrangements for the rest of our time in Newfoundland. It was hard work travelling constantly, sometimes in cars, sometimes in a small boat or a train, with four children and no headquarters. But thanks to the help of friends, we were able to tour a good part of the constituency. We were given enough publicity on the radio to be satisfied that everyone knew we had not forsaken Newfoundland. Indeed the experience of that summer seemed to cement our relations with the constituency and our affection for Newfoundland.

One over-riding impression I gained from that first visit as a member of the Opposition was how many of my constituents and other Newfoundlanders, who had paid little attention to us while I was a minister, went out of their way to be helpful when our luck was down. I learned there is nothing like going into Opposition to teach a politician who his real friends are.

St Laurent resigns as party leader

When we returned from Newfoundland early in August, I visited Mr St Laurent at St Patrick. It was a most disquieting experience. He was obviously deeply depressed, could not be drawn into conversation, and clearly had no interest in his new role. Shortly afterwards, I went to Vancouver for my mother's eightieth birthday. All her surviving children were there, and for a day or two I was out of touch with Ottawa.

It was during this time that St Laurent announced his intention to resign the leadership of the Liberal party. I was not greatly surprised by his decision, but I was hurt that I had not been told in advance. I learned later that his son, Renault, had tried to telephone me. When he did reach me after the announcement, Renault said his father was anxious to see me. After returning from British Columbia, I went to Quebec and spent a day and a night at Renault's summer home on the Ile d'Orleans. St Laurent was clearly relieved that he had made his decision, but was still very depressed. He was brooding about our defeat and placing all the blame on himself. I did not feel my visit did anything to cheer him up, but he did make two decisions.

He asked me to act as his agent with the president and officers of the Liberal federation in organizing the national convention to choose a leader. He said he wanted the convention as soon as possible and did not want to be concerned with detailed arrangements as long as Duncan MacTavish, the Federation president, and I were agreed about what should be done. I suggested we should follow as closely as possible the pattern of the 1948 convention. As the federation still had almost the same staff, the mechanical side of the whole operation would be very easy. St Laurent was a little disappointed that the earliest practicable date was in January 1958. To my great relief he also decided not to have an acting leader of the Opposition. He asked me to take charge of the preparations for his part in the opening of Parliament.

The Queen opened the new Parliament on 14 October 1957, the first time the Canadian Parliament had been opened by the sovereign. The Speech from the Throne sparkled like a Christmas tree, with goodies for nearly every important pressure group across the country and the promise of a 25 per cent increase in universal old age pensions which had already risen by 15 per cent earlier in the year. The new government had got off to a good start.

In every normal session of Parliament, the first debate in the House of Commons is on the Speech from the Throne. This debate is initiated by a private member on the government side, often a new member, who lauds his leader and the government, praises the attractions of his constituency and the virtues of those who voted for him, and then moves that the Commons offer their humble thanks for the gracious speech, normally to the governor general, but in this case to the Queen. The seconder of the motion is another private member, usually speaking the other official language, who makes a similar speech.

The Speech from the Throne is, in actual fact, prepared and submitted to the governor general by the prime minister and is, therefore, open to criticism by the Opposition or, indeed, by any member of the House. By tradition, the leader of the Opposition is the first speaker in the debate after the mover and seconder of the address. It is usual for him to move an amendment to the address of thanks. This amendment is normally critical of the government and, if adopted, constitutes a vote of want of confidence. If the government is defeated in the House, the prime minister has either to resign or to secure a dissolution of Parliament from the governor general, to be followed by an election.

I believed that, if the House voted want of confidence in the government in 1957, Diefenbaker would be happy to ask the governor general to dissolve Parliament and that he would win a decisive majority in an election. I felt it was in the interest of the Liberal party and, in the long run, of the country to remove at once any possibility of a parliamentary defeat of the government and another election at once.

Since the Diefenbaker government did not have a majority of its own party members, the length of its life was dependent, in part, on the Opposition. I thought the Liberal Opposition should not challenge the government and make it count on the smaller parties to save it from defeat. The draft speech I prepared for St Laurent said it would not be appropriate to move the traditional vote of want of confidence, particularly as the government he had headed had recently resigned and he had advised the governor general to ask Diefenbaker to form a government. St Laurent accepted my advice. He added in his speech that, having decided not to move an amendment expressing lack of confidence, the Liberal Opposition would not support any motion of want of confidence moved by any other party or member. The Liberal caucus had agreed to this course. St Laurent's statement assured the government of parliamentary support for the program the Conservatives had put before the electorate.

Our decision not to defeat the government did not prevent us from debating the government's measures vigorously. In fact, until the end of the year 1957, there were a number of lively debates. During the short life of that Parliament, the government did get several popular measures adopted, including an increase in old age pensions and special grants to the Atlantic provinces. Diefenbaker's promises were still believed and his popularity was clearly growing. I felt we should take every precaution to see that the government was given no excuse for an early election.

Pearson takes over

During this period we Liberals were giving more attention to the choice of a new party leader than to Parliament. L.B. Pearson and Paul Martin would obviously be candidates. There was also support for Walter Harris who had not declared himself. After a good deal of soul-searching, I concluded that Pearson alone had any prospect of reviving the party and defeating the Tory government in any reasonable period. Nothing I did in my public life was harder for me than to tell Harris, who was such a close friend, that I hoped he would not be a candidate, since I felt he had no chance of gaining the leadership. I said I thought Pearson was our only hope and intended to offer him my support.

I do not know whether my attitude hurt Walter, but he did not show the faintest resentment, and there has never been any evidence that my decision affected our friendship. My affection and admiration for him has, if possible, grown with the passing years. During the whole Pearson period, it was a matter of deep regret to me that Harris was not brought back into public life, and I made frequent but ineffectual efforts to that end. It remains my judgement that, if Harris had been in Parliament, Pearson would probably have won a majority in 1963, if not in 1962, and that Harris would have been a stabilizing influence in the Pearson government and a great strength in Parliament where he was always thoroughly at home.

While I had a large part in organizing the convention of January 1958, I took little part in the proceedings, except in the policy committee where I was the main author of the Atlantic resolutions which were subsequently implemented in full by the Pearson government. The convention itself went smoothly. Pearson was chosen leader by a substantial margin over Paul Martin.

It had been my intention to give no public indication at the convention of my choice, but I was provoked into a demonstration of open support for Pearson. Martin's committee issued a news bulletin which included a quotation of mine taken from its context to give the impression I was supporting Martin's candidature. I was outraged and, on the spur of the moment, arranged with most of the Newfoundland delegation to march around the convention floor carrying a Pearson banner. I felt very foolish even while doing it. My part in the demonstration cast a shadow over my relations with Paul Martin for some time. Finally, one day, he told me of his resentment, and I expressed the regret I felt. I have always been repelled by the razzle-dazzle of party conventions and was ashamed I had been drawn into it on this one occasion.

One development at the convention was to have the gravest consequences for the Liberal party. That was Pearson's speech of acceptance of the leadership in which he promised to lead this new strong and great party to victory 'and soon'. I was greatly disturbed by what seemed to me an ill-considered and light-hearted repudiation of our announced policy of giving the government a chance to implement its program. Like most others, I interpreted 'and soon' to mean Pearson intended to challenge the government in a vote of confidence at the first opportunity.

I do not think Pearson realized that the first opportunity would come only four days later on Monday, 20 January 1958, the very day he took over as leader of the Opposition. The government had already announced that, on that day, the minister of finance would make a motion to resolve the House into Committee of Supply. That committee is the whole House presided over by the deputy speaker.

A supply motion is the time-honoured occasion for the House to demand the redress of grievances before granting money to the Crown (i.e., the cabinet) to carry on the government. The usual way to demand the redress of grievances is for the leader of the Opposition or one of his supporters to move an amendment to the supply motion in which the grievance is spelled out. Such an amendment is deemed to be a vote of want of confidence. If adopted, the government has to resign or seek a dissolution.

In view of Pearson's defiant challenge, he seemed to have left himself no choice but to make some kind of motion of want of confidence. I discovered that Pearson had drafted no amendment to the supply motion and prepared no speech to support it. I felt someone had a duty to help him. As I was still being paid by the Liberal federation to serve as liaison with the leader of the Opposition, I offered to make a draft of a speech in the spirit of his challenge. The speech Pearson actually delivered was, in fact, little changed from my draft. On reading it again over twenty years later, it seems to me about as good a case as could have been made, if the government was to be challenged at all. Pearson felt, in the light of his speech at the convention, he must make the challenge. I feared that, if he moved a straight vote of want of confidence, the smaller parties, particularly the CCF which had already voted want of confidence in October 1957, would find it hard to vote against it. I believed a defeat in the House was precisely what Diefenbaker wanted. It would give him an opportunity to call another election which he was sure to win decisively. I therefore tried to devise a motion of want of confidence which I was sure the smaller parties would not and could not support.

The motion I drafted complained that trade had ceased to expand, investment had been discouraged, and unemployment had risen drastically; farmers and other primary producers were disillusioned; relations with provincial governments were in confusion; the budget was no longer in balance; there was confusion about defence; and day-to-day expedients were substituted for firm and steady administration. The motion concluded that 'in view of the desirability, at this time, of having a government pledged to implement Liberal policies, His Excellency's advisers should, in the opinion of this House, submit their resignation forthwith.'

I had been right about one thing. No one in the smaller parties would vote for a motion to restore a Liberal government without an election. But I had completely failed to foresee the ridicule which Diefenbaker heaped so overwhelmingly upon the motion. He admitted he had listened on the radio to Pearson's acceptance speech at the convention. He said: 'On Thursday there was shrieking defiance; on the following Monday, there is shrinking indecision.' A torrent followed in which Pearson was figuratively torn limb from limb. It was the most brilliant performance I had ever heard from Diefenbaker. I doubt if a more effective destructive speech was ever made in Parliament.

The best description of the encounter was given in the debate the next day by Colin Cameron of the CCF, who was one of the finest debaters in the House. Of Pearson's performance he said it would have been quite amusing if it had not been tragic. He recalled Shakespeare: 'let us sit on the ground and tell sad stories of the death of kings' – even newly crowned kings. He said there was never such a short period elapse between a coronation and an abdication. There had been a rather tragic scene witnessed the day before. But we had seen something else that was not very pretty to behold. He gave

Diefenbaker 'full marks for a magnificent hatchet job.' At this point the Tories applauded until Cameron wondered if that was the role the prime minister of Canada should play. 'I wondered if he should have rushed with such relish into the abattoir ... When I saw him bring whole batteries of rhetoric, whole arsenals of guided missiles of vitriol and invective in order to shoot one forlorn sitting duck – a sitting duck, indeed, already crippled with a self-inflicted wound – I wondered if the Prime Minister really believes in the humane slaughter of animals.' (Cameron was here referring to a government bill on the order paper to ensure humane slaughter.)

In the light of our later experience with minority parliaments, I am sure Pearson should have moved a straight vote of want of confidence and counted on the minority parties to keep the government in office. I had been far from happy with the motion I had drafted and had none of the pride of authorship ascribed to me by Diefenbaker and others, including many in our own party. Though I never admitted to any part in the drafting, my role was common gossip. After the event I was about as popular in the Liberal caucus as the proverbial skunk at a garden party.

I have often asked myself since why I did anything at all about the situation. I had been given no responsibility to advise Pearson. I suppose, after twenty years as adviser to successive leaders of the party, I had developed the habit of trying to help in emergencies. Certainly my intervention did my own reputation no good. It took me a long time to live down my error of judgement. For the immediate future, the motion was a disastrous beginning for Pearson's leadership.

Neither at the time nor afterwards did Pearson ever utter to me a word of recrimination or blame, which he must have been tempted to do. I went to see him the first thing the morning after the speech to tell him about the arrangement St Laurent had made with the Liberal federation and said I assumed it should be terminated forthwith. He neither agreed nor disagreed, but I saw the president of the federation later in the day and asked to be taken off the payroll.

Another part of Diefenbaker's reply to Pearson was almost as effective at the time. He quoted at length selected extracts from a confidential document prepared for the St Laurent government and circulated to cabinet ministers in March 1957. Diefenbaker alleged this document predicted a down-turn in the economy and an increase in unemployment. He claimed these 'facts had been hidden from the Canadian people by the Liberal Government.' This clever combination of half-truths and charges of deception was vintage Diefenbaker. Stanley Knowles demanded that the whole document be tabled and, when it was tabled later in the day, it was clear that it was a confidential document – a sort of economic weather forecast prepared by civil servants for the advice of ministers.

This so-called 'hidden report' was used by Diefenbaker, despite the solemn undertaking given by incoming prime ministers not to examine, much less publish, the confidential papers of a previous government. Diefenbaker claimed he had just found the hidden report which provided evidence of the deception practised by the Liberals. We expressed great indignation at this act of bad faith in disclosing confidential advice to the previous government and, thereby, dragging civil servants into the political arena. Our protests were ignored by the public. The immediate effect of Diefenbaker's distortions was very damaging.

Pearson's motion was overwhelmingly defeated and the government thereby accorded a substantial vote of confidence which removed any risk of an early defeat in Parliament. This, after all, was what I wanted and expected.

Parliament is dissolved February 1958

We could soon see that Diefenbaker was disappointed that he had no constitutional reason to have a new election. Almost at once there were signs he was seeking an excuse to end the life of the Parliament which had just given him an overwhelming vote of confidence. There was not the slightest excuse, nor the least vestige of constitutional justification, for the dissolution of a Parliament which had been elected only seven months before and in which the government had just won a crucial vote to keep it in office. Yet the governor general apparently raised no question when Diefenbaker asked for a dissolution on 1 February 1958.

The situation in 1926 provided no precedent. The governor general had refused Mackenzie King a dissolution, even though it had become clear no government could count on a vote of confidence in Parliament. Diefenbaker faced no prospect of defeat in Parliament. His action was the closest approach to a claim of absolute power for the prime minister ever made in self governing Canada. Yet such was the state of the public mind in February 1958 that this virtual *coup d'état* was not publicly challenged. I discussed the possibility of doing so with one or two friends, but we all agreed such a challenge would merely be the subject of further ridicule. In any event, my opinion on any question affecting Parliament was not likely to carry any weight at that time.

It was clear to me that I would not be in great demand as a speaker during the election, nor did I seek to campaign outside Newfoundland. I was convinced from the outset that the Liberal party did not have a ghost of a chance to win and that we would have a real fight for survival even in Newfoundland.

Fighting for my political life

In 1957, we had lost the two normally Conservative seats in St John's, but had won the other five easily, one by acclamation. But the surge of Anglo-Saxon Protestant support for the Tories which barely touched Newfoundland in 1957 was bound to affect the five outport constituencies in 1958. Premier Smallwood, who had done very little in the election campaign of 1957, had been outraged by Diefenbaker's attitude to Newfoundland at the conference with the provincial governments in the fall and he devoted almost his full time to the campaign of 1958.

He decided new candidates were needed in two of the ridings and arranged provincial appointments for the former MPs to make way for the new candidates, one of whom was my former executive assistant, Charles Granger. Apart from appearing at two or three meetings to support Granger, I confined myself to my own constituency of Bonavista-Twillingate. For the first time, I had a really serious and prestigious opponent: Gerald Winter was a highly respected merchant in St John's, recently president of the Newfoundland Board of Trade and reputedly assured of a portfolio in Diefenbaker's cabinet. In 1957, I had not held a single public meeting but had simply travelled about the riding talking to voters individually or in small groups, and I had campaigned a good deal outside the province. In 1958, I was fighting for my political life. I campaigned as I had not done before and never had to do again, with meetings in nearly every settlement accessible in the middle of winter.

Fortunately the winter was mild, and it was not too hard to get around. My meetings were exceedingly well attended and I made the same speech at nearly all of them. My theme was a simple comparison of the characters and achievements of Pearson and Diefenbaker, in which Pearson did not suffer. The organizer of many of my meetings told me they were not like other political meetings: it was like being in church! I was not sure whether I should be flattered, but, as he was himself very devout, I knew it was meant as a compliment and that he believed I was being effective.

The campaign was not without incident. I had no help from outside the constituency except for a couple of days when the Newfoundland attorney general, Leslie Curtis, went with me to Twillingate, which was his provincial constituency. In Lewisporte, we hired a small vessel about thirty feet in length with a tiny cabin containing a chair and a narrow bench attached to the side of the cabin. We left Lewisporte about five o'clock in the morning, having had little sleep during the short night after arriving at Lewisporte by train about midnight. We took turns sitting on the chair and stretching out on the narrow bench trying to sleep. After one violent lurch, as we were rounding the rough waters of the Western Head of New World Island, Curtis, who was sleeping, rolled off the bench on to the cabin floor at my feet. He picked himself up and asked me what the devil he was doing there when he could have been sitting comfortably in a warm office in St John's. I never ceased to be grateful for his support.

One day I set out from Gander for Fogo Island in a two-seater Bell helicopter. It began to snow at Gander Bay and we landed in a schoolyard. I went into the school and spoke to the children and asked them, when they went home, to ask their parents to vote for me. It was one of the rare times in six campaigns I made a direct appeal for votes for myself – something I always found difficult to do. Shortly afterwards, the sun came out and we flew on to Fogo Island where I had word passed around I would have a meeting at one o'clock. I then had lunch with one of my main supporters. When we got back to the hall for the meeting the pilot said the weather was closing in and we must get away in seven minutes or we would stay on the island for the rest of the day. The meeting lasted six minutes and was none the worse for that!

As we flew across the water to the nearest point on the mainland of Newfoundland we encountered patches of fog and occasional brief flurries of snow. The pilot asked me if I wanted to go back to Gander or follow the coast to Valleyfield where we could refuel. I opted for the coast, thinking the shoreline would be easier to follow and also hoping the weather might clear so we could fly on across Bonavista Bay to Bonavista town where I had planned a meeting for that evening. We reached Valleyfield without having to land though at times the visibility was not good.

After refuelling we sat around for more than an hour, and then the sky seemed to clear a little and we set out, following the rugged shore, and then across a stretch of water in the direction of Eastport. It began to snow and we could see no land except a piece of very flat rock about 150 feet long. We landed on the rock. After a few minutes the pilot cheerfully suggested the snow might be followed by fog for a day or two. He was a young Manitoban, slim and apparently healthy. I wondered silently whether I would eat him or he would eat me!

Fortunately in ten or fifteen minutes the snow stopped falling and we could see land, two or three small islands and a stretch of the Newfoundland mainland. I asked the pilot if he knew where we were and found he had no clear idea. I pointed to the mainland and said, with more confidence than I felt, that we were close to St Chads and we should head for that bit of coast. Our plastic bubble was partly covered with snow and the pilot said he must clear it off as soon as possible. I said we could land on the wharf at Eastport. When we got over the wharf I suggested we carry on to Happy Adventure where I knew there was a telephone in a shop near the wharf.

While the pilot cleared off the snow, I telephoned my agent in Bonavista and told him we would try to get there that night, but to postpone the meeting until the next day. We then set out following the islands across the south side of the bay to Summerville, intending to follow the coast from there to Bonavista. As we approached Plate Cove we could see a solid bank of fog ahead and turned back to Summerville. My common sense told me we should land there and give up flying for the day, but I hated to give up and suggested to the pilot we could follow the railway line across the peninsula to the Trinity Bay shore and try to follow the road to Port Union.

We managed to follow the railway to the Trinity shore and then began flying just above the road. I noticed a car below going in our direction and thought it might rescue us if we had to land. It was getting dusk, beginning to snow and there were trees ahead close to the road. I suggested to the pilot we turn back and land at a clearing I had noticed. He agreed, with obvious relief. After about half-an-hour the car came along. I stopped the driver and asked him if he would take us to Port Union. He agreed but wondered if I would be willing to ride in his car and told me to look at the rear. It was covered by a large placard advertising the Tory candidate in Trinity-Conception. I said I would ride in the devil's car, if need be. He duly delivered us to the house of a friend in Port Union who gave us a hot dinner and drove us on to Bonavista.

When I arrived I had a conference with my agent and a leading supporter in the town. Both of them advised me not to have a meeting at all, as there would be trouble. I asked whether I would lose any votes if I did not have a meeting. They thought not. I then asked if my supporters would be ashamed of me if there was no meeting. They looked at one another and then both conceded they feared that might be the result. I then said, 'Let us get the Orange Hall but have the meeting in the afternoon' – before the would-be disturbers had imbibed too much courage.

The hall was packed long before four o'clock when the meeting was to start. Fortunately there were a number of school children at the front of the hall, as well as two very noisy drunks. Farther back there were thirty or forty men wearing blue ribbons inscribed 'Vote for Winter.' I had been told they had been paid to break up the meeting. I had an amiable chairman who had no idea how to conduct, much less control, a meeting. I had never felt so lonely in my life. It was the Friday before election day. I realized that news of any disturbance would be all over Canada before the voting started. I remembered the effect of the incident in the Maple Leaf Gardens in 1957, when a young man had rushed up on the platform at St Laurent's meeting and appeared to have been pushed off and injured. I wanted no repetition even on a minor scale.

Before I started to speak the two drunks began interrupting the chairman. My supporters, who were a large majority of the audience, began shouting 'Throw them out.' I managed to stop the shouting long enough to point out that Mr Winter had had a meeting at Bonavista at which everyone had listened to him politely and quietly. I begged them all to give me the same kind of hearing.

This appeal managed to quiet my supporters, but the drunks went on muttering. I said these men have something they want to say; I suggest they come up to the platform and make their speeches. Some of my friends succeeded in getting one of them on the platform where he was stage-struck and speechless. He left the platform and slunk out of the hall. The other went back halfway and muttered away to himself for the rest of the meeting.

I then had to make my speech. I started out by saying that there were a lot of children present and I intended, like the minister in church, to speak to the children before I made my main speech. This device clearly aroused everyone's curiosity and I got a good hearing for a little speech of the most elementary kind on self-government, elections, and the right of every citizen to express his views freely and without interference or disturbance. I could see it had some effect and that I might get through peacefully if I was very brief. I then launched into an abbreviated version of my comparison of the two leaders and the importance of making Mr Pearson prime minister. As soon as I decently could, I stopped and asked everyone to rise and sing 'God Save the Queen' which I had to lead in my monotone, while inwardly thanking God for saving me from a potential riot. That same evening I had a meeting along the shore at Newman's Cove. A few of the possible disturbers turned up from Bonavista, but the audience was so overwhelmingly on my side that the intruders did not dare even to interrupt.

It was with great relief that I went to Gander the next day to go home to Ottawa to vote on 31 March. I never doubted that I would win my seat, but I did not expect the overwhelming victory I actually had. In 1957, my Tory opponent received only about 1,300 votes; in 1958 he received over 4,000.

But I had over 5,000 more votes than in 1957 – in all 75 per cent of the votes cast. Whatever my position in the party generally, I was sure of a solid base in my own constituency. A day or two after the 1958 election I met Diefenbaker in the corridor of the Parliament building. He stopped me and asked me if I was not the only Liberal candidate who had increased his majority. I told him I had not checked the figures for others, but I did know that I had received 5,000 additional votes and his candidate only 4,000 altogether. My own success, however, was small consolation in the light of the overwhelming defeat of the Liberal party across the country.

Election results

On election day, I spent some time with Pearson in his parliamentary office. I asked him whether he had any illusion that we might win the election. He admitted he had none. I believed the best we could hope for was 100 seats and I thought about 80 more probable. Few observers predicted the magnitude of the débâcle – Diefenbaker had won 208 seats. The greatest surprise was that the Tories won 50 of the 75 seats in Quebec. It was the first time since 1887 that the Conservative party had won a majority of the seats in that province. But, at the same time, it was Quebec that had saved the Liberal party from complete annihilation: of the 49 seats we won, 25 were in Quebec. Newfoundland was the only province to give the Liberals a majority. In six provinces no Liberal member was elected. Even in Ontario only 14 were returned; none in Toronto. Only five of the former ministers survived, Pearson, Chevrier, Martin, Lesage, and I; and Lesage decided shortly after the election to leave Parliament to become leader of the Liberal party in Quebec.

Lesage's departure was a substantial loss to our small group. He had become an outstanding debater and was a powerful voice from Quebec. We had worked together closely even before we became ministers in the St Laurent government and I missed him very much. Happily, our personal friendship was never strained by the differences which developed between provincial and federal Liberals when both of us were back in office. There can be no question that his victory in the provincial election in 1960 stimulated the revival of the federal party across Canada, in part by disclosing that Diefenbaker's success in Quebec in 1958 had been a mere 'flash in the pan.'

In 1958, Diefenbaker had a wide choice of able French Canadians as possible ministers. He had enough Senate seats available to create vacancies in the House of Commons for recruits to the ministry. Such a course would have demanded a realization that self-respecting French Canadians must be treated as equals. Diefenbaker had the first real chance since the death of Sir John A. Macdonald to make the Conservative party a truly national party. The chance was thrown away. Diefenbaker was never able to conceal his lack of sympathy for French Canadians, his contempt for his French-speaking colleagues, and his antipathy to what he chose to call the two-nation concept.

Diefenbaker's negative attitude to French Canada was only one of the causes of the weakness of his government and the rapid decline of public support. His suspicion of the whole bureaucracy and his persecution of several civil servants whom he believed, generally wrongly, to be hostile gradually alienated many able and non-partisan public servants and affected morale, which is essential to effective administration of the government.

Perhaps no one, not even Pearson, was in as good a position as I was to know how completely unjustified Diefenbaker's suspicion was. Before entering political life in 1953, I had been a public servant for nearly sixteen years. I had many more close friends among public servants than among politicians. In 1957, it was clear to me that even some of my closest friends were bored with the St Laurent government and welcomed the prospect of new faces and new attitudes. I do not know of a single public servant who, in 1957, was not prepared to work loyally with the Diefenbaker government, though a few – most notably Mitchell Sharp – were disillusioned by Diefenbaker's unscrupulous and unprincipled use of confidential advice given the previous government to score a cheap partisan triumph in January 1958. Howard Green, Donald Fleming, George Hees, Davie Fulton, and Alvin Hamilton (and there were others), who trusted their officials, were served loyally and well, as I am confident all of them would attest. The notion that, in 1957 and 1958, the bureaucracy was Liberal is a myth.

At some cost to our social life, after the election of 1957 I had deliberately cut myself off from close and frequent contact with friends whose careers might be jeopardized by association with me. I am proud to boast that, in my six years in Opposition, I never received any confidential information from a public servant, nor did I ever seek any. Before the Liberal government resigned on 21 June 1957, I had meetings with the senior staff of my department and of the various agencies for which I had been responsible. I thanked them for the loyal support they had given me and expressed the confidence that they would regard it as their duty to give the same loyal support to their new political chief who was there by the choice of the people of Canada. Years afterwards, one or two of those to whom I had spoken reminded me of those meetings and said my words had made a lasting impression on them.

Organizing my life

After the 1958 election, the Liberal party would be in Opposition for at least four or five years. Many observers believed we would be in the wilderness for the next decade and perhaps longer. The prospect was less depressing to me than to others in our small group of survivors in Parliament. I was convinced that Diefenbaker, despite his electoral triumph, was not an adequate leader. The objective of the Liberal Opposition should be to demonstrate to the public that the government was not equal to its task and that our party was a credible alternative.

After 31 March 1958, I personally had four objectives. The first was to be effective in Parliament. The second to maintain my hold on my constituency and increase Liberal support in Newfoundland and the Atlantic region. The third to share actively in party organization, including the development of policy and the revival of Liberal support throughout the country. The fourth, and the most urgent, was to find a way to supplement my parliamentary indemnity with enough income to maintain our family decently.

I was just fifty-two years old when we left office in 1957, and I had known then I could not count for long on the stop-gap arrangement St Laurent had made with the Liberal federation. There was a good possibility I might never be in office again. I had the naive idea of trying to become a lawyer. It was out of the question to think of going to a law school, but I learned that a law degree was not necessary in Newfoundland. They still had the apprenticeship system whereby one was articled to a barrister for a certain period and then admitted to the bar if successful in the examinations. Eric Cook, who was the leader of the bar in Newfoundland and also the president of the Liberal Association, had already become a good friend. I canvassed this possibility with him. He told me that, in Responsible Government days, members of the Parliament of Newfoundland who were articled were not required to work in the office of their principal but merely to pass the examination. He felt the precedent would apply to me and offered to have me articled to him. I accepted his offer and, for a few months, hoped this might be the eventual solution to my problem. I was duly articled to Eric Cook on 21 September 1957 and, from time to time, I read some of the books on which I would be examined.

This long-range plan might have continued, had my allowance as liaison officer between the party leader and the Liberal federation not stopped in January 1958. When the allowance was abruptly terminated at my request after Pearson's ill-fated motion of no confidence, the prospect of being admitted some day to the Newfoundland bar was no answer to my immediate problem. That problem had to be faced as soon as the election campaign was over. The solution arose out of my position as one of Mackenzie King's literary executors.

Shortly after his death in 1950, the literary executors had made a contract with Professor MacGregor Dawson to write King's biography. We had given Dawson access to all Mackenzie King's papers, including his diaries. While giving Dawson the right to read them we retained a total veto on the publication of extracts or paraphrases of the diaries. This condition meant that the literary executors assumed responsibility for the use made of the material. By late 1957, Dawson had completed the first volume of three which were planned. The first volume ended with the year 1923. A second volume was to cover the period until the outbreak of the Second World War, and a third the rest of Mackenzie King's life. The writing of the first volume had taken much longer than expected, and the funds available for Dawson's salary had been almost exhausted by the end of 1955. A final grant was provided by the Rockefeller Foundation to pay the salaries of Dawson and his assistants for 1956. If the biography was to be completed, additional funds had to be found somewhere. On behalf of the literary executors I was able to negotiate an agreement for the sale of the serial rights to the book to the publishers of *Weekend* magazine.

The contract envisaged the completion of the whole biography by MacGregor Dawson. By late 1957, Dawson was in indifferent health and it was clear, early in 1958, that he would not be able to complete the biography without collaborators. In April 1958, the literary executors made an arrangement on 15 May 1958 with Professor Blair Neatby to become co-author. At the time we made the contract with Neatby, I suggested that we might speed up work on the third volume, if someone would read the diaries from September 1939 on, picking out the most significant extracts and connect them with a narrative which could be used as a foundation for the biography. My fellow executors were aware of my financial plight and readily agreed that I should undertake this task experimentally for one year, for which I was to be paid $5,000 in monthly installments. I started on the work at once.

Most of the wartime and post-war diaries had been dictated to a secretary and the transcripts had often not been read by Mackenzie King. Because of my close association with him, I was as well qualified as anyone to detect errors of names and obscurities of meaning, which were not infrequent. I undertook the task with gusto and devoted most of my spare time to this activity which, in a different form, continued through the remaining five years I spent in Opposition.

The arrangement was changed after Dawson's death in July 1958. A new contract was made with Blair Neatby who was to become the sole author of the second volume. As a result of the work I had already done, I had come to the conclusion that we should let Mackenzie King himself tell, through extracts from the diaries, the story of his part in the war and the post-war period. There would be a minimum of paraphrase and explanatory narrative to link the diary extracts together. The other literary executors agreed to have me undertake this task at the same salary, which would continue until 31 May 1960. I decided to call the book *The Mackenzie King Record*. Some time in 1959, the University of Toronto Press convinced me and the literary executors there should be at least two volumes because the material was too interesting and important to be abbreviated and condensed into a single volume. After the first volume was published in October 1960, my income was supplemented by royalties. I continued my work on the rest of the diaries and had completed the selection of the extracts and a first draft of the continuity by the time the Liberal party came back into office in April 1963. Shortly afterwards, I was able to persuade D.F. Forster, who had assisted Dawson at an early stage, to become co-author of the rest of *The Mackenzie King Record*, which eventually extended to four volumes. Being a member of Parliament in Opposition was almost a full-time task — and so was work on the diaries. I had little time for frivolity between 1958 and 1963.

I do not want to give the impression that I spent most of my time in Opposition on *The Mackenzie King Record*. It provided me financial independence, but far more of my time and energy were devoted to Parliament and to Newfoundland. What little was left I used to help with party organization and to visits to other parts of Canada spreading the Liberal gospel according to Pearson. I enjoyed especially visiting universities. But Parliament came first.

Pearson as leader

Pearson must have been distressed by the magnitude of our defeat. He was almost sixty-one years old. The prospect of ending his career as leader of the Opposition was a bleak one, but he gave no inkling of depression to his small band of followers and soon had us at work preparing for the forthcoming session of Parliament.

Pearson wanted experienced advice on how to carry on the Opposition.

The most effective parliamentary opposition in the twentieth century had been conducted by Mackenzie King and his Liberal colleagues between 1930 and 1935. C.G. Power, if not the main strategist for that Opposition, had been its leading tactician. Pearson asked me to find out from Senator Power how they had performed. Chubby was generous with his time in recounting the way the Liberals had operated. He had a collection of contemporary memoranda which he lent me.

The essence of the strategy was that the Opposition should be highly selective in picking issues. They should oppose only those government proposals which were, by their nature, unpopular or those where some issue of principle was involved. Power emphasized it was essential that the Opposition work as a team, and that the leader have a tactical committee of former ministers to decide how the Opposition should behave in the House each day. Back-benchers should be given opportunities from time to time to air local grievances, but there should be no scatter-gun approach. It was of the utmost importance to create a public perception that we had a team capable of governing.

Pearson absorbed this lore quickly. While the issues were different, our methods between 1958 and 1963 were similar to those which Power had described and Mackenzie King and his colleagues had followed from 1930 to 1935.

The new Parliament met on 12 May 1958. When the debate on the Speech from the Throne began, the government asserted that the combined opposition was entitled to have only one speaker in five since we had only a fifth of the membership of the House. We insisted on the immemorial practice of alternating speakers between the government side and the Opposition. The government finally gave way, and the right of the Opposition to participate in debate on equal terms was never questioned again. In this struggle we had the co-operation of the CCF. We made it a rule to co-operate with them as one Opposition whenever possible. I was given the task of briefing their House leader every day about our tactics, and Hazen Argue was equally co-operative with us.

Though our numbers were small, we had substantial debating strength. At its heart were the four privy councillors, Pearson, Lionel Chevrier, Paul Martin, and me. As former ministers, we knew how government operated better than the new cabinet ministers. The four of us were backed up by several members with long service in the House. George McIlraith and Bill Benidickson, who had been parliamentary assistants, were the most prominent on the English side. Among French-speaking members from Quebec, Maurice Bourget, who had been a parliamentary assistant, Lucien Cardin, Jean Paul Deschatelets, and Guy Rouleau were knowledgeable and good speakers. Hedard Robichaud from New Brunswick was equally effective in French and English and particularly useful in debates affecting the Atlantic region. He and I worked together closely and easily.

Our eight-man Atlantic caucus was active and effective. Chesley Carter had been elected in 1949 and was thoroughly at home in the House. He concentrated on Newfoundland issues and matters affecting veterans. Herman Batten, elected, as I was, in 1953, did not confine himself to questions affecting Newfoundland but was helpful in general debates. Charlie Granger, though first elected in 1958, was thoroughly familiar with Ottawa because of his service from 1949 with Gordon Bradley, the first minister from Newfoundland, and later with me. Jim Tucker also elected in 1958 took some time to find his feet in Ottawa, but he was a dependable back-bencher. From New Brunswick, Roy McWilliam's membership dated from 1949: his greatest quality was solid common sense and his contributions to the House business were always well-timed and useful. Hervé Michaud, the third New Brunswicker, was a quiet back-bencher who spoke rarely but was always on hand for votes. Our deliberations as a caucus were frequent and generally reinforced by the attendance of Allan MacEachen of the leader's office.

Of our fifteen MPs elected in Ontario, eight were from northern Ontario and four from Ottawa and the valley. Two of the three from the rest of the province were from the Niagara peninsula and the third from Windsor. The southern Ontario heartland was otherwise unrepresented by Liberals. Apart from Pearson, Martin, McIlraith, and Benedickson, the most outstanding Liberal from Ontario was Jack Garland who weighed over 500 pounds and carried this weight well in caucus and the House. Jean Richard could be effective when he was in good form. Dr Bill McMillan was a good debater, especially on financial questions.

From the Quebec members, we drew our whip, Alexis Caron. Sam Boulanger had an agricultural background and was our official spokesman in French, but he did not speak English easily and Paul Martin often spoke for the party on agricultural issues. Though never at a loss for words, Paul was no agricultural expert and the Liberal Opposition was seriously handicapped in this field. Two new members from Quebec were good debaters: Yvon Dupuis, who was an outstanding orator in the House and a rabble-rouser in the country, and Gabriel Roberge, who was especially effective on legal questions. If he had not lost his seat to a Social Crediter in 1962 he would probably have become a cabinet minister instead of a distinguished superior court judge.

Despite our depleted ranks, the Liberal Opposition was able to hold its own in the House. Under Pearson's leadership, the back-benchers were never ignored. The party caucus was kept fully informed of strategy on which discussions were often lively. Pearson was once criticized in caucus for not being belligerent and partisan enough. I replied to this criticism by saying that, Diefenbaker to the contrary, Canadians did not really like their leaders to be hell-raisers and expected their prime ministers to speak for all Canadians. I suggested the hell-raising should be left to others in the caucus who would be ready and able to do their part.

Pearson met with the front-benchers almost every morning to discuss tactics in the House. At these meetings, to which other members were often invited, we decided what questions to raise and which government measures to oppose vigorously and which were popular and should be allowed to pass quickly. These meetings were attended by Pearson's advisers on policy, Maurice Lamontagne and Allan MacEachen.

Lamontagne had been a professor at Laval University. He was anathema to Premier Duplessis. He had come to the more congenial atmosphere of Ottawa as assistant deputy minister of northern affairs while Lesage was minister and had subsequently joined the Privy Council staff as economic adviser to St Laurent. After the election of 1957, Lamontagne resigned from the Privy Council Office and became principal economic adviser to the leader of the Opposition during St Laurent's brief tenure of that position. He stayed on with Pearson. Lamontagne performed invaluable service in connection with federal-provincial relations, before, during, and after Diefenbaker's federal-provincial conference in 1957. He had been one of the architects of equalization and he was at least as knowledgeable about federal-provincial relations as the public servants advising the government. Unlike them, he enjoyed the full confidence of those he was advising. Lamontagne was an indispensable adviser to Pearson on Quebec, but his lively intelligence ranged over the whole field of public policy. He failed to win election to Parliament in 1958 and continued to be an adviser to Pearson until he gained a seat in Parliament in 1963.

Allan MacEachen had been a member of Parliament from 1953 to 1958. In Parliament from 1953 to 1957, he had been a relatively quiet back-bencher who gained an undeserved reputation for indolence. But as one of the two surviving Liberal members from Nova Scotia in 1957 he performed most effectively in that short Parliament. His defeat in 1958 by a few votes was a great disappointment to all of us and especially to me as a senior member from the Atlantic region. I had formed a high opinion of MacEachen's abilities and felt we needed a Nova Scotian voice in the heart of the parliamentary opposition. I suggested to Pearson that he invite MacEachen to join his staff. Despite some reservations on the ground that MacEachen had a reputation for laziness, Pearson agreed. No happier choice could possibly have been made. MacEachen soon became a master of parliamentary tactics and his knowledge of the rules of the House was unrivalled. But we came to depend upon MacEachen for much more. He and Lamontagne contributed as much to the development of Liberal policy as any of us in the caucus. Without them it would have been harder to convince the public that the Liberal Opposition represented a viable alternative government.

Pearson chose Chevrier as House leader for the Opposition. I was expected to assist Chevrier and to act for him whenever he was absent. Chevrier and I were a good combination. I cannot recall a single occasion when we failed to work together in complete harmony. Pearson's own leadership in the House was generally limited to broad strategy. He always backed us up in our decisions on day-to-day tactics.

Pearson was to prove more effective as a leader of the Opposition than any other leader in this century except Mackenzie King. Considering the magnitude of the task he faced in regaining office, Pearson, in my judgement, was, in that role, every bit the equal of Mackenzie King. He was highly successful in many careers but, in my view, his most outstanding achievement was his leadership of the Opposition from 1958 to 1963.

Before Parliament met we were briefly tempted to make an issue of the government's light-hearted spending of money that Parliament had not voted. We quickly decided that, after the landslide victory, to try to censure the government for contempt of Parliament would not arouse the public and might expose us to ridicule. We felt we would be wiser to find an issue which would be more durable.

Parliament opens

When the new Parliament met on 12 May 1958, the Diefenbaker government had as great an opportunity to implement its program, almost without opposition, as any in our history. No party leader before or since had made so many promises of action as John Diefenbaker had, though Brian Mulroney challenged that record in 1984. We in the Opposition expected a Speech from the Throne filled with a copious and dynamic legislative program. Instead only a few specific measures were forecast: bills were to be introduced to authorize construction of the South Saskatchewan dam and a railway to the Northwest Territories, and to revise the Broadcasting Act to take from the Canadian Broadcasting Corporation the authority to regulate radio and television broadcasting and vest it in a new body to be called the Board of Broadcast Governors. A Bill of Rights was to be introduced. Attention was drawn to a forthcoming Commonwealth trade and economic conference to be held in Canada.

In view of Diefenbaker's huge majority, Pearson felt that a straight motion of want of confidence would be a denial of the verdict in the election. But he did not want to leave the field free to the eight CCF members led by Hazen Argue, fearing they might move a motion it would be embarrassing to vote for or against.

Pearson decided to base his motion on Diefenbaker's promise to divert 15 per cent of Canadian imports from the United States to Britain. The British government had responded to the proposed diversion by an offer to negotiate a complete free trade area between Canada and Britain. This offer had flabbergasted the Diefenbaker government, which never replied to it in public. By May 1958 Diefenbaker was already denying that he had ever proposed a 15 per cent diversion.

In his speech, Pearson carefully documented Diefenbaker's repeated promises to divert trade to Britain and his subsequent repudiation of the policy. The subject was a shrewd choice which underlined Diefenbaker's vacillation and the hollowness of his pro-British pretensions. This difference in attitude to Britain between government and Opposition was to remain an issue throughout all four years of the 1958 Parliament.

We Liberals were modest about our expectations in this first session. At the outset, Diefenbaker could do no wrong. The polls indicated his popularity had increased after the election. We realized that little or nothing was to be gained by confrontations with a popular prime minister. We quickly sensed that Diefenbaker was, in the public mind, the whole government. None of his ministers had a substantial political base of his own, none of them had ever served in a cabinet before, and only two or three were known except in their own region. As an Opposition we felt we should do our best to keep it that way by exposing their mistakes and their weaknesses and doing nothing to help them build up any positive reputations.

My own view was that the greatest weakness of the government was the multiplicity of Diefenbaker's promises. Throughout the 1957 campaign, he had made an incredible number of unrealistic or unrealizable promises. I thought one effective way to oppose the government at the start was to keep reminding the public of these promises. I gathered the best press reports I could find, had them reproduced by the Liberal federation, and bound in red cardboard in a volume entitled *Diefenbaker's Promises, 1957*. A copy was given to every Liberal member and to anyone else who was interested. We made use of the volume in the debates before Parliament was dissolved. After the election, I compiled a volume of the 1958 promises. Copies were also made by the Liberal federation for every Liberal member. Most of us kept these volumes in our desks in the House of Commons and took them out on every appropriate occasion. They proved to be one of the most effective tools of Opposition for the whole period the Tories were in office.

Of all Diefenbaker's promises, the most damaging to the government, and to him as its head, was his promise that, as long as he was prime minister, no one in Canada would suffer from unemployment. This promise was made four or five times during the 1958 campaign. Diefenbaker's *'no one will suffer from unemployment'* became one of the unforgotten and unforgettable Canadian political phrases. It was in the same class as Mackenzie King's costly statement in 1930 that his government would not give a Tory provincial government 'a five-cent piece' to spend on relief of the unemployed and R.B. Bennett's prophetic undertaking in 1930 'to cure unemployment or perish in the attempt.'

I noted with interest in Donald Fleming's memoirs (vol. 2, p. 145) the words: 'Diefenbaker's path was strewn with promises. This was one of the crosses I had to bear.' Later on Fleming observes that Diefenbaker 'could not resist seeking the applause that could be expected when he proclaimed that no one would suffer from unemployment as long as he was Prime Minister, whether it meant a balanced budget or not.' Fleming added: 'This was obviously promising far too much. To me it was axiomatic that one should not promise more than one could deliver.'

In the session of 1958 and, increasingly, through the next four years, the Liberal Opposition made unemployment the basic issue. Unemployment did not result in the acute hardship of the depression years, thanks to unemployment insurance and the development of social welfare, but the prolongation of unemployment at a much higher level than it had reached since the thirties gradually eroded support for the government. This erosion was hastened by the proposals the Liberal Opposition developed for dealing with the problem.

I expected the Liberal party to recover and eventually to regain office, but did not dare to hope it would happen as soon as it did. It would be a mistake, I believed, to mortgage the future by advocating policies or making promises which would embarrass us when we were again in office. Pearson felt the same way. He refused to advocate policies merely to get temporary applause.

In the 1950s and early 60s, the daily oral question period had not yet begun to eclipse all other proceedings in the House. The media, still dominated by the press, actually paid attention to the debates on legislation and other public business. I concentrated on debating and seldom asked questions except on subjects for which I was Opposition critic. I felt the question period should be left as much as possible to back-benchers who had few other ways to get publicity. I heeded advice from experienced politicians never to engage in debate with back-benchers. It was a mistake, I felt, to seek confrontation with ministers who could get little publicity on their own. But I welcomed every chance to clash with Diefenbaker, and even created a few.

I spent a great deal of time in the House and was soon more at ease than I had been as a minister. In speaking, I rarely had a prepared text, but often only a few notes on the back of an envelope or an order paper to keep me on the rails. During my whole time in Parliament, I was nervous before I had to initiate a debate. I preferred not to be the first speaker but to have someone to reply to. I learned to listen carefully to any speaker I was going to follow, in order to deal systematically with the points raised. In Opposition, debating for me quickly became a game, occasionally played merely for its own sake!

Debate on relations with Britain did not end in 1958 with Pearson's motion on trade diversion. Prime Minister Macmillan visited Canada and spoke to Parliament in June 1958. I liked his speech. My closest friend on the government side of the House was Jim Macdonnell. He told me how thrilled he had been by the speech. I commented that Macmillan was the first British prime minister who had not uttered a patronizing word about Canada and who had treated this country as a genuine equal of Britain. I was filled with admiration of his attitude and have remained an admirer ever since.

Diefenbaker was not happy with the visit. He accompanied Macmillan when the British prime minister was interviewed by the CBC. Macmillan asked in advance what questions would be put to him. When he was told the first question would be about the British free trade offer, Diefenbaker intervened. The press reported that he said, 'No, no, you cannot ask that question.' The question was not asked in the interview.

On 16 June Pearson raised a question in the House about the instruction Diefenbaker had given to the CBC. Later in the day we made it the subject of a grievance. Diefenbaker denied that there had been any interference and diverted attention by dredging up alleged incidents of interference with the CBC by the St Laurent government. We were led into replying to these charges instead of pressing our own case. However, on this occasion, Pearson did manage to leave the impression that Diefenbaker had tried to influence the CBC on behalf of the government.

In a later debate in the session, I returned to relations with Britain, and pronounced a sort of epitaph on Diefenbaker's 15 per cent diversion of trade to Britain. Once in every generation, I claimed, it seemed to be possible for the Tory party 'to excite the people of this country by stirring up feeling against the United States and by parading a great affection for Great Britain ... We had that in 1911; we had it in 1930, and we have had it again in the last two years ... the pattern does seem to go on.' Each time, when the chips are down, Britain is forgotten by the Tories.

The difference between the Tory and Liberal attitude to Britain arose two or three years later in an even sharper form when Diefenbaker and his ministers opposed Macmillan's attempt to negotiate Britain's entry into the European Common Market.

The Broadcasting Act

In the session of 1958, the new Broadcasting Act was the most controversial government measure. The act was designed to remove the power of the CBC to regulate private broadcasters and to place the regulation of all broadcasting in a new body to be called the Board of Broadcast Governors. This was a fundamental change of broadcasting policy.

Public financing of broadcasting, started by the Bennett government in the early thirties, was supported by all parties in Parliament. When the CBC was established in 1936, the basic principle was accepted that public broadcasting should be as independent of control by a minister or the cabinet as are the Supreme Court or the Chief Electoral Officer.

The CBC was created by Parliament in the heyday of Mussolini's fascism, Hitler's nazism, and Stalin's brutal dictatorship. All these totalitarian regimes were bolstered up by incessant radio propaganda. Many believed it would not be possible to have a publicly owned broadcasting system which would remain free of control by the government in office. In the United States, broadcasting under public ownership was widely feared as a threat to freedom itself. Fortunately, in the British Broadcasting Corporation, there was an example of a public broadcasting system which had been kept, from the outset, independent of the government of the day.

Under the Canadian legislation of 1936, independence of government control was to be assured by the appointment of a board of the CBC consisting of men and women selected for their integrity, broad experience, and independence of mind and character. The CBC was to have, like the BBC, an assured source of revenue which required no annual parliamentary vote of funds.

These safeguards secured public broadcasting from partisan control by the government in office for twenty years. During the period when Davidson Dunton was head of the CBC a tradition of independent and objective control of broadcasting was firmly established. Unfortunately the assured sources of revenue, initially from licence fees and, later, from excise taxes earmarked for the CBC, proved by 1956 to be inadequate. A commission was appointed under Robert Fowler to recommend a new system of assured financing and to review broadcasting policy.

In addition to the problem of providing assured revenue for the CBC, another problem in broadcasting developed in the 1950s. That problem involved the scope of broadcasting by privately owned stations. The CBC in 1936 had been modelled largely on the BBC, but the Canadian corporation was not given a total monopoly; many private stations were already in operation in Canada. It was decided that our national broadcasting system should include private stations but that they should be complementary to the CBC and not in direct competition with public broadcasting. On this principle, it was quite logical that the CBC should regulate all broadcasting and determine the degree to which the system should include private stations.

As the private stations became more numerous, more influential, and more profitable in larger centres, they began to regard the CBC as a competitor. The private broadcasters argued that it was a denial of natural justice to have one competitor regulate another. The Tory party in opposition accepted this position and promised to establish an independent regulatory authority for broadcasting. Even in the Liberal party there was growing support for such a change.

Once the Diefenbaker government, with its overwhelming mandate, decided to establish a Board separate from the CBC to regulate broadcasting, our caucus felt it would be futile to oppose the change. We decided instead to concentrate on keeping the CBC free of control by a minister or the cabinet. It became Liberal policy to implement a scheme of financial independence recommended by the Fowler commission, and to uphold the principle that public broadcasting should be subject to review only by Parliament and never by the cabinet.

In 1958, as the session went on without any sign of the broadcasting legislation, we in the Opposition suspected it was being held off in the hope of rushing it through at the end of the session without much debate. Under the rules at that time, there were six occasions in a session when the Opposition had the chance to air grievances and move votes of want of confidence. This was done by moving amendments to what were called supply motions. We decided to use one such occasion to complain about the delay and to set out the policy we Liberals felt should be the basis of broadcasting legislation.

Pearson and I had been closely associated with the development of broadcasting policy from the beginnings of the CBC, so it was agreed we should take the initiative in the debate. In a comprehensive speech Pearson reviewed the history of public broadcasting and indicated what changes we would support and what safeguards we felt should be maintained. In a supporting speech, I identified three problems which should be faced in the new legislation. The first was to decide to whom, where, and under what conditions private licences for television were to be granted; the second was to provide a method by which public funds were to be provided for the CBC; and the third was to determine who was to control the content of broadcasts. These were the main points we debated later when the legislation came before the House.

That debate did not begin until 18 August, when the members were already getting weary of the long session. In the preliminary stage, Pearson tried to have the legislation postponed until the following session. This suggestion was waved aside, as was my suggestion that the broadcasting bill be sent to a select committee where representations could be made by public bodies and interested individuals and witnesses could be heard.

The minister of national revenue, George Nowlan, was in charge of the legislation. He declined to agree to send the bill to a select committee on the ground that there seemed to be no objection in principle to the proposed new set-up.

In a lengthy reply to Nowlan, Pearson set out the objections of the Opposition. We feared the proposed act would weaken the concept of a single national system of broadcasting. We felt it might weaken the independence of the CBC and lead to political interference through direct financial control of broadcasting by the government. Pearson foresaw the danger of conflict between the new Board of Broadcast Governors and the board of the CBC. He objected strongly to the unprecedented proposal that the president and vice-president of the CBC should be appointed *during pleasure* for a period of seven years. Appointment during pleasure left the government free to remove the person appointed at any time and without notice; appointment for a period of years meant the person appointed could not be removed except for cause. An attempt to combine the two was nonsense.

We were never able to find out who was the author of this contradictory notion. We fully expected the government to change it in committee. Pearson insisted that the independence of the CBC from control by the government could not be assured unless the president had a fixed term longer than the maximum life of a single Parliament. He announced that the Liberal Opposition would not vote for second reading of the bill, because the objections he had raised had not been met. I echoed the criticisms Pearson had made, laying particular emphasis on security of financing for the CBC. We voted against second reading of the bill and later proposed several amendments to sections of the bill one of which would have deleted the words 'during pleasure' and applied 'during good behaviour' to the tenure of the president and vice-president of the CBC. Nowlan declined to accept this amendment, which was later made by the Senate and agreed to by the government on the last day of the session.

The broadcasting legislation got through the House quickly. Part of the reason it passed relatively easily was Nowlan's conciliatory manner. He was the member of the cabinet who got along best with the Opposition. We were not willing to press him very hard, because we knew he was one of the few ministers who unreservedly supported public broadcasting.

Diefenbaker also realized public broadcasting was popular, but it was soon widely known that he was hostile to Alphonse Ouimet who had succeeded Davidson Dunton as head of the CBC. There was widespread opposition to the CBC among the Tory members based on a theoretical preference for private enterprise. Even some of the Liberals in Parliament were lukewarm about the CBC.

Pearson and I, as the spokesmen of the Opposition on broadcasting, never wavered in our support of the principle of nation-wide public broadcasting and of the CBC as an independent agency. R.M. Fowler had told me, in 1957, after the royal commission he headed made its report, that there was no doubt that a majority of Canadians felt CBC broadcasts were a large part of their lives. Although we did not object to the existence of private broadcasting, we continued to insist there be only one system and no private networks in radio. As for television, we were relieved that the government had retained the original television policy of permitting only one station in each city, so long as television was not available nation-wide. We had the consolation of a promise from Nowlan that a special committee would be set up in the next session to review broadcasting, including the operation of the new act.

We had tried hard to have Parliament provide the CBC with an assured budget for a period of years longer than the life of a single Parliament, instead of by annual grants determined by the cabinet. The object was to prevent a financial squeeze on the CBC by the government. We were not successful while Diefenbaker was in office. When we became the government I was disappointed that we never carried out our undertaking to provide long-term financing for public broadcasting. I personally kept trying until my very last day in the cabinet. My last official act as a minister was to attend a meeting of a cabinet committee which was drafting a new broadcasting act. My pleas fell on deaf ears.

Neither the Pearson nor the Trudeau government attempted to cut the CBC budget, but the danger was always there. Recently two steps were taken which strengthened my view that the independence of public broadcasting is not adequately protected. In 1984 an arbitrary cut was made in the CBC budget without reference to Parliament. The Mulroney government appointed patronage officials to watch over the administration of government departments and agencies on behalf of the minister. The independence of public broadcasting from control by government was threatened by the appointment of one of these 'political commissars' to check up on the management of the CBC.

Apart from royal commissions, the only public body which scrutinized the operations of the CBC in the past was a select committee of the House of Commons operating in public. The governmental interference with the operation of public broadcasting in 1984 was fortunately the subject of widespread public protests. A task force has since been appointed to review broadcasting, but in private not in public, though public agitation seems to be forcing the task force to listen to representations.

There are signs that the minister of communications is now considering the problems of broadcasting seriously and sympathetically with a view to maintaining its national character. But it continues to be my opinion that independence from any danger of partisan control of public broadcasting will never be safe until the CBC has an assured long-term budget that cannot be altered by the government of the day.

The BC ferry crisis

During the 1958 session, the government was faced with a problem which could not have been foreseen. The only ferry service between the British Columbia mainland and Vancouver Island was interrupted by a strike on 16 May. The ferry service was part of the Canadian Pacific system and therefore under federal jurisdiction. The government allowed the strike to drag on for two months. By then, all hope of a negotiated settlement had disappeared. Public indignation was rising.

On 23 July the government announced it intended to introduce legislation to end the strike. We Liberals discussed in caucus what our attitude should be to back-to-work legislation. Some members wanted to oppose it outright, but most of us, including Pearson, did not think straight opposition would be defensible. We knew the government would bring up the precedent of 1950 when the Liberal government had ended a nation-wide railway strike by legislation. There was one substantial difference. The Diefenbaker bill proposed to order the employees back to work at the old wages, whereas in 1950 the Liberal legislation had awarded the workers the highest wage rates the railways had offered during negotiations. In addition, our bill had provided for compulsory arbitration of the difference between the wage rates awarded in the law and the demands of the union negotiators.

We were convinced that outright opposition to back to work legislation in the BC ferry dispute would have outraged public opinion in the province. A conciliation board had recommended a wage settlement that the union negotiators had accepted but Canadian Pacific had rejected. We decided to support the back-to-work legislation only if it included some increase in wages; our recommendation was to give the workers the settlement proposed by the conciliation board. Several of us in Opposition discussed our position with officials of the Canadian Labour Congress. By doing so, we earned some goodwill in the rank of organized labour. When the government rejected our proposed compromise, we voted against the bill to send the workers back without any increase in pay.

Most of us in the Liberal Opposition believed back-to-work legislation would be needed in the future. We did not want a Liberal government to be embarrassed by a bad precedent which we would have set by outright opposition.

The government resorted to back-to-work legislation again in 1960. The railways and their unions failed to agree on new wage contracts and a strike was called for 3 December. The government tried without success to get the union leaders to postpone the strike deadline until 15 May 1961. They were also unable to get the presidents of the railways to accept a settlement proposed by a conciliation board which the unions were ready to settle for. The excuse for delaying the deadline for a strike until 15 May was that the royal commission on transportation presided over by M.A. MacPherson was expected to make a report which the government hoped would recommend a permanent solution of the railway problem. When persuasion failed, the minister of labour, Michael Starr, introduced a bill called an 'Act to Provide for the Continuation of the Operation of Railways.' This bill prohibited a strike before 15 May 1961.

Pearson made our position clear in a brief speech following Starr. He said a Liberal government would have introduced legislation to make the strike unnecessary by requiring the railways to accept the settlement recommended by the conciliation board. The Liberal Opposition was against compelling men to continue to work for less than that report had recommended. We believed the railways were in a position to pay the higher wages for the short period until 15 May 1961, when the government would have the opportunity to consider the report of the MacPherson commission.

The legislation prohibiting a railway strike was to expire on 15 May 1961. Ten days before the deadline, on 5 May, the railways and the unions announced they had reached an agreement. Chevrier noted that the agreement was precisely on the terms suggested by the Liberal Opposition during the debate on the compulsory legislation in November.

We asked the government whether any commitment had been made to enable the railways to finance the wage increase. We believed the government intended to recompense the railways for the wage increase by legislation. Leon Balcer, the minister of transport, denied there was any such intention. It was not until the very last day of the session in September 1961 that the House learned how the increased wage bill of the railways was to be paid. An item was included in the supplementary estimates to provide $50 million to be paid to the railways until the government had completed its consideration of the MacPherson report. This was an obvious wage subsidy. It fooled no one. It was still being paid when I became minister of transport and was not terminated until the National Transportation Act came into force in 1967.

It never occurred to me that the next back-to-work legislation would be introduced by the Pearson government when I was minister of transport. I was glad then that we had not yielded in opposition to the temptation to oppose such legislation outright.

Atlantic affairs

My activities in Parliament while we were in opposition were not confined to national issues. As the only former Liberal cabinet minister from the region, I tried to take the lead in every debate of special concern to Newfoundland or the Atlantic provinces. All Liberal members from Newfoundland and New Brunswick were encouraged to take part in these debates. We concentrated especially on fisheries and public works.

On the public works estimates on the evening of 19 June 1958, I made a speech which seemed to entertain the House. I took the minister, Howard Green, on a hypothetical cruise on our schooner, the *Millie Ford*, along the coast of my constituency from Twillingate to Bonavista. I managed to refer to every wharf, breakwater, or other marine work that was being sought in each outport or settlement. I spoke without notes and named over seventy of them from memory. It was politically helpful to have the name of every place on the coast in my riding recorded in *Hansard*, and the speech received appropriate publicity in Newfoundland!

The following morning I was telephoned from the parliamentary press gallery and asked if I had a picture of my schooner. I said that I had none at the office but several at home. I assumed the picture was wanted to illustrate my speech of the previous evening. But that was not so. To my horror, I

Reprinted with permission – The Halifax Herald Limited

was told the *Millie Ford* had been wrecked the previous day in a storm off Cape Race, fortunately with no loss of life. The whole family was devastated by the news. In time we realized the loss did have its consolation. As long as I was in opposition we could not have afforded to use the schooner for a political tour. The marine insurance covered the full cost of building a modest summer cottage which we still own at Traytown on Bonavista Bay. This was a well-located headquarters for the riding.

There was a serious regional problem about coal. Coal was the basis of the economy of Cape Breton Island. The market for coal began shrinking in the 1950s. To stimulate the use of coal, the St Laurent government in 1957 offered subsidies for new thermal plants to produce electric power for Nova Scotia and New Brunswick. In the election campaign, St Laurent had promised the government would support the existing level of coal production, but would not encourage any increase. The Tories charged that St Laurent wanted to leave the coal in the ground. Diefenbaker promised a Tory government would expand the production of coal to produce electric power.

By the middle of 1958, stock-piles of coal were building up in Cape Breton, while thermal plants to produce electricity were using oil as fuel instead of coal because the oil was cheaper. The St Laurent government had promised that, if oil became cheaper than coal, the federal government would subsidize the price of coal to assure its use in producing electricity. The Diefenbaker government acquiesced in the use of the cheaper oil.

We decided to attack the government head-on for its neglect of the coal problem. We charged it with failing to avert the shut-down of coal mines in Nova Scotia and with retreating from Diefenbaker's specific promise to ensure the use of coal in thermal plants. In the debate I argued there was no excuse for using oil instead of coal in the Maritimes and declared it continued to be Liberal policy to ensure the use of coal. I would have liked to go further. When we had been in office, I had tried to persuade my colleagues to provide special aid to make Sydney a modern industrial centre which would lift the economy of the whole region. In opposition, I was seeking the same goal, but with no greater success. The problem was still with us when Pearson became prime minister, and it is worse today.

On 30 August 1958, Diefenbaker announced that the government was proposing, through a supplementary estimate, to meet, as an emergency, the shortage of farm income on the prairies by payments through the Wheat Board to western grain producers, of one dollar per acre up to 200 acres per farm. The amount to be provided for that purpose was forty million dollars. The proposal was supported by Pearson, though he questioned whether it was large enough. He said the plight of the western grain producers was a regional problem of national importance. Pearson pointed out that there were other primary producers who would relate this assistance to their own difficulties. He was, he went on, 'thinking particularly ... of the fisherman who had also had his hard times, and who perhaps will look with a certain amount of envy' to the assistance for the grain producers.

Ches Carter intervened briefly when the supplementary estimate for the acreage payments was being debated on 6 September to repeat Pearson's reference to the fishermen. Carter said we did not object to the acreage payments, but he pointed out that the fishery had failed in 1958 in many parts of Newfoundland. We hoped the same consideration and assistance would be given to the fishermen as to the farmers. I echoed Carter in a single sentence.

After touring my constituency in the fall of 1958, I wrote the prime minister on 21 October that I had 'found the failure of the cod fishery which is the mainstay of more than half the population of the North East coast of New-foundland is of even more serious proportions than earlier reports had led me to expect.' I estimated that up to two-thirds of the fishermen would not have enough stamps to entitle them to unemployment insurance, which had saved a serious situation in the winter of 1957–58. I said it was 'no exaggeration to say that half the fishermen on the North East coast of Newfoundland will be forced to go on relief in the coming winter unless action is taken by the Federal Government to treat this failure of the cod fishery as an emergency situation calling for action similar to that taken by the Government to assist the prairie grain farmers who experienced a crop failure this year that is certainly no more serious for them than the 'crop failure' in the cod fishery is to the fishermen of Newfoundland.'

I reminded the prime minister that on 30 August in proposing the vote of forty millions for the grain farmers he had stated that his government's 'concept of a national policy is based on the belief that the national welfare demands positive action to meet the basic causes of distress and maladjustment in particular industries and regions.' I went on to give my opinion that 'the situation of the fishermen of Newfoundland this year calls urgently for pos-itive action to meet acute distress in the fishing industry.' 'The simplest way to meet this problem would be for the government to use the agency of the unemployment insurance commission which has the necessary machinery and, through the commission, to provide every full-time fisherman with the mini-mum contributions to entitle him to unemployment insurance. This method would ensure that assistance went to those who actually had a failure of the fishery.' The government could re-imburse the Unemployment Insurance Commission for the cost of the relief.

I told Diefenbaker I was sending a copy of my letter to all MPs from fishing constituencies in the Atlantic region and to the ministers of fisheries and labour and the minister from Newfoundland.

I concluded by saying I could not emphasize too strongly that the 'crop failure' in the fishery called 'for an early statement of positive action by the Federal Government, if many thousands of fishermen are not to be driven to accept relief in order to provide for their families in the coming winter.'

The only result of my appeal was considerable and generally favourable publicity in the media in Newfoundland and some elsewhere in the Atlantic region. The government took no action. Other appeals for the fishermen fell on equally deaf ears throughout our years in opposition until the final session before the 1962 election, when the government provided another substantial payment to the grain farmers and a miserable winter works program for fishermen.

In 1959, I initiated a debate on a motion regretting the failure of the government to keep its election promises to the people of Atlantic provinces. In a long speech I listed Diefenbaker's unkept promise to the region and contrasted that record with the program the Liberals intended to implement when we regained office. I am proud to recall that every proposal in the Liberal Atlantic program was carried out by the Pearson government.

The coal problem came up in 1961 in an acute form when the Bras d'Or mine in Cape Breton was on the point of closing. On 1 May the government brought forward a measure to provide financial support to keep that mine open. Unluckily for them, Dosco, the leading coal producer chose that day to announce that it would close three mines at Glace Bay on 31 May.

We supported the help proposed to keep the Bras d'Or mine open and recommended the extension of similar help to save the Glace Bay mines. That plea met no response. I happened, primarily for some other reason, to be in Sydney and Glace Bay on the day the mines closed. The next day I was back in Ottawa, when the estimates of the Dominion Coal Board were up for debate. I described the sad scene in Glace Bay the previous day and reported that another mine was to close on 1 August. The coal problem in Cape Breton, I contended, had become a national emergency.

While speaking I was frequently interrupted by Tory back-benchers taunting me about St Laurent's coal policy in 1957. I replied that I was talking about 1961, but if they insisted on history I would recall the promises made all over Nova Scotia in 1957 by Diefenbaker that a Tory government would increase coal production. Instead of an increase, production had declined ever since the Tories took office. Despite systematic interruptions, I did manage, before my time expired, to recommend that the problem be tackled by using coal, in a big way, for the production of electricity.

Since my reference to Diefenbaker's promise had been ignored, I brought a copy of the 1957 Tory advertisement into the House the next day and read the promise that a Conservative government would increase the production of coal – one more unkept Diefenbaker promise.

Another essentially regional issue arose in 1961, when the government brought forward a general overhaul of the Fisheries Act. The changes were not contentious. We Liberals used the debate, instead, to urge the government to get ahead with the extension of the exclusive fishing zone from three to twelve miles offshore – another Diefenbaker promise of 1957. The government claimed that it was trying to get international approval. Pearson agreed that international agreement was preferable, but, if it could not be secured quickly, a Liberal government would not hesitate to extend the limit to twelve miles unilaterally. All five Liberal members from Newfoundland spoke in support of Pearson.

Early in 1962, Frank Howard of the CCF-NDP introduced a bill to extend the exclusive fishing zone to twelve miles. It was opposed by the government on the ground that negotiations were still on to secure an international agreement. I congratulated Howard on his moderate presentation, and contrasted the hesitant attitude of the government with the very different attitude taken by Diefenbaker in a speech at Yarmouth on 25 March 1958, in which he had promised a firm stand against foreign trawlers. I then repeated the Liberal policy as set out by Pearson in Parliament in 1961 that multilateral agreement was preferable, but unilateral action should be taken if necessary. Being a private member's bill, Howard's bill did not come to a vote. No action was achieved until we got back in office.

An even more immediate fishing problem in 1961 was a substantial surplus of salt fish and a depressed price. I recalled another unkept Diefenbaker promise made at Charlottetown, Prince Edward Island, in 1958 to place a floor price under fish. Once again, the government ignored the problem. I spoke, as I usually tried to do, on matters relating to Newfoundland after most of our other Liberals had spoken, feeling they needed the publicity more than I did.

Questions were raised in 1961 by Tory members about the suitability of fishermen being covered by unemployment insurance. I took a proprietary interest in unemployment insurance for fishermen which I had persuaded my colleagues in the St Laurent government to initiate. The parliamentary secretary to the minister of labour, in reply to the critics in his own party, claimed the Diefenbaker government had brought fishermen under the act. I rose at once to correct this statement. When interrupted, I declared the statement was false. The act, I noted, had received royal assent in August 1956, ten months before the Diefenbaker government took office. When Starr asked what my attitude was to continuing unemployment insurance for fishermen, I replied that I was a member of the government that had put unemployment insurance for fishermen into the law and I would fight to the very limit of my capabilities to keep it there.

One matter of special interest to Newfoundland in 1961 was the decision of the United States government to close the leased military base at Pepperrell in St John's. A dispute immediately arose as to whether the title to the base should revert to the provincial or the federal government. Throughout this dispute I was consulted frequently by Premier Smallwood. Diefenbaker announced in Parliament on 23 January 1961, that the question of ownership would be referred to the Supreme Court.

The terms of reference had still not been settled in July. I asked whether some arrangement could not be made to use the property rather than leave it unoccupied. On my own initiative, I suggested that the reference to the court be abandoned and title vested in the province. Diefenbaker replied, politely for once, that when the Court had spoken, each government would know what its legal rights were.

I did not abandon the idea of an out-of-court settlement and persuaded Smallwood to have the provincial government propose to Diefenbaker that the federal government take over whatever facilities were needed for defence or other federal purposes, and that the rest of the buildings on the base, including particularly the hospital and the housing, be taken over by the provincial government. On that basis, an amicable division was made which has served very well ever since.

Just before announcing the election on 17 April 1962, Diefenbaker announced that the government had decided to build a causeway between New Brunswick and Prince Edward Island, on which he claimed studies had been authorized in January 1958. The proposed causeway was also to become a concern of mine before any action was taken.

During the session, I had also raised a question which became of great concern to Newfoundland after I became a minister again. The hydro-electric development of Churchill Falls in Labrador was to be done by Brinco, a private corporation. Privately owned corporations which developed power were subject to federal corporation-income taxation, whereas provincial hydro authorities, being agents of the provincial crown, were exempt. If the privately owned power producers were similarly tax-free, the price of power would be lower, and Brinco would be more likely to find customers to justify starting construction. I asked in 1962 whether consideration was being given to placing privately owned utilities on an equal basis with government-owned utilities by removing the federal tax. My plea got no response, but action was subsequently taken by the Pearson government and was an essential factor in getting the agreement between the governments of Newfoundland and Quebec which made the great power project at Churchill Falls a reality.

Moving from a mega-project to a parochial subject, I made my annual plea to the government to build a post office at Hare Bay, which was the most populous place in my riding without a publicly owned post office. Hare Bay got its post office when the Pearson government achieved office. There is no doubt in my mind that the frequent attention given by the Liberal Opposition to the Atlantic region helped to build support for the party in the 1962 election.

The tide begins to ebb: 1959

The parliamentary session eventually closed on 6 September 1958 to the relief of government and Opposition alike. During that first session, the public honeymoon with Diefenbaker was not over, even in Quebec. After Jean Lesage's resignation, the Liberal candidate for his seat lost in the by-election; the Liberal party had gained no measurable additional support when the session ended. But the Liberal Opposition had developed an effective parliamentary strategy. We had become competent in debating as a team. Though not a great debater, Pearson was clearly captain of the team. We were in a good position to take advantage, in future sessions, of political issues in which there was widespread public interest.

The government, despite its huge majority, emerged from the session without a single major achievement except for the Broadcasting Act. The session itself had not been managed effectively. Most of the ministers had not been impressive in the House. If the Speech from the Throne was thin, the closing one was even thinner.

As for myself, I felt I had got the feel of Parliament in a way I had not done while the St Laurent government was in office. I once told St Laurent that his one weakness as a politician was his failure to make politics exciting. This was one fault I tried to avoid. Despite many – perhaps too many – and varied interventions in debate, I did not seem to bore the House. Without making any conscious effort to cultivate the media, I got plenty of publicity and was frequently the subject of cartoons. Unlike many members on both sides of the House, I was not intimidated by Diefenbaker. I accepted being in Opposition cheerfully and tried to get as much fun as possible out of the relative irresponsibility of being out of office. My hope of eventually being in government again remained high. Diefenbaker would prove to be an inadequate prime minister and I felt sure the public would find that out. Our job as an Opposition was to look like a better alternative. I was sure we were on the right road, but I expected the road to be much longer than it turned out to be.

As soon as the session ended, I turned to my second priority; my constituency and Newfoundland. By dragging the session on into September, Parliament had deprived our family of the summer in Newfoundland. 1958 was the only year, in my fourteen in Parliament and since, that Margaret and I missed spending much of the summer on Bonavista Bay. In September 1958, I went to Newfoundland alone and made a tour of my constituency. Once the tour was completed, I settled down in Ottawa to my fourth priority, working on *The Mackenzie King Record*.

But I did not entirely neglect the third priority: to spread the Liberal gospel. In November I was in Halifax to speak to the annual meeting of the Nova Scotia Liberal Association, and from there I went on to Newfoundland for ten days during which I took part in the ceremony opening a new road in the north-eastern part of my constituency. This road made a number of settlements more accessible. I made a second visit to Nova Scotia before the end of the year, and in the next five years I managed to visit most parts of the country as part of our missionary efforts on behalf of the Liberal party.

The second session of the 1958 Parliament opened on 15 January 1959. Once again, the legislative program was very thin. Specific proposals were made for a Bill of Rights, crop insurance, and a national energy board. A temporary measure was forecast to deal with increases in freight rates, and the extension *for one year* of the increase made in 1958 in the provincial share of income tax revenues was promised. Compared with the 'vision' offered in the elections of 1957 and 1958, the Speech from the Throne was a mere shadow. There was no comprehensive plan to deal with unemployment which the government claimed it had already taken steps to reduce. The honeymoon was over.

The spirits of the Opposition began to revive at the end of 1958 when the Liberals won a by-election. Paul Hellyer was elected in Toronto-Trinity and we once again had a voice in Toronto. Hellyer had become associate minister of national defence in the St Laurent government at the very end of its term. He was very knowledgeable about defence questions and became an effective military critic. We needed such a critic early in 1959 when Diefenbaker brutally terminated the construction of the Avro-Arrow. The A.V. Roe company had developed a new fighter aircraft under contract with the Department of Defence. Its quality was unquestioned, but it was a moot question whether production could be justified on the limited scale needed to meet Canadian requirements. The government could hardly be blamed for examining the pro's and con's with care. But the sudden and brutal action by Diefenbaker himself of ending the Avro-Arrow program could not be justified. The cancellation of the Arrow contract resulted in the loss of a highly skilled technical labour force. This loss was a great shock. The lack of alternative employment in Canada increased resentment. The disappearance of the Arrow marked the beginning of serious erosion of support for Diefenbaker in Metropolitan Toronto. Hellyer was effective in the debate on the Arrow and a valuable reinforcement to the Opposition.

Before the 1959 session began, the government was faced with an embarrassing incident. Charles Van Horne, a rambunctious Tory member from northern New Brunswick, attacked the prime minister in a broadcast. Van Horne had been elected to Parliament in 1955. He quickly became one of the noisiest critics of the St Laurent government. Diefenbaker had praised Van Horne extravagantly in the 1957 election campaign. In a speech, at Campbellton, in Van Horne's riding, he said Charlie Van Horne had made a contribution to Parliament worthy of the finest traditions of representation in the House of Commons. He counted him an exceptionally good friend and appealed to the audience by saying, 'I want you to send Charlie Van Horne back to the House of Commons. This party wants him.'

Van Horne had proclaimed in his broadcast that Canada deserved something better than the mediocrity of the Diefenbaker government. We decided to have a little fun at Diefenbaker's expense. Pearson concluded his speech in the debate on the Speech from the Throne with a reference to Van Horne's revolt. Following Pearson's lead, I dealt with Van Horne in my speech. I reminded the House that it was usual for the prime minister to choose recently elected members to move and second the address in reply to the governor general's speech. I expressed surprise that the numerous new members had been passed over and the honour given to members elected more than once. But I was not surprised he had not chosen Van Horne for the honour. Van Horne, I observed, had been assigned a new seat on the front bench at the far end of the chamber. He had not yet been purged, but he was so near the door 'that one more little push would put him out.' The prime minister, I assumed, had, in Gilbert's words, 'a little list' of those who 'never would be missed.' I was sure 'Charlie's name heads all the rest.'

Diefenbaker was doubtless vastly relieved when Van Horne resigned from the House in January 1961. Among his 207 followers, there were several who were an embarrassment to the government, but none was so irritating as Diefenbaker's friend 'Charlie.' But the government soon had more than a single disgruntled member to worry about in 1959.

After the cancellation of the Arrow contract, the position of the government continued to deteriorate. Unemployment was greater and, for many, more prolonged than in 1958. The Opposition made more effective use of the economic situation in attacking the government. We rang the changes on Diefenbaker's promise that so long as he was prime minister no one would suffer from unemployment. In his opening speech, Pearson gave an impressive catalogue of the government's sins of commission and more frequent sins of omission. His motion of non-confidence stressed the failure of the government to deal with mounting unemployment.

The RCMP in Newfoundland

While I had little part in the Arrow affair, I had a major share in two controversies in 1959 of direct concern to Newfoundland. The first arose out of a strike by loggers who cut pulpwood for the paper mill at Grand Falls in central Newfoundland. From the early days of paper mills in the province, both loggers and millworkers belonged to trade unions which bargained collectively. There had been a long history of labour peace in the industry. Wages in Newfoundland were higher than the average wages in the Maritime provinces or Quebec, where the loggers were largely unorganized. In 1956, the International Woodworkers of America sent organizers from British Columbia into Newfoundland to wean the loggers away from existing unions.

The IWA recruited a majority of the loggers and secured legal recognition as the exclusive bargaining agent. The new union failed to negotiate a wage contract and the Anglo-Newfoundland Development Company refused to accept the majority report of a conciliation board. A strike was called in the winter of 1958–59. The strike was quite legal.

But, shortly after the strike began, a number of acts of violence were committed by supporters of the IWA. Several independent contractors who were also engaged in logging and who had no part in the dispute were prevented by force from trucking their logs to the mill. IWA supporters also raided some of the logging camps and expelled loggers who were not willing to strike. At least one raid made during the night in cold weather forced loggers from the camp to walk without winter clothing a considerable distance to the nearest settlement. Leaders of the IWA also directed loggers to lock themselves in the camps and stay there, using property and provisions belonging to the company.

For the first time, violence and lawlessness in labour disputes had been introduced into Newfoundland. It was because of this violence and lawlessness that the premier of the province decided to intervene. Smallwood made a province-wide radio broadcast, in which he denounced the illegal acts of the IWA and the violence which had followed. He declared the IWA was useless to the loggers. He invited them to repudiate the IWA and to join a new union which he himself offered to assist them in organizing. He appealed to the loggers to let him know whether they wished to follow his advice and whether they wanted his help in forming a new union. The response to this broadcast was extraordinary. From all sections of the province, there was a tremendous expression of approval.

On the mainland, labour leaders and their sympathizers denounced Smallwood's action. The Canadian Labour Congress joined in this outcry. Charges began to appear, especially in the *Toronto Star* that the RCMP, under their contract to serve as the provincial police, were engaged in strike-breaking.

The question of strike-breaking came up in Parliament on 10 February 1959, when Hazen Argue, the House leader of the CCF, asked Davie Fulton, the minister of justice, about disturbing reports that the RCMP had marched 125 strikers ten miles in sub-zero temperatures and held them incommunicado for thirty-six hours. Argue asked for an assurance that the police were not being used for 'what are commonly called strike-breaking activities.' Fulton replied that he did not have a complete report, but that the police were performing their responsibilities for local law enforcement under contract with the government of Newfoundland and under the direction of the attorney general of the province.

While there were only a few more questions in Parliament, developments outside Parliament almost caused a split in the Liberal Opposition. Pearson had received several demands that he repudiate Smallwood. One or two of his advisers were urging him to speak out. Pearson was also influenced by a letter from Claude Jodoin, the president of the Canadian Labour Congress, enclosing a statement to the press made on behalf of the congress. Jodoin said the congress would like Pearson's 'clear assurance that the views expressed by such a prominent member of the Liberal Party as Mr. Smallwood are not the official views of the Party.' Pearson replied that 'the policy in labour matters of the national Liberal Party – for which I speak – is clear and unchanged. It is firmly based on, and will continue to be based, on free collective bargaining.' He added that the Liberal party would oppose any effort to weaken the right of a union certified for the purpose to bargain collectively within the law.

In a letter to Smallwood, Pearson enclosed the exchange of correspondence with Jodoin. The letter began: 'My dear Joe.' Pearson said he would have preferred not to have become involved in any way in these difficulties with the IWA, difficulties which were matters for 'provincial handling.' He explained that pressure on him as the leader of the national Liberal party was great and increasing and he felt he had to say something at once. He considered it necessary, in answering Jodoin's letter, to state established Liberal policy in the matter of collective bargaining in a purely factual way. He had thought, he said, of putting in an additional sentence in the letter to Jodoin, stating that his dispute was a provincial matter exclusively and that, as national leader, he was not concerned with it, but felt that would have been interpreted in many quarters as evasion. Pearson added that, throughout, he had been in close touch with the Newfoundland Liberal members, and especially with me, and we had kept him fully informed of the details and difficulties of the situation in Newfoundland.

Pearson sent a copy of these letters to the Newfoundland Liberal members. I cannot recall whether I saw the letters he wrote to Jodoin and to Smallwood before or after he sent them, but I do remember well one conversation we had in which I said I would like to tell him what I would do if I were leader of the national Liberal Party. He interrupted to say that, in such a case, I would support the Newfoundland government. I replied that I would do nothing of the kind. A national leader, I felt, had no mandate to interfere in action being taken by a provincial government within its own exclusive jurisdiction. As a member for a Newfoundland constituency, I considered I had the right to support the Newfoundland government and, if necessary, would do so. I did not question the right of individual Liberal members to take exception to Smallwood's conduct, though I hoped none of them would condemn it. But I did not believe a national party could survive if the national leader condemned a provincial Liberal government for action which was entirely within its constitutional jurisdiction. As for myself, I told Pearson I hoped to avoid saying anything at all, and, if silence was not possible, to express myself moderately to avoid weakening the unity of the Liberal Opposition.

I hoped my advice would restrain Pearson from any public criticism of Smallwood. Pearson would, I knew, continue to be under strong pressure, particularly in response to the next step Smallwood was going to take. Smallwood had told me that he proposed to introduce legislation in the House of Assembly to decertify the local unions of the IWA in Newfoundland. One of the IWA locals was engaged in a legal strike against the Anglo-Newfoundland Development Company of Grand Falls; the other was provoking illegal strikes against private contractors who were cutting wood for Bowaters, the paper mill at Corner Brook. The legislation decertified both locals of the IWA and it was denounced by the IWA and its supporters and sympathizers inside, and especially outside, Newfoundland. Smallwood was charged with outlawing or suppressing the union. This description was not legally correct.

Decertification does not destroy or even 'outlaw' a union. What it does is to remove the exclusive right of the union to bargain collectively. The exclusive right to bargain collectively is a monopoly given to a union to bargain with the employer for all the employees, whether they are members of the union or not. The IWA local had been certified as the exclusive bargaining agent once it had recruited a majority of the loggers for the Grand Falls mill. Certification, of course, gave the union no licence to break the law or to take the law into its own hands. The illegal acts of violence were the justification offered in the legislature for the bill to decertify the locals of the IWA. The new law did not end the legal existence of the unions. In fact, both locals continued to maintain pickets long after the IWA was decertified. The legislation also opened the way for another union to achieve certification if it could recruit a majority of the loggers.

Decertification was not an arbitrary act by the premier or the government of Newfoundland. It was done by an act of the legislature of Newfoundland which the members of the Opposition as well as the supporters of the government approved without a single dissenting vote. And it had the overwhelming backing of public opinion throughout the province.

At the same time, the House of Assembly passed another bill Smallwood had not told me about in advance. This bill amended the provincial Labour Relations Act to permit the Newfoundland cabinet by order-in-council to dissolve any trade union in the province which was the local or branch of a union outside the province in which, in the opinion of the cabinet, a substantial number of the superior officers or agents had been convicted of any heinous crime, such as trafficking in narcotics, manslaughter, extortion, embezzlement, or perjury. Fortunately, no attempt was made to invoke this arbitrary power given to the cabinet and the law remained a dead letter. It was, however, very objectionable in principle and I would never have been able to defend it. Luckily I never had to.

The loggers strike was raised again in Parliament on 10 March 1959. In a question to Fulton, Argue asserted that the police had escorted strike-breakers through a picket line. The Speaker at first objected to the question, on the ground that, in reply to a similar question earlier in the session, the minister of justice had said the policing was a matter within provincial jurisdiction. Fulton interrupted to say the question referred to a different incident and offered to reply. He said a report had been made to him that a road-block had been placed on a public road and that the RCMP, acting under the terms of the contract with the provincial government, had sent a patrol to ensure that the obstruction was removed. He added that the RCMP had not escorted anyone through picket lines, as had been alleged. The next day, Fulton made a lengthy and detailed statement regarding the conduct of the RCMP in which he reported on an incident at Badger where a policeman who belonged to the Newfoundland Constabulary, not the RCMP, had been seriously injured. Fulton said there was no foundation for the charge that the police had been used as strike-breakers, and that he was satisfied the police had acted within the limits of their duty to enforce the criminal law.

Pearson accepted Fulton's statement and expressed satisfaction that the RCMP had not been concerned in any way, shape, or form, with strike-breaking activities. Pearson's reference to the absence of strike-breaking, though perfectly proper, made me vaguely uneasy, because I knew Pearson was under increasing pressure to dissociate himself from the action taken by the government of Newfoundland.

Two days later, there was a rumour circulating in Ottawa that the government of Newfoundland had asked for reinforcements for the RCMP in the province and that the minister of justice had refused to send them. When the House met I asked Fulton whether he had stopped the reinforcements requested. He evaded a direct answer by saying that the authority of the attorney general of Canada was required before reinforcements were sent and that authority had not yet been given. Several exchanges followed, including a question as to whether Fulton had received any communication from the attorney general of Newfoundland. Fulton replied he had been in communication with the attorney general the previous night. I then asked the prime minister if he had received any communication from the premier of the province. Diefenbaker answered that 'the close relationship between the Government of Newfoundland and the honourable gentleman would no doubt provide an answer to his question.' It was widely rumoured that the cabinet was divided over the request for reinforcements. The question would have to be resolved over the weekend.

On Monday, 16 March Diefenbaker informed the House that the government had replied to two telegrams from the premier of Newfoundland. One telegram asked the prime minister to support the request of the attorney general that fifty additional constables of the RCMP be sent to Newfoundland; the other asked the federal government to appoint a judicial inquiry into the labour situation in the province.

Diefenbaker stated that, while the government had no intention of infringing on matters under provincial jurisdiction, he felt impelled to say that 'the premier of Newfoundland has greatly aggravated the present situation in that province by intervening in a labour dispute in a way which apparently goes beyond the usual role of government.' He added that 'the result, as might have been anticipated, has been a violent reaction on the part of the workers concerned.' He announced that 'under the circumstances we have concluded that it would be provocative and likely to cause further outbreaks of violence to authorize the sending of further members of the RCMP at this time.' He stated that the RCMP had performed its duty with fairness and efficiency. He promised that, if they were subject to or encountered intimidation or threats by law-breakers, the government would reconsider its decision.

Diefenbaker saw no necessity of setting up a judicial inquiry, as requested by Smallwood, and suggested instead that the danger of disorder and violence would be reduced if all concerned would agree to a cooling-off period of, say, two weeks.

Fulton followed Diefenbaker with the announcement that he had received and accepted the resignation of the commissioner of the RCMP. He informed the House that, pending the arrival of the anticipated reinforcements of the RCMP twenty-five members of the Newfoundland Constabulary, a provincial force which normally policed St John's, had been sent to central Newfoundland. Fulton argued that mere availability of potential reinforcements was not the only factor he, as minister of justice, had to consider in deciding whether the request should be met. He said that he had also to consider the over-all responsibilities of the RCMP and the necessity 'to maintain its full integrity and its ability to discharge that duty on a national basis.' His lengthy and complicated justification for refusing the fifty constables requested was casuistical and unconvincing. Nicholson had resigned because he considered the refusal a clear breach of the contract to have the RCMP police the province.

In his comment which followed immediately, Pearson regretted the resignation of the commissioner and deplored the refusal of the government to establish the commission of inquiry Smallwood had requested. Pearson said Fulton had given his own interpretation to a paragraph in the contract that, on the face of it, seemed very clear. Pearson implied there was an obligation to send the reinforcements, but he did not categorically condemn the decision of the government not to send the additional police requested.

He noted that strong differences of opinion had developed about measures taken by the government and legislature of Newfoundland and said he wished to repeat a statement he had already made 'that the policy of the national Liberal Party in labour matters had been and will continue to be firmly based on the right of free collective bargaining through unions chosen by the workers themselves.' On the basis of information he had received, he would be unable, as leader of his party, to agree with certain of the procedures in Newfoundland or with specific provisions of the provincial legislation. He declined to yield to pressure to be more definite. He repeated his objection to the refusal of the federal government to appoint the judicial inquiry requested by the premier of Newfoundland.

How Newfoundland
Liberal MPs reacted
to Pearson

From the beginning of the controversy over the loggers' strike, the five Liberal members from Newfoundland had consulted regularly about what position we should take and, until 16 March we had all refrained from making any public statements. When we met again after Pearson had spoken, we were all unhappy about his failure to condemn outright the refusal to send reinforcements and, even more, about his reference, which seemed to us gratuitous, to the measures taken by the government and legislature of Newfoundland.

In order to avoid misunderstanding in Newfoundland of our position, we drafted a statement for the press which set out our support of the government of Newfoundland. The statement read:

The Newfoundland Liberal Members of the House of Commons at Ottawa have from the outset supported the emergency action of the Premier, the Government and the House of Assembly of Newfoundland in their determination to uphold law and order and to preserve the continued operation of the pulp and paper industry which provides employment and a livelihood for one third of the people of Newfoundland.

The present situation, being a provincial matter, could not, under the rules of the House of Commons, be debated at an earlier date. However now that it has been brought up in the Parliament of Canada by the Government, we wish to remove any doubt, both in Newfoundland and Ottawa, as to our support of the Premier's stand.

We were deeply shocked by the unwarranted and inexcusable failure of the Government of Canada to honour its pledge to provide RCMP reinforcements to Newfoundland during this emergency and we resent, as all Newfoundlanders will resent, the shocking and provocative attack by the Prime Minister of Canada on the action of the Premier of Newfoundland in seeking to maintain law and order in the province, while at the same time refusing to set up the public inquiry that Mr. Smallwood requested so that all the facts might be obtained and placed before the people of Canada.

In deciding to issue this public statement all five of us were conscious that it might result in a split in the Liberal Opposition. We saw Pearson and showed him our statement before making it public. He asked whether it might result in a split in the party. I replied that it might, but that would depend on the attitude of others. The criticism in our statement had been directed solely against the government. Pearson asked us to say nothing the following day about a possible split and we agreed not to.

The statement was issued at eight o'clock that evening. Shortly afterwards I was invited to go on a television broadcast called 'Press Conference' the next evening (17 March). I agreed at once. I woke up at 4 a.m. that Tuesday morning and made a note of every embarrassing question I would ask if I was a member of the panel, and decided on how I would reply to all but one of them. That question I hoped to avoid. When I told Pearson about the proposed broadcast, he asked me to reconsider and excuse myself. I said, if I did that, I would be considered a coward in Newfoundland: he would have to hope I would say nothing to create any further difficulty.

The *Ottawa Citizen* that afternoon announced sensationally that the Newfoundland Liberal MPs had formally repudiated Pearson in our statement which the paper reproduced in full. It reported that Pearson had known about the statement before it was issued and said that the 'difference of opinion' was 'regrettable' but that it was nothing tragic.

In the broadcast the first question was how wide the split was with Pearson. I said there was no split at all. Mr Pearson had been quoted in the *Citizen* as saying there was a difference of opinion about the procedure and the legislation in Newfoundland. I felt that was almost an exaggeration. Mr Pearson had only said there were some things he couldn't approve. Those of us from Newfoundland felt we must make it very clear that we were supporting the government of Newfoundland in taking action in what we believe to be an emergency.

When asked why we waited so long, I replied we felt the situation was a matter entirely for the provincial government and the provincial legislature. The Newfoundland members did not want to take part in a controversy on the mainland.

Asked whether our statement was a repudiation of Mr Pearson and his views, I pointed out there was not one word in our statement that suggests any thought of repudiation. All five members from Newfoundland were deeply appreciative of the statement Mr Pearson made the previous day, of the sympathy he showed for Newfoundland, the understanding he showed for Newfoundland, which was in such marked contrast to the attitude of the prime minister and of the spokesman for the CCF.

Asked if there were no real differences of opinion between Mr Pearson and the five Newfoundland members, I replied that I did not think the matter was of any concern to the federal Liberal party. I was not elected, and Mr Pearson was not elected, and neither was any other member of the House of Commons elected, to look after the provincial affairs of Newfoundland. We were elected to the Parliament of Canada to look after federal matters.

Two very important questions had come into the federal arena the previous day. One was the question of sending reinforcements to the police in Newfoundland. On that, our whole party was completely united in favour of carrying out the solemn obligation of Canada. And on the question of having an inquiry to bring out the facts, and all the facts, we were all completely united.

One of the panelists asserted that Pearson had said he did not agree with part of the Newfoundland legislation and that we had differed with him and said we agreed with the legislation. I said I did not like the legislation and I was sure Mr Smallwood did not like it. There would not have been such legislation if almost everyone in Newfoundland had not believed there was an emergency affecting the economy of the province. The legislation which decertified two locals of the IWA was not legally necessary. I had with me a copy of the Newfoundland Labour Relations Act and read the section which gave the provincial cabinet power to exclude an employer or employee or any class of employers or employees from any of its provisions.

Asked why there had been new legislation, I said Mr Smallwood had discussed this very question with me. They could have decertified the locals by order-in-council under the existing law, but he felt so important a departure from the usual practice should be brought before the representatives of the people in the legislature so that every elected member could express his opinion. Surely it was better to have so important a decision made by the legislature than by the cabinet?

When asked what the emergency was, I replied that one third of the people of Newfoundland derived their living from the pulp and paper industry. The industry's costs were high and its existence should not be jeopardized. The level of wages of the loggers was higher than it was anywhere else in Canada east of Ontario, substantially higher. That has been stated over and over again and never contradicted.

In a conversation which I did not think was private, about this very matter, on the night of the press gallery dinner, I had asked Stanley Knowles why it was that the IWA chose to go right from British Columbia to Newfoundland, which had the highest wages in the east and which was completely unionized, instead of to Quebec or the Maritimes where the wages were lower. Knowles had replied that was a hard question to answer.

Asked whether I would support legislation to decertify a union, I replied I would not support legislation that interfered with the normal operation of free collective bargaining unless there was a clear emergency. The Liberal Opposition had supported such legislation, which was introduced by the

Diefenbaker government the previous summer, to restore the ferry service to Vancouver Island, because we felt, when there was no other steamship ferry service there, it was essential to the life of the island. I didn't feel I could refuse to support it though I didn't like it.

I recalled that Mr Pearson was a member of the St Laurent government at the time that the legislation was passed in 1950 to send the railway employees back to work. That was something it was very disagreeable for him to do, but there had come a point when the public interest had to be placed first and that point, we members from Newfoundland believed, was reached over the loggers' strike.

In reply to the question as to whether Smallwood was trying to protect the mills, I said he was protecting the livelihood of one third of the people of the province. In the mill at Grand Falls, all four unions of mill workers, representing many more men that the loggers who were involved in the strike, all of them belonging to international unions, all of them affiliated with CLC, all supported Mr Smallwood.

When charged with approving of Smallwood's legislation, I replied: 'No, I support the action of the government.' The strike had gone on for 43 days before Mr. Smallwood had said a single word about it, and during those 43 days many Newfoundlanders were interfered with by the members of this union when they were seeking to go about their lawful business along the roads of the province.

After some discussion about picketing and violence, I was asked if I did not think that the companies had something to do with the action taken by Smallwood. My response was that 'I was convinced that Mr. Smallwood took this action because he sincerely believed, as I believe, that the industry itself was in jeopardy, that there was a very grave danger of one or both of these mills being closed, and that if a mill closed, it might be a very long time before it reopened.'

Asked if I did not think the IWA was adhering to the law, I replied: 'No. They were breaking the law. They were flagrantly breaking the law. Members of the IWA were assaulting my own constituents.'

One of the panelists then said that the law said they could picket, they could organize, without the support of all the loggers. I responded that the law did not say that they could go into a lumber camp in the middle of the night and turn people out into the snow without being warmly clad, when it was twenty below zero. I fully supported the view that trade unions, like everybody else, should have to obey the ordinary fundamental law of the country.

It was next suggested that the police had used weapons and clubs against defenceless workers who were not armed. I said I believed those stories to be entirely untrue. I was convinced that the police had acted in a perfectly proper manner, and that, on no occasion, did the police use any force until force had been used by others.

When the chairman of the panel asserted that Smallwood had legislated a union out of existence I objected that this statement was not correct, that the IWA still had a legal existence in Newfoundland, that it had headquarters there, and that the headquarters had been protected by the police. People still belonged to this union.

The chairman of the panel then said; 'But it cannot bargain with the two paper companies.' I pointed out that the union never had the right to bargain with one of the companies. In the case of the other company, the union was given a privilege, a monopoly, to bargain for all the workers. That was what certification meant. Certification was not a right – it was a privilege. When the union abused that privilege, the privilege had been taken away by the Legislature.

Asked whether the commissioner of the RCMP had been right to resign, I said there was no question about that in my mind. I thought the government had acted very improperly and that I would hate to be, as Fulton had become, the first minister of the Crown in Canada to break a contract signed by the government.

After some exchanges about whether a contract had really been broken, I said I was convinced it had been broken, and I explained why. The administration of justice, under section 92 of the British North America Act, was the exclusive responsibility of the province. In Quebec and Ontario, where they have provincial police, there could have been no interference by Mr Fulton or Mr Diefenbaker with the administration of justice. But they had presumed to interfere with the administration of justice in Newfoundland by repudiating the contract. Refusing the police reinforcements denied to the province what it had the right to have under a contract with Canada. Under the contract the RCMP was to provide the police necessary to enable the province to discharge its constitutional duty to administer justice.

I was reminded that Fulton had argued that the decision whether to send reinforcements included the right of the minister of justice to decide whether the reinforcements were refused to protect the integrity of the force. I asked: what does that argument mean? If you analyse that argument, it means that he is saying that, in Newfoundland, or Manitoba, or British Columbia, he can decide what police are necessary to administer justice in the province, though he can't do it in Quebec or Ontario. And surely that's not what our constitution means.

That broadcast was the greatest test I had faced in my public life. I had persisted, despite the request of our party leader that I call it off. If the effect had been bad, it would almost inevitably resulted in an open split in the Liberal Opposition in Parliament.

I was vastly relieved when the broadcast ended. I felt it had gone well and believed it would prevent a split. I told the panelists, as soon as the lights went off, that they had not asked me the one question which would have embarrassed me. The chairman said he had started to put the question and I had interrupted and diverted attention to another subject. The question I had feared was my attitude to the second bill passed by the Newfoundland legislature, which would have permitted the cabinet to outlaw any local in Newfoundland of an international union whose leadership was involved in criminal or scandalous activity outside the province. I could not have defended such arbitrary power and I would not have tried. Fortunately I had avoided that embarrassment.

The reaction to the broadcast was greater than I had dared to hope for. I never received so much 'fan mail' for any other broadcast in my life. Mr St Laurent telephoned me from Quebec to congratulate me, but – what was even more important – Pearson was completely satisfied. At the Liberal caucus next day I was warmly received and we went on unitedly to attack the government for its failure to send police reinforcements.

I had only one regret about my broadcast, and that was the reference to my conversation with Stanley Knowles. Knowles had not been elected to the Parliament of 1958 and he spent the four years absence as an official of the Canadian Labour Congress. On 18 March H.W. Herridge of the CCF stated in Parliament that he had spoken to Knowles who had contradicted me and said it was a private conversation. Herridge felt my reference to it was unethical and expressed regret that I was not in the House that day to defend myself.

The next day (19 March), on a question of privilege, I said the word I should have used was 'confidential' not 'private,' because the conversation was certainly private in the sense that it was not public debate or discussion. But I did not regard it as confidential and I would still like to know why the IWA had jumped all the way from British Columbia to Newfoundland and ignored several provinces where the loggers did not have unions and were not as well paid.

The member of the Newfoundland Constabulary who had been injured at Badger died a few days after the night of the broadcast and the violence stopped quickly, but the public outrage increased.

At the time I believed that Fulton intended to send the RCMP reinforcements and that he had yielded to pressure from Diefenbaker. Donald Fleming in his memoirs confirms this. He says he gave Fulton his full support as did a committee of the cabinet appointed to consider the matter, but that, in face of Diefenbaker's intransigence, the cabinet decided the reinforcements should not be sent. Fleming adds that, after the meeting, Fulton asked him to join in telling the prime minister they would resign if the reinforcements were not dispatched at once. Fleming was not willing to go that far.

I thought, at the time, that Fulton should have submitted his resignation. I believed, if he had, Diefenbaker would have caved in. Whether Fulton would have got his way or had his resignation accepted, it was and still is my opinion that his chances of succeeding Diefenbaker as party leader and perhaps as prime minister would have been greatly strengthened. Like Mackenzie King, I had a good opinion of Fulton, and was sorry he had not stuck to his guns.

Newfoundland and term 29

The second controversy relating to Newfoundland overlapped the RCMP crisis, and involved the interpretation made by Diefenbaker of term 29 of the Terms of Union of Newfoundland with Canada. To understand why this difference reached a crisis in 1959, a brief explanation of the background is required.

It had not been possible during the negotiation of the Terms of Union in 1948 to settle finally the amount of the annual subsidy from the federal to the provincial government to be included in the Terms of Union, which became part of the Canadian Constitution. Accordingly, annual transitional grants on a diminishing scale until 31 March 1961 were agreed on. Provision was made, in term 29, for the appointment of a royal commission within eight years of the union 'to recommend the form and scale of additional financial assistance, if any, that may be required by the Government of the Province of Newfoundland to enable it to continue public services at levels and standards reached subsequent to the date of Union without resorting to taxation more burdensome, having regard to capacity to pay, than that obtaining generally in the region comprising the Maritime Provinces of Nova Scotia, New Brunswick and Prince Edward Island.'

The St Laurent government had appointed this royal commission under the chairmanship of Chief Justice McNair, a former premier of New Brunswick, on 21 February 1957. The commission naturally aroused great expectations in Newfoundland. Though he was leader of the opposition at the time, Diefenbaker had apparently paid no attention to the appointment of the McNair commission. When he visited Newfoundland two months later, during the 1957 election campaign, Diefenbaker got off on the wrong foot about term 29 and he was never to get back on the right foot. The day he arrived in St John's, he was interviewed on television by Don Jamieson, the leading broadcaster in Newfoundland. Jamieson naturally asked Diefenbaker about the royal commission on term 29. Apparently Diefenbaker failed to realize, or had forgotten, the connection of the commission with the Terms of Union – he dismissed Jamieson's question by saying there were far too many royal commissions. I was watching the broadcast. I shall never forget the expression on Jamieson's face. It was the only time I ever saw him completely at a loss for words.

Diefenbaker, after he became prime minister, called a conference with the provincial premiers for November 1957. The only concrete proposal his government made at the conference was to provide additional grants to the three Maritime provinces. Newfoundland was to be excluded. The excuse for the exclusion of Newfoundland was that that province would be taken care of by the recommendations of the McNair commission on term 29.

The McNair commission was not concerned with the fiscal arrangements then in force; its sole purpose was to deal with a problem which had not been settled when the Terms of Union were negotiated. Premier Smallwood was furious. Lamontagne and I helped him to prepare a cast-iron case for Newfoundland to share in any additional fiscal grants to the Atlantic provinces. Diefenbaker backed down and agreed to include Newfoundland. The special grants did get Diefenbaker some support in the 1958 election in the three Maritime provinces, but his lack of understanding of the purpose of term 29 and his attempt to exclude Newfoundland from the special grants incurred Smallwood's hostility, which was mixed with a generous measure of contempt.

The McNair commission presented its report on 1 May 1958. It recommended that the annual payments of the interim grants to Newfoundland for the period 1 April 1957 to 31 March 1961 be increased to eight million dollars and that there should be an annual grant of eight millions thereafter. When the report was published, Smallwood attacked the award as totally inadequate and made uncomplimentary personal references to the commissioners.

The foundation for the confrontation in 1959 had been laid in 1958. On 15 August Pearson asked Diefenbaker what the government intended to do about implementing the recommendation of the McNair commission. Diefenbaker replied that, in view of Smallwood's criticism, the federal government would have to give the fullest consideration to the matter. When I asked whether that meant no action at the 1958 session, Diefenbaker replied that the lack of support in Newfoundland for McNair's recommendation made the fullest consideration by the government necessary.

On learning of the exchange in Parliament Premier Smallwood introduced a resolution in the Newfoundland House of Assembly which was seconded by the leader of the Conservative opposition and adopted unanimously. The resolution was in the form of a message to Diefenbaker. The message congratulated him on promising a study of the McNair award which was regarded in Newfoundland as inadequate. The resolution asked the federal government, meanwhile, as an interim measure, to pay Newfoundland the amount recommended by the commission. Smallwood told me in advance about the resolution of the legislature. He stressed the urgent need of the province for additional revenue. I suggested to Pearson that the Opposition should support the Newfoundland request. Pearson agreed that I should see Diefenbaker and tell him that, if the government would introduce a measure to meet the request made unanimously and urgently by the legislature of the province, the Liberal Opposition would support it and commend the government for meeting the need of the province.

My visit to Diefenbaker on this mission was one of only two occasions I was ever in his office. He told me he had read the report of the McNair commission, but could not make head or tail of it, and did not see how the government could act immediately. He then kept me nearly half an hour talking about other things. When I got up to leave I repeated my message and added that, if the government did not act, I intended to speak at length in support of Newfoundland's request in the House that day. Diefenbaker repeated his refusal. My speech that day laid the foundation for the confrontation on term 29 which the government had to face in the 1959 session of Parliament.

The Opposition did not stop there. I returned to the attack the next day and was supported by three of the Newfoundland members. We were backed up strongly by Pearson. The refusal of Diefenbaker to meet the reasonable provincial request was resented in Newfoundland in 1958, but the feeling aroused was not comparable to the outburst in 1959.

The question of the McNair award was raised in Parliament in 1959 only a few days after the crisis over the RCMP reinforcements. On 23 March Pearson asked the prime minister whether the recommendation of the McNair commission would be accepted before the tenth anniversary of the Union with Newfoundland on 31 March. Diefenbaker replied that an announcement could be expected before that date.

The announcement came on 25 March. Diefenbaker said legislation would be introduced to provide for the payments recommended by the McNair commission up to 31 March 1962, and that they would be 'in final and irrevocable settlement of the provisions of article 29 and the contractual obligations of the union consummated in 1949.' I could scarcely believe my ears. I turned to Pearson at once and handed him a note on which I had scribbled the words 'final and irrevocable settlement." In his comment, Pearson welcomed the statement that payments were to be in the amounts recommended by the McNair commission. He regretted the government had not acted sooner. Pearson hoped he was not misinterpreting Diefenbaker's statement that no further obligation would exist after 31 March 1962. He said such an assumption was quite unwarranted. Pearson's immediate reaction created an issue over Newfoundland between the government and the Liberal Opposition which was to last as long as Diefenbaker was prime minister.

To make doubly sure there was no misunderstanding, I asked Diefenbaker later that day whether what he proposed was regarded by the government as a 'complete discharge of the obligation under section 29 of the Terms of Union' by legislation which would expire on 31 March 1962. Diefenbaker replied: 'That is so.' He added that any consideration in 1962 would be in the context of the larger situation of the nation as a whole. I asked, as a supplementary: 'Does the Prime Minister realize that every person in Newfoundland will regard this as another breach of a solemn contract?' Diefenbaker replied that he did not think I was speaking for all the people. I retorted: 'You will see.' And he did!

Because Parliament then adjourned for Easter, there was no immediate reflection in Ottawa of the uproar in Newfoundland over Diefenbaker's repudiation of term 29. There the disapproval was universal. The House of Assembly unanimously condemned the federal government's decision, and a majority of the members of the small Conservative opposition left the party and formed a new group called the United Newfoundland Party. Diefenbaker's minister from Newfoundland was embarrassed in St John's and the other Tory MP, James McGrath, was known to be considering withdrawing his support from the Diefenbaker government.

When the session resumed on 6 April I raised a question of privilege about a statement in the St John's *Daily News* of 26 March attributed to the minister from Newfoundland on his arrival in St John's for Easter. Browne was quoted as saying: 'There are 22 other members in the Cabinet of Canada and I cannot expect to push my opinions down their throats.' My point of privilege was that, in view of the collective responsibility of the cabinet, the House was entitled to know whether the minister had concurred in the cabinet decision about term 29. Browne made no reply.

The next day I asked Browne to comment on a statement of his reported in the St John's *Daily News* on 31 March that he was going to Ottawa 'to tell the Prime Minister of the strong feelings here about his Term 29 decision.'

I also asked Browne to report to the House how the prime minister had responded. The Speaker ruled my question out of order. I next asked, whether since his return from Newfoundland, Browne had made any representations to the prime minister on the subject. Diefenbaker objected to this question, which was also ruled out of order. I then put a third question as to whether the reason the minister had left Newfoundland so precipitately was that he did not wish to defend his leader. Of course, there was no reply, but my questions had served their purpose.

During the rest of the 1959 session, we in the Liberal Opposition took every available opportunity to recall the way the Diefenbaker government had treated Newfoundland. In a speech on the budget on 15 April I said the ultimate in bad faith had been seen in Parliament recently, when the prime minister had taken it upon himself 'to alter or seek to alter the terms of the agreement upon which two nations were joined together into one nation.' I recalled telling the House just before the Easter adjournment that every Newfoundlander would regard this as a betrayal. The prime minister had replied that I could not speak for all Newfoundlanders. Having been in Newfoundland during the recess, I could now speak for 'the Newfoundlanders, all but one of them.' I concluded my speech by saying there was one other question about which not only the people of Newfoundland but the people of all Canada were concerned. When, on that Black Monday, Diefenbaker 'took the side of the law-breakers against those who were maintaining law and order, he did more to destroy confidence in his government than by any other act he has done or is likely to do, and it seems to me that of all the acts of bad faith which will be held against this government that will, for all time, be the worst.'

Smallwood had not been too pleased about Pearson's public disagreement with some of the procedures and legislation regarding the loggers' strike, but he was delighted with Pearson's forthright attitude over term 29. I took advantage of this enthusiasm to get Smallwood to agree to introduce an amendment to the provincial Labour Relations Act. I explained that the law giving power to the cabinet to dissolve unions by order-in-council was similar to Duplessis's notorious padlock law and that neither Pearson nor I could possibly defend it. The amendment I suggested substituted a provision which would require the attorney-general of the province to satisfy the Supreme Court of the province that the union locals to be dissolved were affiliated with unions headed by convicted criminals.

Pearson was pleased by this initiative and Smallwood duly introduced the bill into the House of Assembly. However, when the leader of the opposition in the legislature objected to the change, Smallwood agreed not to proceed with it. In a message on 5 April he regretted any embarrassment he might have caused Pearson by failing to go ahead with the amendment. He explained that, when the leader of the opposition objected, he felt he should not destroy the unanimity which had existed in the House of Assembly. He hoped to review the whole act later and, meanwhile, gave the assurance that, while he was premier, if any objection was taken, the government of the province would put no obstacle in the way of officers of the union bringing the matter before the law courts for adjudication.

If the loggers' strike and the RCMP reinforcements ceased to be an active parliamentary issue, the same was not true of term 29. We in the Opposition brought the question up at every available opportunity. On the tenth anniversary of the Union on 31 March 1959, I appealed to the government to reverse its position on term 29. On 2 May I moved a vote of want of confidence in the government in which I referred to the repudiation by the Tory government of term 29. W.J. Browne, the minister from Newfoundland, replied to me on 3 May claiming that the government had carried out the recommendations of the McNair commission. He said he resented my statement because the government had undertaken to review the financial relationship with the government of Newfoundland before 31 March 1962. Since my purpose in raising the question was to keep it in the public mind, particularly in Newfoundland, I was glad to have Browne on record in defence of Diefenbaker.

I took advantage of the report of a speech Donald Fleming had made in Newfoundland early in July to ask him, on 7 July whether it was correct that he had stated the government intended to restore the rights of the province under term 29. Fleming asserted that the government had respected the law. When I commented that, in other words, the minister did not undertake to restore the rights of Newfoundland, he became indignant and claimed there had been no repudiation. I was pleased to have the Tory attitude repeated.

The debate on the resolution stage of the legislation about term 29 began on 13 July. The grants would expire in March 1962, but Fleming gave an undertaking that the needs of Newfoundland would be reviewed before that date, at the same time as the equalization payments and Atlantic grants came up for review. Pearson replied immediately. He pointed out that term 29 was an integral part of the solemn agreement which brought about the union, that no time limit was set by term 29, and that no time limit was set on the payments recommended by the McNair commission. He admitted that it might be desirable from time to time to review the finances of Newfoundland as well as of the other provinces, but said that such a review should not reduce the obligation to pay at least the eight million dollars annually indefinitely into the future. When Diefenbaker interrupted to ask whether Pearson interpreted the recommendation 'as requiring the payment in perpetuity of the amount in question, $8 million.' Pearson replied that there was no other interpretation to the words 'thereafter, $8 million per annum.' He concluded by appealing to the government to accept the recommendations of the royal commission 'until both parties to the act of union agree to their change.'

Argue for the CCF took the same basic position as Pearson. Two Liberal members also spoke in the same sense. James McGrath, the only private member from Newfoundland on the Conservative side, made a long unconvincing speech in support of the government. Two other Liberal MPs, Tucker and Granger, spoke next. As no one else rose, I asked whether the minister from Newfoundland was not going to speak. Fleming asked: 'What about?' Browne did not rise. When the chairman said 'carried,' I said 'No' and added that, if the minister from Newfoundland was without voice, 'I as the one remaining Member from Newfoundland who had not yet spoken, will certainly not be without voice.' In my speech I gave a detailed account of the origins of term 29 to refute points made by Fleming. My speech concluded debate on the resolution stage. At a later stage of the debate, Fleming based the government's case mainly on St Laurent's comment in 1949 that Parliament would not be legally bound to accept the recommendation of the royal commission. Pearson agreed that there was no legal obligation, but said there was something more important than legality 'and that is the moral and constitutional responsibility of this government to take no action which would interfere with the implementation of Term 29 ... unless the changes made to Term 29 are made by agreement between the two parties to the contract.' He made a pledge that when 'the responsibility is ours again we shall remove this injustice. We shall correct this violation of a contract and we shall make sure once again that the act of union is honoured in all its parts and is carried out as it must be carried out in letter and in spirit.' And this undertaking was duly carried out by the Pearson government.

Diefenbaker followed Pearson with a long discursive speech which barely dealt with the bill, attacked Smallwood for his criticisms of the McNair commission and earlier criticisms, in 1957 of the St Laurent government. He expressed resentment at Pearson's charge of a breach of faith by the government.

In reply to Diefenbaker I said I could not enter into all the aspects of his 100 per cent diversion from the subject. When Diefenbaker had no answer to an argument, he changed the scene, shifted the scenery with great skill and produced effects which sometimes took people in until the third or fourth performance. The House was getting well past the third or fourth performance.

Diefenbaker, like Fleming, I said, had made a good deal of St Laurent's statement in 1949 that the government was not legally bound to accept the recommendations of the commission. St Laurent had also said both sides had felt the union was being entered into in a spirit of fairness, and that it was not necessary to make binding stipulations about what would happen to the report of the commission, because it was expected that men of honour would be dealing with the terms of union and that they would not be interpreted by police-court quibbling.

Term 29 to a Newfoundlander was almost the equivalent of the language rights in the constitution to a French Canadian. Diefenbaker interrupted to ask whether I remembered that St Laurent had said the language rights could be changed by a majority in Parliament. I said I remembered that very well, but also remembered what else he had said – that no man of honour would ever do it. We could not believe any government would fail to respect the Terms of Union with Newfoundland. Pearson interjected that no person of honour would do that.

No one could believe, I added, that any Canadian government would propose legislation to repudiate the terms of the British North America Act. Yet that was what was before the House that day. That was why every Newfoundlander, except one or two, resented bitterly the action being taken by the Diefenbaker government. I doubted if the government had ever understood the meaning of term 29. I recalled Diefenbaker's broadcast interview in Newfoundland in 1957 when he had been asked about the McNair commission and replied that there were too many royal commissions! Fleming interrupted to ask me to point to any words in the bill which took anything away from Newfoundland. I said there was no fulfilment of an obligation; there was a 'ratting' on the obligation. I added that was why Fleming had a very uneasy conscience about it.

The attitude of the CCF was even more damaging to the government. Their members had condemned the Newfoundland government, and Smallwood in particular, in almost violent language about the treatment of the IWA. When they attacked the Diefenbaker government so soon afterwards over term 29 in even more violent terms, the attack was almost sensationally effective.

Frank Howard spoke first for the CCF. He reminded the House of his own dislike and distaste for the premier of Newfoundland, but said he did not believe in retaliation, but in proceeding on a basis of fairness and justice. He said, if the government had any sense of decency and honesty, they would withdraw the bill and submit one in keeping with the solemn pledge and promise made to the people of Newfoundland. He used strong language to condemn Fleming and Diefenbaker for declaring political warfare, with their legalistic terms and their twisty, forked-tongue interpretation of words, in order to justify the awkward position they were in. He believed it was 'a betrayal of trust bordering very closely on treason.' He concluded that the CCF believed political and economic justice should be provided for the people of Newfoundland, 'not political tom-foolery and backstabbing,' and on that basis the CCF intended to oppose the bill.

Charlie Granger made an impressive speech. He concluded: 'In Term 29, the nation of Canada and the people of Newfoundland pledged their mutual faith in each other and left it for other people of similar good will to complete the union which they had begun. It is a pity that this final part of the creation of a mighty modern nation which should be a bright moment in our history should be tarnished by bad faith. It is degrading to see those who are walking with history attempt to reduce a great moment in a nation's development to the lowest common denominator in dollars and cents.'

'But,' Granger added, 'the final act is not yet over. The time will come, and come it will, when those of us on this side of the House will be in a position to rectify the wrong being done today and justice will be done to the province of Newfoundland by a Liberal Government of the future.'

Donald Fleming closed the debate in a lengthy speech threshing the same old straw. His main point was that the bill specifically included an undertaking to review dominion-provincial fiscal and financial relations before 31 March 1962. In that review, he said, Newfoundland could put forward its position with all other provinces. Where there were any special circumstances, New-foundland could be assured they would be considered. Throughout the debate Fleming argued that this proposed review was a substitute for the fixed annual payment recommended by the commission. The debate dealt largely with the meaning of the phrase 'thereafter $8,000,000 per annum' which was the last line of the McNair report. First I, then Pearson, and finally Carter tried to get amendments accepted which would have required the payments of eight million dollars to continue annually until the federal and Newfoundland governments agreed on any variation. All our amendments were ruled out of order, and Fleming declined to have such an amendment moved by the government.

During the debate, Fleming asserted that, except for the subsidies provided in the British North America Act, no province had anything in black and white 'to define its financial relations with the Dominion' beyond 31 March 1962. I replied that this statement was not correct. I reminded him of the subsidies paid to the Maritime provinces since 1935. These subsidies were for the purpose of enabling those provinces to provide services comparable to those of other provinces, just as the award under term 29 was to do for Newfoundland. These subsidies had been recommended by a royal commission presided over by Sir Thomas White and were called the White subsidies. In 1942, they were provided for by statute for an indefinite period. Fleming was clearly embarrassed. He tried to refute my point by saying the White subsidies had been included as one item with the constitutional subsidies. With reference to the McNair award, I replied: 'just as this should be.'

Fleming had promised that a proposed review would look after New-foundland after 31 March 1962. Pearson replied that the eight million annual payment was intended to give Newfoundland security and that, instead of this security for the future, the people of Newfoundland were being told that 'big brother' would look after them.

In his memoirs, Donald Fleming disclosed that he had proposed that the eight million per annum should be paid until 1967, but the cabinet had decided to end the payments in 1962. He also notes that in presenting the legislation he avoided using Diefenbaker's phrase; 'final and irrevocable' settlement. He recalls that after the bitter debate in 1959 the storm passed and was succeeded by relative quiet for several years, 'but it left considerable local damage behind.' That was an understatement: Newfoundland was lost to the Tory party as long as Diefenbaker was its leader.

Federal-provincial relations

The confrontation over term 29 was only the most acute aspect of federal-provincial relations for the Diefenbaker government. Almost from its formation, relations with the provincial governments were a recurring embarrassment. The original cause of embarrassment was the Tory opposition to the tax-sharing and equalization legislation of 1956, and Diefenbaker's denunciation of the measure as undermining the principle of federalism itself by 'the centralization complex' of the St Laurent government which he promised to change for a better plan of tax-sharing. To do so he undertook that, once in office, he would convene a conference with the provinces in the fall to establish a healthy balance of revenues between the federal and provincial governments 'not in a spirit of arrogant domination' but 'in a spirit of unity.' On the platform with Premier Frost, he promised Ontario would get an additional tax share of one hundred millions.

The promised conference had met in November 1957. Diefenbaker insisted on calling the conference 'dominion-provincial' rather than 'federal-provincial.' For the next five years, the government spread the designation 'dominion' on new public buildings and everywhere they could find to use it. Diefenbaker considered 'dominion' more British than 'federal.' Apparently no one told him there was no French equivalent of the word 'dominion' or he did not care.

The conference was not a success. Far from getting one hundred million,

Premier Frost was merely promised another conference in 1958. Premier Small-wood was alienated by the unsuccessful attempt to exclude Newfoundland from the proposed special grants to the Atlantic provinces. He was not appeased when Diefenbaker backed down and agreed Newfoundland should share in the grants. The provision of the Atlantic grants, no doubt, won Diefenbaker some support in the other three provinces. In accord with our strategy of supporting good legislation, we Liberals supported the grants.

We were surprised when Diefenbaker, instead of setting a date for a second conference in 1958, sent a telegram to the premiers in January, advising them that Ottawa was unilaterally increasing the provincial share of the personal income tax under the tax-sharing arrangement from 10 to 13 per cent in the coming fiscal year. When Parliament was dissolved on 1 February we under-stood why this concession was made without waiting for a conference.

Soon after the 1958 Parliament met it became clear that Diefenbaker was reluctant to call another conference. We believed the cabinet could not agree on what, if anything, to propose as a substitute for the tax-sharing and equalization plan put in place by the St Laurent government in 1958. It was our view in the Opposition that neither Diefenbaker nor Fleming really understood the background of the tax-sharing and equalization plan. We had the good fortune to have those in our midst who did. Pearson had the expert advice of Maurice Lamontagne, one of the architects of equalization. And my first task when I joined the prime minister's office in 1937 was to keep track of the work of the Royal Commission on Dominion-Provincial Rela-tions which had recently been set up. From that moment, I had been familiar with every twist and turn of federal-provincial tax-sharing.

The arrangement of 1956 was the first peace-time tax-sharing plan in which the government of Quebec participated. All the premiers accepted the new principle of equalization, though their governments were always eager to get a larger share of taxes. We could not understand why the Tories had been so unwise as to oppose the plan.

Early in the session of 1958, Pearson introduced a motion condemning the government for the delay in calling a conference and demanding an assurance that the government would maintain or improve the existing equalization formula. Pearson's motion did not arouse any great public interest, no doubt because tax-sharing and equalization arrangements are inherently complex and not easy to present in a simple fashion. But we realized how vital tax-sharing and equalization were to national unity and how important it was to keep the Liberal party on the right side of the issue. Beyond increasing the provincial share of income tax to 13 per cent, the government made no other change in 1958.

Fleming was commendably eager to persuade the government of Quebec to allow the universities in that province to accept federal grants which were being paid in all the other provinces. Premier Duplessis had been adamant in his opposition, but the political scene changed in Quebec after Duplessis died in 1959. Paul Sauvé, his successor as premier of Quebec, was an attractive personality with a positive rather than a negative attitude to Ottawa and the rest of the country. The Diefenbaker government, and particularly Donald Fleming, had great hopes of developing co-operation with Sauvé which would give the Conservative party some genuine strength in that province. Fleming succeeded in reaching an agreement with Sauvé which made federal university grants acceptable to the government of Quebec. Before he could introduce legislation to implement this agreement, Paul Sauvé died suddenly at the end of 1959. His successor, Antonio Barrette, an old Duplessis war-horse, was no leader, much less a saviour of federal conservativism.

The federal measure in 1960, to embody the new method of providing university grants to Quebec, also renewed for one more year the increase in the provincial share of personal income tax from 10 to 13 per cent without making any other change in the tax-sharing and equalization legislation of 1956. Speaking on the legislation, I expressed satisfaction that the opposition of the Quebec government to grants started by a Liberal government had finally been overcome. I expressed equal satisfaction that the government was continuing the plan of equalization established by the Liberal government, with a small increase in the provincial share of the personal income tax.

Pearson made a splendid debating speech on the federal-provincial bill. At one stage he was being interrupted frequently. Theogène Ricard sat in the Tory rump on the Opposition side of the House next to the Liberal front bench and two seats away from me. Ricard often kept up a stream of half-articulate interruptions when Liberals were speaking. When he started interrupting Pearson that day, I half-rose and, with a gesture, interjected in a loud voice: 'Down Fido.' The whole House was amused.

More important than the debate on university grants and tax-sharing were developments outside the House which affected federal-provincial relations. Four provincial elections were held in June 1960.

The first one was in Nova Scotia on 7 June. Premier Stanfield was returned to office with an increased majority and the leader of the opposition, former premier Henry Hicks, lost his seat as did his most effective colleague, Gordon Cowan. This was the only provincial election campaign outside Newfoundland in which I participated. I did so against my own better judgement. The intervention of someone from Ottawa with no connection with the province might, I feared, be resented and do more harm than good. I agreed to take part only if my objections were reported to Henry Hicks and he specifically authorized the invitation, which he did. I spoke at three or four large and enthusiastic meetings, and I thoroughly enjoyed the experience. So far as I could tell, my intervention caused no resentment, but neither did it improve the results.

Believing our fortunes were rising, we Liberals in Opposition were depressed by the result in Nova Scotia. Our spirits revived a little when the Liberals improved their position against the CCF in the Saskatchewan election the next day – and not one Tory was elected in Diefenbaker's home province. Our outlook improved on 20 June when the Liberals under Jean Lesage's leadership won a resounding victory over the Union Nationale in Quebec. The defeat by Louis Robichaud of the Tory government in New Brunswick on June 27 made us feel the tide was really turning.

A federal-provincial conference had been called for late July. Before the conference met, Jean Lesage invited Maurice Lamontagne and me to Quebec to go over his opening speech. My main task was to ensure that the English text corresponded as precisely as possible with the French.

During the whole time Jean Lesage was premier of Quebec our personal relations remained very friendly. At no time did I share the annoyance or indignation many Liberals in Ottawa felt because Lesage behaved like a provincial politician, often differing with the federal Liberal party. So long as he was premier, his was the outstanding provincial voice in federal-provincial relations; often he was much better informed about issues being discussed than the federal ministers, partly because of his wide earlier experience in Ottawa.

At the conference in July, Diefenbaker undertook to continue the tax-sharing principle established in 1956 by the St Laurent government. At a second conference in October 1960, the government proposed amendments to the principle which pleased none of the premiers. We joined the chorus of provincial protests by moving in Parliament in January 1961 a motion condemning the government for repudiating the principle of equalization. At a further conference in February 1961, the provincial governments were presented with a proposal which drastically changed the basis of tax-sharing. This new formula was to be applied to the tax-sharing and equalization arrangements which were to replace for five years those which would expire on 31 March 1962.

With minor changes made after the conference the legislation for tax-sharing was introduced in Parliament on 11 July 1961. Fleming predicted that the amended proposal would usher in a new era of co-operation on more equal terms. In reply, Pearson noted how far short the proposal was from the additional $100 million Diefenbaker had promised to Premier Frost for Ontario in 1957. He criticized the change in the basis of equalization. None of the premiers, he noted, was satisfied, not even Mr Frost, though Ontario would fare relatively better than any other provincial government.

In my speech, I said how pleased I had been, in July 1960, to hear Diefenbaker pledge his government to maintain the Liberal principle of equalization, and how depressed I was when it was repudiated. The new tax-sharing legislation included a grant of the eight millions a year awarded to Newfoundland by the McNair commission, but the payment was to be limited to the five years from March 1962, instead of being made permanent as McNair had recommended. I repeated the Liberal pledge to have the McNair award paid indefinitely as a matter of right, and not for a limited period as a matter of grace.

I pointed out that an analysis of the new proposals indicated a net gain to Ontario of 18 million and the total cost to the federal treasury for all ten provinces was only 17 million. The big losers would be Alberta and British Columbia; there would be no change for Manitoba, Saskatchewan, and Quebec, and very little for New Brunswick; it would be somewhat better for Prince Edward Island and Nova Scotia; and better for Newfoundland only because the McNair award was included. The richest province, Ontario, was the only net gainer. In the debate we undertook to restore the principle of equalization accepted by all the provincial governments in 1956.

Equalization, we felt, was one of the greatest Liberal achievements. It has proved to be an essential part of the cement of confederation. The principle is enshrined today in the new constitution.

The Trans-Canada highway

One aspect of federal-provincial relations was of special concern to Newfoundland. That was the shared-cost program for the construction of the Trans-Canada highway. The length of the proposed road across the island was far greater in proportion to population than the highway in any other province. There was, in 1959, not a continuous road of any kind from St John's to Port aux Basques. The whole of the gap was in my constituency. Early in the session of 1959, the minister of public works introduced a bill to raise the ceiling placed in the original legislation on federal expenditures on the Trans-Canada highway. Howard Green made a careful and detailed statement of the progress already made across the country. Two of our Newfoundland members, Charles Granger and Herman Batten, drew on the information the minister had provided to show how much greater the burden

was to Newfoundland than to any other province. I spoke about the dispro-
portionate burden on the Maritime provinces and put on the record the
resolution adopted at the Liberal convention of 1958 committing a Liberal
government to pay 90 per cent of the cost of completing the highway in the
four Atlantic provinces.

One of the Tory members from Quebec objected to the bill because he
claimed federal participation in financing the Trans-Canada highway in-
fringed provincial autonomy. He pointed out that Premier Duplessis had
refused to have Quebec share in the program for that reason. I said I could
assure the House that the government of Newfoundland did not regard the
project as any threat to the autonomy of that province. It was clear all members
of the Opposition were prepared to vote for the bill and that several Tory
MPs from Quebec would not. We accordingly insisted on a recorded vote.
No one voted against the bill, but several Tories from Quebec were con-
spicuously absent from the House when the vote was taken.

The government was obliged to introduce another amendment to the
Trans-Canada highway bill in 1960 – this time to extend the time permitted
for completion of the road and to increase again the maximum federal contribution. In the meantime David Walker had succeeded Howard Green as
minister of public works, and Walker did not have as easy a time with his
bill. Pearson spoke first and appealed for special assistance to the Atlantic
provinces. Granger and Batten spoke effectively about the special problem
for Newfoundland. Later, I quoted statements made by ministers when they
were in opposition urging the federal government to make a greater contribution to the cost of the highway. George Hees had urged, in 1956, that the
federal government assume the whole financial responsibility for the construction and 'stop playing around with makeshift methods.' I repeated our
commitment to pay 90 per cent of the cost of completing the road in the
Atlantic provinces and made the argument against 50–50 shared-cost programs
which were unfair to the poorer provinces and put relatively little burden on
the wealthier.

Walker was frequently offensive in his references to members of the Opposition. This was his usual practice in debate. Later in the session, when he
was defending his estimates, we in the Opposition decided to give him a
hard time. Hédard Robichaud and I took turns asking a series of questions
about Diefenbaker's promise in 1957 to construct a canal across the isthmus
of Chignecto. Walker became confused and contradicted earlier statements
made by Diefenbaker and George Hees. Chevrier and I led him to contradict
statements he himself had made in 1957 about the construction in Hull of the
Government Printing Bureau which he had tried to show was scandalously
extravagant. Later in the day Robichaud and I continued the harrassment.

At the end of the evening Bourget and Caron took over until eleven o'clock. After the House rose for the day, Walker told me he was so exhausted he would have collapsed if the questioning had gone on for another half-hour. To be fair to him, I think he learned a lesson about Parliament that day and he was not always so outrageously offensive afterwards.

The pace of construction of the Trans-Canada highway proceeded slowly especially in the Atlantic provinces and, above all, in Newfoundland. In 1962, the final link in the road in British Columbia became passable and Diefenbaker presided at a ceremony in the Rogers Pass in September, originally described as the official opening of the complete Trans-Canada highway. I protested to Diefenbaker in writing that, far from completion, the route of the highway in Newfoundland had not yet been finally settled. In his maiden speech in Parliament in October 1962, Richard Cashin described the ceremony in British Columbia as the so-called opening of the so-called Trans-Canada highway and pointed out what a disproportionately high burden there was on the government of Newfoundland. That situation changed once the Liberals were back in office. Almost the first act of the Pearson government was to make provision for payment from Ottawa of 90 per cent of the cost of completing the Trans-Canada highway in the Atlantic provinces.

Premier Smallwood had signs put up all along the highway reading: 'We'll finish the drive in 65, thanks to Mr Pearson.' And a paved highway across the province was in place at the end of the year 1965.

The National Gallery

The resignation of Commissioner Nicholson of the RCMP in 1959 was not the only resignation to embarrass the Diefenbaker government. In March, Alan Jarvis, the director of the National Gallery, resigned.

The public profile of the National Gallery had begun to rise after the publication of the Massey report on the arts and the subsequent increase in financial support for the gallery. As the minister for the gallery, Walter Harris had put a new act through Parliament giving the board of trustees greater independence. He had also accepted the recommendation of the trustees for the purchase of a collection of European paintings on a scale far beyond any previous acquisition. After succeeding Harris as minister in 1954, I was in-strumental in having Alan Jarvis appointed as director of the National Gallery

79

when the post became vacant. Thanks largely to the work of Jarvis and his travels throughout the country, the gallery was mobilizing much wider public support.

In 1958, the board had, on Jarvis's recommendation, contracted to buy a painting by Breughel, after informing the ministers immediately concerned. The price was on the same scale as that paid for European paintings when Harris was minister. It was therefore unlikely that the purchase would have been criticized by the Liberal Opposition. The ministers immediately concerned apparently believed there was enough money available in the estimates prepared by the Liberal government to cover the cost. They had indicated no disapproval, and a contract was made for the purchase. The Treasury Board then discovered that Parliament had not yet voted the necessary funds, and that the contract could not be carried out unless Parliament was asked to vote money specifically for the purpose. At this point, the minister of finance refused to ask for such a vote and the contract had to be cancelled. The director of the National Gallery believed the government had authorized the contract which had to be repudiated. He resigned in protest.

Pearson had already learned about the difficulty. He raised a question about the proposed purchase during the debate on the estimates of the National Gallery on 12 March 1959. In his statement, Pearson asserted that the acting minister (then Fulton) had authorized the offer to purchase on 2 May 1958, in the belief that funds were available, and the director had proceeded accordingly. I took the matter up the next day and said it appeared from Pearson's statement, which the minister, now Ellen Fairclough, had not contradicted, that the government was prepared to buy the picture so long as they thought the purchase would not come to the notice of Parliament, but that, when they found they would have to come to the House, in a straightforward manner, and ask Parliament to vote the money, they backed down on their commitment. I called it a shocking and shabby business and a repudiation of the good name of Canada. Fulton accused me of working up a frenzy over nothing. I retorted: 'just a repudiation of a contract.' Pearson then proceeded to cross-examine Fulton about the facts. Between us we made both Fulton and Ellen Fairclough look foolish.

The whole affair would have made little impact on the general public if Jarvis' resignation had not taken place at almost the same time as that of the commissioner of the RCMP. The shabby treatment of the gallery by the government alienated a large section of the artistic community.

In the session of 1960, Ellen Fairclough initiated the discussion of the National Gallery estimates by describing in glowing terms the opening of the new building by the prime minister before a distinguished gathering of some three thousand persons. I spoke after the minister, and said it was a great satisfaction to me and, I thought, to all members of the previous administration who had authorized the building of the new gallery, to see the completion of the great project we had planned, organized, and started. At that gala white-tie opening by the prime minister, I said I had been asked by one of those present: 'What do we have a governor general for?' The question had come from a person who knew the original gallery had been opened by the governor general, the Marquess of Lorne, for whom the new building had been named. I wondered whether the opening of the Lorne building was not one of sufficient national importance to have warranted the presence of the governor general.

I deplored the absence at the opening of Alan Jarvis, who had perhaps done more by his hard work and enthusiasm to get the kind of support for the gallery which it had achieved throughout the country. His name had not been mentioned in any of the speeches at the opening on what should have been a non-partisan occasion.

Despite the move to the new building in 1960, the malaise in the National Gallery resulting from Jarvis's resignation had not diminished in 1961. My friend, Donald Buchanan, who held a senior post in the gallery, resigned in protest against its administration. His resignation caused no great stir, but when the gallery estimates were before the House I expressed my great regret that he was no longer there. Donald Buchanan, in my opinion, had contributed as much to the development of appreciation of the arts as 'any living Canadian, bar none.' I felt he had 'made a contribution to our cultural life that is almost unique.' I hoped he would not leave Canada, but would find some other useful field for 'his great energies and his sensitive appreciation' of Canadian culture. I am happy to say that Donald's memory is still cherished in the Canadian artistic community in 1986.

'Heads will roll'

After 1958, there was no further broadcasting legislation during the Diefenbaker period, but the subject did not disappear. The special committee promised by George Nowlan caused nothing but embarrassment for the government in 1959. Nowlan himself was the only articulate Conservative who supported the CBC and the principle of public broadcasting. The French-speaking Tories were constantly sniping at the CBC because they believed Alphonse Ouimet, the president of the corporation, and many of the Radio-Canada broadcasters, were not friendly to the Diefenbaker government. A number

81

of western Tories were virtually stooges of the private broadcasters in a campaign to weaken and, if possible, destroy the CBC. Nowlan got most of his support from the Liberal members of the committee and particularly from me. He himself was a stalwart defender. Without him as minister, public broadcasting would have been damaged seriously.

I recall vividly an occasion in the committee when a Tory member from Quebec asked Ouimet a question in French. Because there was no interpreter present, the questioner suggested that Ouimet answer in English. I saw at once what would happen if he did: certain members of the press would report that, when Ouimet was asked a question in French, he, like the rest of the Ottawa establishment, had replied in English. I insisted the reply be given in French. The proceedings of the committee were held up for nearly an hour while an interpreter was found.

In the latter part of the session of 1959, Ouimet was ill and the vice-president, Ernest Bushnell, was acting for him. During this period, the government got into serious trouble. In 1959 the CBC had a program, immediately after the eight o'clock morning radio news, called 'Preview Commentary.' A member of the press gallery was invited each morning to comment on some item in the news. Inevitably some of these commentaries were critical of the government and, at times, of the prime minister. Bushnell decided on 15 June to cancel the program. Three senior members of the staff of 'talks and public affairs' submitted their resignations and issued a public statement charging that the cancellation of the program was the result of 'clandestine political influence' on the CBC.

Pearson tried to have the ordinary parliamentary business interrupted for an urgent debate. After hearing arguments on the question of urgency, the Speaker refused to accept Pearson's motion. Nowlan was then asked in the question period whether he had made any representations about the program. He categorically denied that he had. The next day, more questions were asked. The answer to all questions was given that day by the prime minister. He refused any comment and said the questions should be directed to the board of the CBC.

On 19 June Nowlan made a bare announcement that the board of directors had decided to reinstate 'Preview Commentary' and that all the employees had resumed their work except the three who had formally resigned. They wished their resignations to stand until after they had appeared before the parliamentary committee. I commented that Nowlan was right and wise in not giving an opinion on the issue and that I hoped no attempt would be made to prevent the committee from finding out the truth.

At the committee F.W. Peers, the supervisor of talks and public affairs, gave a detailed account of the various meetings and consultations in the CBC which had led him and his two colleagues to reach the conclusion that there had been political pressure on Bushnell to cancel the program and to do so promptly. It was widely rumoured in the press that Bushnell was told, if the program was not cancelled, 'heads will roll.' The impression was general that the pressure had come directly or indirectly from Diefenbaker. A chance remark made to me by Nowlan in the corridor convinced me that neither Diefenbaker nor Nowlan had brought any direct pressure on Bushnell, so I discouraged any further attempt in the committee to find out who, if anyone, had told Bushnell that heads would roll.

It was generally believed that there had been political interference. Once the CBC board decided to restore the program, there seemed to be no advantage in pursuing the matter. The resignations and the public outcry were likely to discourage any future attempt at political interference.

The most serious problem in broadcasting in 1960 was the prolonged strike of French-language broadcasters in the CBC for whom René Lévesque became the leading spokesman. He received wide publicity in Quebec, and made a welcome recruit to the provincial Liberal party, where he began his political career in 1960. The apparent indifference of the government to the fate of the French-speaking broadcasters contributed to the impression that most Conservatives were unfriendly, if not hostile, to French Canadians. The Liberal Opposition on the contrary demonstrated interest and concern.

In 1960, the board of directors of the CBC elected one of its own members, R.L. Dunsmore, as chairman in place of Alphonse Ouimet, though Ouimet remained president. The law clearly stipulated that the president should also be chairman of the board. I charged that the CBC board had broken the law and declared that, before the estimates passed, the House was entitled to have an opinion from the deputy minister of justice as to the legality of the action of the board. The government refused to produce the opinion. It was widely believed there had been political pressure on the board to humiliate Ouimet because Diefenbaker disliked him. (In 1963, when the Liberals were back in office and I was the minister who reported on broadcasting, I secured a legal opinion that Dunsmore's election was a breach of the law. Pearson then agreed that Ouimet should be restored to the chairmanship.)

In the debate on the CBC estimates in 1960, I repeated the argument that, to assure the CBC's independence from the government in office, it should be provided an income fixed by Parliament for a period of years and not an annual vote determined by the government of the day. I maintained that broadcasting by a public agency was essential to the preservation of Canada as a separate country. Most private broadcasters, in my opinion, had a sense of public service, but it was beyond the capacity of anyone who had to put up his own money to establish the kind of national network that was necessary to keep the country Canadian.

The Diefenbaker government abandoned the policy that, until the whole country was served by television, there should not be more than one TV station in any one place. One of the first centres to receive alternate service was Toronto. In 1961, the private station in Toronto was having financial difficulties. On 7 September, I asked Nowlan about a news story that a substantial interest in the private TV station in Toronto was to be transferred to US interests. He said he had not seen the story. In the debate on the estimates for the Board of Broadcast Governors, I criticized an interim decision of the board to give the American Broadcasting Corporation a minority interest in the Toronto station unless there was an equally satisfactory offer from experienced Canadian broadcasting interests. Any such Canadian offer was to be received by 25 September, only three days after the day I was speaking. Whether my objection had any influence on the decision, ABC failed to get an interest in the Toronto TV station.

There was little reference to broadcasting in the House in 1962. But on one occasion Nowlan gave a good reply to a Tory member who wanted the government to interfere with a specific CBC program. Nowlan replied that, if any government started to interfere with CBC programming, it would be laying the foundation for either a fascist or a communist state. Public broadcasting owed a great deal to that broad-minded and courageous Tory minister.

Immigration and citizenship

As the former minister of citizenship and immigration, I was the critic of the department in Opposition. I did not have long to wait for something to criticize. The first occasion arose over a new regulation which entitled a Canadian citizen to sponsor a relative as an immigrant. The restriction applied only to immigrants from certain specific countries.

This new regulation was made by order-in-council on 19 March 1959, the day after the House had passed the immigration estimates. The order was not made public before Parliament rose for Easter. Publication of the discriminating order aroused indignant protests from the leaders of the Italian community against whom it was obviously directed. When Parliament reassembled after the Easter recess in 1959 the protests were reflected by a question from a Tory member of Italian origin on 7 April. Diefenbaker gave a reply in which he suggested that the discrimination was the result of changes in the immigration regulations made when I was minister. I said his charge was untrue. Withholding publication of the regulation until after Parliament had adjourned constituted contempt of Parliament.

The agitation in the Italian community intensified. On 10 April and again on 14 April I asked in the question period why the minister did not end the fuss by withdrawing the order which I described as unnecessary and inhuman. In a later speech, I suggested the reason the order was passed was that the government got into a panic when it realized that, in 1958, there had been more immigrants of Italian origin than British immigrants. Ministers felt they had to do something to change the trend. In restricting the number and relationship of the persons who could be sponsored, the new regulation worked great hardship upon many other communities, particularly people from Poland who were being allowed to emigrate for the first time in many years. The minister did not need to make a long speech in reply; all she needed to do was to come into the House and admit her mistake and say this stupid and inhuman regulation had been revoked.

A week later, on 22 April Ellen Fairclough spoke on the budget. She denounced me at length for my description of the order and said I had done many cruel and inhuman things when I was minister. After dealing at length with my sins, she stated the Immigration Act was being reviewed with the intention of bringing in new legislation. She then announced that the regulation was being revoked because its purpose was being misrepresented by Liberal propagandists. I thanked her for taking my advice to rescind the order. This clumsy and unsuccessful attempt to restrict Italian immigration helped, of course, to maintain Liberal support in the Italian Canadian community.

I was less successful in 1959 in another immigration matter. All children born in Canada are natural-born Canadian citizens, unless foreign citizens residing in Canada register their children at birth as citizens of their own country.

Early in my administration of Immigration I had been responsible for deporting immigrants who had young children born in Canada. I stopped the practice once I realized that young children, though Canadian citizens, were being condemned either to exile from their native country or separation from their parents when the parents were deported. I complained about the deportation, by the Diefenbaker government, of immigrants with Canadian-born children. Ellen Fairclough replied, citing instances where this had happened when I was minister. I retorted that it was wrong then, and two wrongs did not make a right.

I protested again on 6 May 1960, about the decision of the government to deport a Chinese woman who was the mother of a Canadian citizen. I asked if it was the policy of the minister to deport parents of infant Canadian citizens. When the minister said the question was too broad to permit a simple answer, I asked if the minister intended to deport the mother of this Canadian citizen and she replied 'Yes.' I was surprised this incident aroused so little attention except in the Chinese Canadian community.

I carried on a running campaign through the Diefenbaker years to remove from the law discrimination between natural-born Canadian citizens and citizens who had been naturalized. Under the Canadian Citizenship Act, the government had the authority to revoke the citizenship of citizens not born in Canada, for certain limited reasons. As minister of citizenship, I had, on a very few occasions, used this power to revoke citizenship. The most notable was the revocation of the citizenship of Fred Rose, the member of Parliament mentioned in the Gouzenko disclosures. His citizenship was revoked only after he had been convicted of espionage and left Canada for some time. I had used this power with great reluctance, because I realized that the existence of the legal power to revoke citizenship, however rarely used, created a feeling among some who were not born in Canada that they were second-class citizens. I had come to the conclusion that the capacity to revoke citizenship was not a power the government needed to protect the public interest and that it should be removed from the law.

Late in the session of 1958 the government had introduced a bill to amend the Canadian Citizenship Act to make some minor changes in the law. I got our caucus to agree to my trying to amend the government's bill to provide that naturalized citizens should have equality of rights and status with natural-born citizens. We tried without success to get the bill changed. I could never understand why, on the very day Diefenbaker moved first reading of his proposed Bill of Rights, the government refused to accept a proposal which would have given all Canadians equal rights as citizens.

On 19 January 1959, I introduced my own bill to give all citizens equality of status. Only a few bills introduced by private members reached the top of the order paper and were debated for the one hour provided for such bills. In 1959 my bill was actually debated. Once more I was surprised, as I had been in 1958, that the government did not accept a proposal so fully in line with Diefenbaker's theoretical opposition to discrimination and his championship of human rights.

I introduced a bill containing the same proposal in every session while we were in Opposition, but none of the others ever reached the top of the list for debate. After the enactment of Diefenbaker's Bill of Rights, I introduced these bills as amendments to the Bill of Rights. I was pleased, when we got back into office, that the Pearson government had legislation passed to end this discrimination against citizens who had become Canadians not by birth but by choice.

Diefenbaker and the Speaker

Diefenbaker's choice of Roland Michener as Speaker of the House of Commons in 1957 had been a very happy choice for Parliament. His re-election as Speaker in the Parliament of 1958 was generally acclaimed. As Speaker, Michener was scrupulously non-partisan, scholarly, and full of common sense. But by 1959 Diefenbaker began to show his resentment of Michener's insistence that the prime minister, like other members, obey the rules of the House. On 25 May, Diefenbaker's treatment of the Speaker shocked even his own supporters.

The incident arose during a debate on the estimates of the Department of Labour. A few days earlier a Liberal member had asked Starr if he would table the minutes for 1958 of a meeting of the Advisory Committee of the Unemployment Insurance Commission, as Starr had already done in the case of minutes of meetings held when the Liberal government was in office. Starr said this was a reasonable request, but suggested the Opposition should follow the usual procedure which involved putting a motion on the order paper asking for the tabling of the document. That was done. On 25 March the Opposition was both surprised and indignant when Starr opposed the motion, which was voted down. Pearson raised a question of privilege in which he demanded to know how Starr justified a change of mind about an undertaking he had given the House. The Speaker was in the middle of making a ruling about Pearson's motion when I interjected the phrase 'deprived of debate by trickery.' My interjection aroused the prime minister who interrupted the Speaker to ask me to withdraw the statement. After a couple more exchanges, I asked if the prime minister would say what he would like withdrawn.

Diefenbaker began to reply with a reference to my 'being about to write the history of Mr. King' when the Speaker interrupted him: 'I am afraid the Prime Minister is introducing another point of order in the middle of the first one. The Prime Minister is asking for a statement to be withdrawn. If he would allow me to deal with the first matter, then I would ... ' Diefenbaker interrupted him angrily: 'Mr. Speaker, will you allow me to finish now?' Diefenbaker continued in defiance of the Speaker. Pearson then replied to Diefenbaker. The Speaker went on to rule that Pearson had not raised a valid question of privilege.

Michener then said that the prime minister had raised a question that had not yet been disposed of. Diefenbaker then repeated his demand that I withdraw my interjection; 'deprived of debate by trickery.' I said there was no dispute that we had been deprived of debate. 'Whether it was by trickery or by some other means I imputed no motive to any individual.' If the Speaker considered it was wrong to say the House had been deprived by trickery, I would withdraw the word 'trickery,' but only if the Speaker said so. The Speaker ruled that, unless a statement was offensive by charging a member with some reprehensible conduct, it was not unparliamentary, but added that since the whole discussion was about the minister of labour, an inference might be drawn. He would feel much better if I would indicate I was not charging the minister with trickery. I replied that I never intended to charge him with trickery. I was quite willing to withdraw the word 'trickery' and substitute 'maladroitness.' That ended the incident so far as I was concerned. I was very anxious to make sure my behaviour was in sharp contrast to Diefenbaker's offensive attitude to the Speaker. This was by no means the only time Diefenbaker showed resentment towards Michener, but he never succeeded in intimidating the Speaker.

The defiance of the Speaker was frequently recalled especially in the media. For example on 9 February 1960, the *Ottawa Citizen* commented that Diefenbaker's boasted reverence for Parliament had some times 'been displayed in a rather peculiar fashion. There was the time he told the Speaker of the Commons to sit down.' The next day in the House Diefenbaker protested that the statement he had told the Speaker to sit down was a breach of privilege. He said: 'That statement is untrue and a breach of the privileges of this House in its reflection on both the Speaker and myself. At no time did I ever tell or invite you, Mr. Speaker, to sit down.'

On 11 February, the *Citizen* acknowledged that the sentence could have been more precisely worded but added: 'Yet the substance is sufficiently accurate.' The *Citizen* then reproduced the record from Hansard of 25 May 1959, where Diefenbaker had interrupted the Speaker with the words: 'Mr. Speaker, will you allow me to finish now?' Press reports of the incident stated that the Speaker had resumed his seat.

On 12 February the *Citizen* reproduced contemporary reports of the incident from the *Globe and Mail*, the Toronto *Telegram*, the *Calgary Herald*, and the Canadian Press which had all expressed shock at Diefenbaker's angry interruption of the Speaker. The *Citizen* added that in an editorial yesterday it had admitted it was 'technically incorrect' in saying the prime minister had 'told the Speaker to sit down,' but 'correct in substance.'

The defiance of the Speaker was never again quite so blatant, but Diefenbaker's all too obvious resentment of the Speaker's impartiality continued throughout the years of the Parliament.

To the end of 1959

The atmosphere in the House changed late in 1959 with a change in the House leadership. On 4 June after his usual procrastination, Diefenbaker appointed Howard Green to external affairs in succession to Sidney Smith who had died suddenly in March. Green remained minister of public works as well until the departmental estimates were adopted. Warm tributes were paid to Green by spokesmen of both Opposition parties. Pearson expressed the fear that with two portfolios Green would have to give up the leadership of the House. That did not in fact happen at once. David Walker was appointed minister of public works on August 20. Walker was one of Diefenbaker's closest friends. I often referred to him in private as 'the beloved disciple.' He was not beloved in the House, however, where he had already earned a reputation as one of the nastiest debaters, though he was friendly enough outside the chamber.

Though Green remained as House leader for the rest of the session, Gordon Churchill substituted for him more and more often as the session went on. Churchill never achieved the degree of co-operation Green had won. The change did not expedite government business.

The 1959 session had not been a happy one for the government. There was very little constructive achievement to report in the closing Speech from the Throne. The brutal cancellation of the Avro Arrow; the immigration regulation which offended the Italian community; the treatment of Newfoundland; the resignation of the commissioner of the RCMP; the resignation of the director of the National Gallery; the 'heads will roll' fiasco; and Diefenbaker's rebuke of the Speaker had all hurt the government. In most cases, the Opposition had, in debate over these and other embarrassments, helped to create the impression that the administration was not competent and that the prime minister often acted impulsively and, at times, vindictively.

More damaging to the government was the background of unemployment. This had been the main subject of Pearson's opening speech in the session. The failure to reduce unemployment was the prime public grievance against the government. We kept the subject to the fore in debate.

By mid-July, the Opposition was as eager as the government to get the session ended. Once we felt the session should end, Chevrier and I helped Churchill substantially in getting the remaining essential business through speedily. The House finally rose on 18 July 1959.

As soon as the session ended, our whole family, except for our elder daughter, Jane, who had a summer job in a chemical plant in Quebec City, left for Newfoundland for the rest of the summer. A close Newfoundland friend, Edgar Baird, had recently built a summer house at Traytown on the shore of Bonavista Bay. I had persuaded him to lease a part of his land to us and to have a cabin built on it to our specifications. When we reached New-foundland, we went to Traytown to inspect our new summer home. We were delighted with the progress. Shortly afterwards, we embarked on the coastal steamer *Bonavista* to visit settlements, not accessible by road, in the northern part of my constituency.

After our tour, we returned to Traytown and camped in our new house while it was still under construction. Later in the summer we visited Bonavista and other settlements in the southern part of the constituency. For the first time it was possible to travel by road. Part of the Trans-Canada highway through the Terra Nova national park had been opened. A ferry had been established crossing Clode Sound to connect with roads south of the park. As well as having a lovely place for the family's summers, Traytown was a headquarters equidistant from Bonavista and Twillingate, the two extremities of the constituency. When we left Newfoundland at the beginning of Sep-tember to take the children back to Ottawa for the opening of school, we were already looking forward to spending the summer of 1960 in our com-pleted house.

During the fall of 1959 I spent most of my time working on *The Mackenzie King Record*. Notwithstanding my preoccupation with the book, I did a good deal of politicking in the latter half of 1959. What I enjoyed most were visits to universities where I always felt at home, and where the Liberal party was noticeably gaining support. Among other engagements, I made a speech to the Canadian Club of Fort William about Louis St Laurent. I called my speech 'The Greatest Living Canadian.' I was flattered when the *Globe and Mail* reproduced much of the speech without credit to me in 1973 as an obituary on St Laurent's death.

1960: Unemployment

The parliamentary session of 1960 began on 14 January and lasted until 10 August. No striking new legislation was forecast in the Speech from the Throne. It was a long session but the least difficult for the Diefenbaker government, although unemployment continued to plague the country and to wear down support for the government.

In a broadcast on 4 February Michael Starr declared that the recession was over. He claimed that the policies of the government had provided more jobs for Canadians than at any other time in our history. He promised measures necessary to continue this economic expansion and to move closer to the goal of full employment.

The main debate on unemployment came late in the session on the estimates of the Department of Labour. Unemployment was clearly not declining. Paul Martin was the main spokesman for the Opposition. Chevrier and Pearson also made effective speeches. Pearson and Martin demanded that the minister of labour give the House the forecasts of unemployment for the coming winter prepared by his economic experts.

Later in the debate I quoted from Starr's claim in his February broadcast that the recession was over, and then said that surely this optimistic forecast had not been made until he had first examined the views of the economic advisers of the government. The House had a right to a straightforward and careful answer to the question Pearson and Martin had already asked. That question was: what was the considered joint forecast of the government's economic advisers on prospective employment and unemployment for the winter of 1960–61?

Starr replied that the situation was difficult to assess so far in advance and that he had, in fact, received no forecasts. I then asked whether it was more difficult to make forecasts in 1960 than it had been in 1957. Starr said he did not know why I had asked about 1957. I reminded him that, in January 1958, the prime minister had used an estimate which was already a year old to accuse the St Laurent government of having concealed the prospect of unemployment. I contrasted Diefenbaker's charge with Starr's statement that unemployment was difficult to assess months in advance.

We did not really expect to be given any forecasts of future employment and unemployment, even if any existed. But we were trying to keep reminding the public of the scandalous use Diefenbaker had made in January 1958 of the confidential advice on economic prospects for 1957–8.

We asked for forecasts of unemployment at least once in every session of the Parliament of 1958. On 18 June 1958 I had moved for the tabling and publication of the 'Canadian Economic Outlook for 1958.' Diefenbaker opposed the motion on the ground that the document was confidential. Later in 1958, extracts from that forecast appeared in the press. Diefenbaker and Churchill, who was then minister of trade and commerce, were obviously embarrassed, but they refused to confirm or deny the accuracy of the leaks. Pearson decided to devote a motion of want of confidence to the 'hidden report.'

He contended that Diefenbaker's disclosure of the 1957 forecast had exposed the confidential advice of public servants and thereby dragged public servants into the political arena. He stated that fear of publication of their advice would inevitably impair the quality of such advice. We had obviously embarrassed the government in Parliament. We were slow to learn that it is rarely possible to revive a subject and get the same effect the second or third time round. Trying to do so is like trying to warm up cold porridge. But we kept on trying.

At the end of 1958, Pearson secured an authentic copy of the 'Economic Outlook' for that year. On 23 January 1959, he told Parliament that the National Liberal Federation had had copies of the 'hidden report' reproduced and distributed to MPs and the press. This turning of the tables had little public effect, but embarrassing the government in Parliament gave us a good deal of satisfaction.

The subject came up again at the beginning of the session of 1960, when I asked the prime minister how soon the 'Canadian Economic Outlook for 1959' would be published. Pearson interrupted with a facetious offer to have the document circulated by the Liberal party if the government would make it available. Diefenbaker did not reply.

In 1961, in response to motions for production of the reports for 1959 and 1960, the government agreed to produce the 1959 report but refused the report for 1960, on the ground it related to current matters. Later in the session, George McIlraith asked about the current report. George Hees, who was by then minister of trade and commerce, replied that the procedure currently being followed was to have reports prepared frequently for the minister. McIlraith then asked whether there was one comprehensive annual report similar to the former 'Canadian Economic Outlook' and Hees said 'No.' He explained that the reports were no longer regularly circulated to other ministers, whereupon I retorted that the minister was now keeping his colleagues in the dark. Apparently he was afraid to circulate the reports for fear copies might be found after a change of government and used as Diefenbaker had used the 1957 forecast.

In the debate on the Labour estimates in 1960, when I was deploring the level of unemployment, Starr interrupted me to say he had the greatest confidence in the country, though I seemed to lack it. I said I did not lack confidence in the country, but in the government. I was sure the country would survive this government as it had survived the previous Tory government. I then asked the rhetorical question: why do we have to suffer Tory governments once in every generation? That – and similar remarks at other times – led to accusations that I had claimed the Liberal party was the natural governing party – a claim I never made at any time.

The Opposition supports
reforms

One really constructive measure dealt with in 1960 was the consolidation and revision of the Canada Elections Act. The proposed changes were considered first in a committee. R.A. Bell was the chief spokesman for the Conservatives and I was the senior representative of the Liberal Opposition. Bell and I worked together to try to avoid partisanship. The committee's report was a really non-partisan effort. The debate in the House was led for the government by Bell. I was the first Liberal speaker and devoted most of my speech to advocating radical improvements in election machinery for the future. My main proposal was that the expenditures of candidates and political parties in election campaigns should be severely limited, and that these expenditures should be paid for out of the public treasury and not out of campaign funds. I believe this was the first time such a reform had been suggested in Parliament. I made it clear the suggestion was my own and not yet the policy of the Liberal party.

The final debate was confined to a discussion of a possible change in the voting age. Hazen Argue for the CCF tried to get the voting age reduced from 21 to 18. We had already discussed the question in the Liberal caucus, and Paul Hellyer had spoken eloquently for the change. In the committee, I had opposed reducing the age. I had no objection in principle and agreed to support in the House whichever position the caucus wished to take. Pearson pointed out in the House that the Liberals on the committee had been divided on the question: one had spoken against reducing the age, another had spoken for it. He announced that the Liberal Opposition had decided to support the change and would vote for Argue's proposed amendment.

Diefenbaker replied immediately and sought to humiliate me by suggesting that, as spokesman of the Liberals in the committee, I had now been repudiated by my leader. He opposed the amendment because its adoption would delay the passage of the bill, but expressed willingness to consider the proposed change on another occasion. I spoke right after Diefenbaker to explain my position.

I did not think any question of principle was involved. Extending the vote to those over 18 would not make Canada more democratic or less democratic. I confessed that the reason I had not supported the change earlier was that at the age of 18 I was a hereditary Conservative; at the age of 21 I had seen the light and become a Liberal. Such a change was not infrequent in western Canada in the 1920s. What was more uncommon in western Canada in those years was another conversion such as that of a much more distinguished member of the House than I was. While I was advancing, another gentleman was receding. (Everyone knew Diefenbaker had started out his political career as a Liberal and had become a Tory because he had failed to get a Liberal nomination.) It seemed to me, I continued, there was a tendency, once one had cast a vote, to become more identified with a party than before one had cast a vote. Giving the vote at 18 might cause many voters to remain in their hereditary position instead of forming more mature views. I did not think mine a strong argument and had no problem about changing my position. My explanation ended that discussion. After some debate the proposed amendment was defeated and the bill passed unanimously.

I was delighted with the improvements we had made in the law. Somewhat later I was disconcerted to discover that, because we had repealed the old act and enacted a new statute, all the returning officers automatically lost their positions and the government was free to exercise wholesale patronage by appointing new ones where it chose to.

Two attempts were made to replace the returning officer in my constituency. In one case an actual appointment was made and the new returning officer, who was a personal friend of mine, came to Ottawa to discuss his duties with me. He subsequently decided he did not feel equal to the duties and resigned. Another man was approached who was also friendly to me; he also consulted with me. I explained what the duties were and encouraged him to accept, but he declined because he felt the duties were too complicated for him to undertake. The government then had to go back to the original returning officer whom they had ignored and beg him to take the position again. When I learned of this, I encouraged him strongly to accept, as I had always found him both efficient and impartial – and I wanted nothing more. The whole episode taught me something about the perils of patronage.

Another reform we supported was the government's legislation to give status Indians a vote in federal elections. This went beyond what the Liberal government had done when the Indian Act was revised in 1952, while Walter Harris was minister of citizenship and immigration. Under that act, Indians living on reserves could acquire the right to vote only by giving up their exemption from taxation of income earned on the reserve. A mere handful of Indians had done so in the subsequent eight years. I had never been happy, while I was minister in charge of Indian affairs, about this limitation of the right to vote of status Indians and welcomed the decision to remove the limitation. The Liberal Opposition, I announced, would support the bill. We were taking a position which differed from our position in 1952, but we were happy to do so.

The Opposition also approved the proposal of the government to have judges of the superior courts retire at the age of 75. This was the rule for judges of the Supreme Court of Canada, but the British North America Act provided that superior court judges be appointed for life and this rule could be changed only by the British Parliament. We supported the proposal for this change in the constitution, but argued that the change should apply only to future appointments and should not be applied retroactively to judges who had accepted appointment for life. Their compulsory retirement would, we maintained, be a breach of contract. I felt keenly about this injustice, as I regarded it, but our caucus generally was opposed to making it a big issue. We were not successful in getting the government to make this change in its resolution. When the Pearson government sought a similar constitutional amendment to provide for the retirement of senators at age 75, the change applied only to future appointments.

The Bill of Rights

For Diefenbaker, the highlight of the session of 1960 was the enactment of the Bill of Rights. The Liberal party had never supported Diefenbaker's advocacy of a Bill of Rights while he was in opposition. I personally had never had, and still do not have, any enthusiasm for bills of rights. Human rights, I believed, are likely to be protected more effectively by an elected Parliament than by appointed judges. Despite the misgivings of a few members, we decided in the Liberal caucus we could not afford politically to oppose the principle of a Bill of Rights which, in fact, many Liberals favoured. Our attitude should be one of support for the bill in general; we should seek to improve it in detail and urge some moderating amendments to the War Measures Act which Diefenbaker's bill did not propose to touch. Paul Martin was our main spokesman and he was particularly effective in dealing with this difficult subject.

In the debate I limited myself mainly to a detailed refutation of Diefenbaker's claim that he had spoken out for the Japanese Canadians during the war. If the prime minister could find anything he had said in Parliament during the years of war in protest against the treatment of Japanese Canadians, I said I would be pleased to be told about it. Diefenbaker tried to weasel out of the situation by asking me if I would say that December 1945 was in 'the days of war.' I replied: 'No, I do not.' Our exchange did not restrain Diefenbaker from claiming for the rest of his life that he had protested in wartime the treatment of the Japanese Canadians.

In the first volume of his memoirs, Diefenbaker states: 'The course taken against Japanese Canadians was wrong. I said it over and over again. It was considered unbelievable that I would take this stand.' It was unbelievable because it never happened! In a review of this first volume I pointed out that 'Hansard does not record one word of protest by Diefenbaker about the treatment of the Japanese Canadians during the war.'

He repeated the claim somewhat defensively in his second volume where he said: 'It has been critically remarked in relation to the first volume of these memoirs that there is nothing in Hansard to indicate my position on the question of the banishment of the Canadian Japanese from the west coast of British Columbia during the second world war.' Instead of citing a case where he had spoken in wartime, he referred to a question of privilege he raised in Parliament on 23 April 1947. I looked up the Hansard later and found his question of privilege had nothing to do with a protest in wartime.

By 1976, Diefenbaker had repeated this myth so often he probably believed it himself. In my review of his second volume I repeated that there is no record of one word said by Diefenbaker in Parliament 'in opposition to the treatment of the Japanese Canadians while the war was being fought.' I added: 'It is hard to understand why he goes on pretending he did. He has a record of opposition to racial discrimination in the years since the war which is honoured even by his political opponents. Surely that should be enough.'

The Kingston conference

The most important event in 1960, from the point of view of the Liberal party, was the Thinkers Conference at Queen's University in Kingston, organized by Mitchell Sharp at Pearson's suggestion. The Thinkers Conference was not an official Liberal function. A number of those who attended were not members of the party and, in some cases, not Liberals. Among the leading participants were Sharp, Bud Drury, Maurice Lamontagne, John Turner, Bob Fowler, Tom Kent, and Frank Underhill, one of the founders of the CCF. To me, the most attractive new face was Jean Marchand's. I had not met him before.

The Kingston conference was modelled on one held at Port Hope in 1933, which had been organized by Vincent Massey. That conference was a large factor a generation earlier in reviving and rejuvenating the Liberal party in Opposition. There were striking differences. In 1933, Mackenzie King had viewed some of the young people and their ideas with suspicion bordering on alarm. In 1960 Pearson was attracted by young people and open to new ideas. In 1933 Vincent Massey was an official Liberal who had been briefly a cabinet minister; in 1960 Mitchell Sharp was not yet a member of the party and had, until 1957, been a non-partisan bureaucrat. But the effect was the same. The Kingston conference, like Port Hope, attracted new people to the party and advertised the room available for new talent. Indeed, because the defeat in 1958 was so much more devastating than the defeat in 1930, there was more room at the top in the Liberal party in 1960, though the prospect of office seemed more remote.

I was present throughout the conference but took little part in the discussions and spent most of the time listening. Mitchell Sharp had asked me to speak at the closing luncheon and to give my impressions of the conference. Several other speakers gave their impressions during the final morning session. At the luncheon, in addition to giving my own reaction to the conference, I raised two or three political issues facing Canadian society which Liberals would have to consider in shaping future policy. I felt there seemed to be no appreciable dissent among eggheads or among comfortable, liberally minded, middle-class Canadians about the desirability of maintaining relative independence for Canada. When I was younger, there were still many Canadians who did not want independence. In 1960, Canada was a more solid and united country. It would be difficult either to fragment Canada or to persuade us to join another country.

Though all of us in the conference wanted an independent Canada, politicians had to realize that, just as French Canadians were indissolubly mixed up with other Canadians and could not get away from the rest of us no matter how many separatists they might generate, so, for better or worse, we Canadians were inseparably mixed up with the United States. That was the biggest brute fact of our existence. We could have just as much independence as we were willing to pay for. In the twentieth century, no country had independence in any absolute sense – not even the United States.

There was another fact about Canada I thought was recognized far more clearly than ever before. It was accepted sometimes reluctantly and almost as a necessary evil. That fact was that, as far ahead as we could see, we were going to continue to have a dual culture in Canada. I believed it was wrong to do all the public business in Ottawa in English. There was no doubt, in time, there would be a steady increase in the use of the French language in the official life of the country.

Because our society was smaller and more intimate, I believed we had done a slightly better job than the Americans of reconciling the various races in our population. But I had no patience with the view that we Canadians were superior to Americans. There were times when the United States was resented in Canada, but individual Americans rarely were. I had tried never to lose an opportunity to express my gratitude for the enlightened attitude of the American governments under Truman and Eisenhower. The United States had turned a very difficult corner by abandoning isolation and assuming the biggest share of the burden of defending liberalism in the world.

Though some of us were honest enough to admit that Canadians were no better than Americans, we still wanted to have our own national society *because it was our own*. For me, that was a sufficient reason. And liberally minded Canadians wanted that national society to be a liberal society.

I quoted from an article of mine published in the *Canadian Forum* in April 1935 called 'The Decay of Liberalism.' The theme of the article was that when liberalism ceased to be radical it ceased to be vital. I considered the debate between those who want to get government out of business and those who want to put more government into business was a sterile debate. What the country needed was more initiative and more enterprise. Liberals should not care too much where the initiative came from, so long as it was directed to useful and constructive ends. We needed more private initiative, more corporate initiative, and more government initiative. I was afraid of Liberals getting stuck in the mud; just as I was concerned about government in the clouds, such as we then had in Ottawa.

The Canadian Labour Congress, in my view, had replaced the CPR as the greatest aggregation of private power in the country. Instead of trying to stroke this new tiger, we had to realize it was a tiger, and that, like the CPR, which has been pretty thoroughly tamed, this tiger would have to be tamed too. To me the saddest thing about much of modern industry was that a high proportion of those who earned their living in industrial plants did not enjoy their work but got all of their satisfaction away from the workplace.

To give the workers a sense of genuine participation, I believed they would have to share in the control of the workplace. Most people wanted to work at something that they had some creative part in. Another problem was the sharing of income. There was a growing gap between the income of industrial workers and the financial rewards of farmers and fishermen. Some way had to be found to shift the emphasis in industry from ever-rising wage rates to the maintenance of real income. We had no answer at all to that problem.

Several participants at the conference had referred to the St Laurent government as conservative and managerial. In my view, no government had been more innovative. I listed several of the innovations. To applause, I reminded the audience that our present leader had been a member of the St

Laurent government the whole time. Pearson's contributions included the major role in the solution of the Suez crisis, and a substantial part in the creation of NATO, and support for the UN role in the Korean conflict.

In conclusion, I recalled that Mitchell Sharp was a one-time public servant and that modern efficient government was not possible without brains in its public service. I thanked Sharp for assembling this impressive conference at Pearson's invitation. The conference was one of the best measures of the difference between the approach to government of liberally minded people and the approach of the visionaries then in office.

The Kingston conference did not engender as many new ideas as Port Hope had done, but I realized that Sharp had gathered together an impressive group of bright new people attracted by the spirit Pearson had infused into the Liberal party. Several of those present at Kingston were subsequently elected to Parliament and some became ministers in the Pearson government.

The Kingston conference, not an official Liberal function, was followed in early January 1961 by a Liberal rally in Ottawa. The emphasis of the rally was on youth. Paul Hellyer, who was the youngest privy councillor, presided. I was not active in the general proceedings of the rally, but busied myself in making sure every item in the resolutions of the national convention of 1958 relating to the Atlantic provinces was included in the new Liberal program. The rally was a huge success and stimulated Liberal activity throughout the country, particularly among young people. The resolutions adopted at the rally brought the Liberal program up to date.

Away from Parliament

My legal career was aborted in 1960. On 23 March, I received a letter from Alex Hickman, the secretary of the Benchers of the Newfoundland Law Society, raising the question as to whether I was performing my duties as a law clerk articled to Eric Cook. Eric Cook was indignant and inclined to protest, but I welcomed the excuse to drop my articles. I arranged to do so during a visit to St John's on 20 April for the opening of the session of the House of Assembly.

The parliamentary session ended on 10 August 1960. By that time I was already in Newfoundland with the family. The construction of our house at Traytown was finished. There were enough new roads to make it worthwhile to have a car to visit many places we could not reach in earlier summers. As well, we travelled as a family along the coast in the northern part of the constituency on the *Sylvia Joyce*, a cabin cruiser lent to me with great generosity by Ken Goodyear of Grand Falls. We had similar voyages on the *Sylvia Joyce* in succeeding summers for several years; they were greatly enjoyed by the family.

In addition to almost full-time attendance in Parliament during the session and frequent participation in debates, I devoted many hours to *The Mackenzie King Record*, latterly to the proofreading of the first volume which was published in the fall of 1960. Publication came not a moment too soon, as my salary from the Mackenzie King estate ran only until 31 May. By fall, I needed the anticipated royalties to supplement the family income.

Margaret and I were in Toronto for a party to launch *The Mackenzie King Record* on 11 October. Later on, after a few days' visit to my sister in Washington state, I arrived in Victoria where I was met by the press. The first question I was asked was what I thought of Diefenbaker's comment on my book. I asked what he had said, and was told he had described *The Mackenzie King Record* as the greatest work of fiction of the year. There could, I replied, be no better judge of fiction than Diefenbaker.

One occasion I particularly enjoyed that year was the official opening of the Confederation Building in St John's. Louis St Laurent was invited to cut the ribbon inaugurating the building in which the House of Assembly of Newfoundland was to sit, and he asked me to accompany him. It gave me great pleasure to watch him emerging from almost complete retirement and receiving such a warm welcome.

The session of 1960-61

The parliamentary session of 1960 had been noteworthy for the passage of Diefenbaker's Bill of Rights, which undoubtedly gained the prime minister some renewed support. That session was perhaps the least onerous and the least damaging for the Diefenbaker government. That could not be said of the session of 1960–61.

That session opened on 20 November 1960 and adjourned for Christmas on 21 December. On the opening day four new members were introduced who had been elected in by-elections. The only Conservative was Hugh John Flemming who had recently been defeated as premier of New Brunswick and who became the first minister of forestry – a department with almost no function and which had been created for him. Judy LaMarsh had been elected in Niagara Falls to succeed a Liberal who had died; she was to prove a powerful debater and a tower of strength in the Liberal Opposition. Gaston Clermont, a Liberal, had won back the seat Henri Courtemanche had vacated in western Quebec. The Tories had lost Peterborough to Walter Pitman, the first member elected as a member of the NDP, a result which shocked both the Tories and the Liberals. Pitman was to prove an excellent debater and a substantial reinforcement of the Opposition.

The Liberal Opposition adopted a tactic to surprise the government. We decided not to move the usual non-confidence motion on the Speech from the Throne; the CCF, now the NDP, moved one which was disposed of the same day. We understood the government had expected a long debate on the Speech from the Throne and did not have its legislation ready. This tactic was not original. The Liberal Opposition had once done the same thing in the 1930s when Mackenzie King was leader: the Bennett government had no legislation ready. The tactic worked again in 1960. The government had no important business to introduce.

Donald Fleming, in an early speech, claimed the parliamentary session was being started in the fall so there could be early action by the government on economic problems, especially unemployment. No action was taken on these problems before Christmas. When Fleming presented his budget on the last sitting day before the Christmas recess, he reversed himself: there was no emergency about unemployment. The month before the recess was not completely wasted because the government had to deal with a threatened railway strike. That problem would have been an adequate reason for an early beginning of the session without the pretence that the government had an urgent program to deal with the economy.

The work of the session really began in January 1961 and the first business was the debate on the budget which had been presented in December. I spoke early in the debate and, in contradiction to Fleming, asserted that the country and the Opposition felt there was an emergency about unemployment. The subject was so important I proposed to do something I had not done before in the House: that was to 'follow my notes closely' (the traditional euphemism for reading a speech). The statement was couched in colourful and extravagant language about the emergency and the plight of the unemployed. Before I had completed the statement, Fleming exclaimed: 'Why can you not tell the truth?' I went on briefly with my reading and then said: 'I cannot go on, sir. I have three more pages, but every word I have just read – and I have read it, sir: I confess it – was uttered in this House by the Honourable member for Eglinton [Fleming]; every word.' I admitted I had read the statement because I was not as capable as Fleming of painting such a vivid picture of doom and gloom as he had done in 1955 when unemployment was not much more than half as great as it was in 1961.

His colleagues and the supporters of the government barely tried to conceal their amusement at Fleming's discómfiture. The Opposition members did not try. I doubt if any other speech I made in Parliament received as much publicity.

The Coyne affair

The controversy over James Coyne, the governor of the Bank of Canada, was the most sensational issue in the session of 1960–61. The Coyne affair, as it came to be called, had a long background. Under the Bank of Canada Act, it was the duty of the bank to maintain the value of the Canadian dollar, to the extent that could be done by monetary measures. In the middle 1950s, the bank had taken action to restrain the expansion of credit which was beginning to assume inflationary proportions. The restraint resulted in a rise of interest rates which those opposed to the action of the bank called 'tight money.' The Tory Opposition, with Fleming as the main spokesman, had attacked the policy of tight money. With his usual vehemence, Fleming asserted that the government was responsible for monetary policy.

Even while the St Laurent government was in office, there was already some discontent on the Liberal back-benches over tight money. When un-employment began to increase late in 1957, some members of each party blamed the increase on tight money and higher interest rates. After the Diefenbaker government had been in office for a few months, there was a decline in interest rates. Fleming and Diefenbaker claimed credit for the decline. But when interest rates rose again a bit later, Fleming reversed himself and declared that monetary policy was the exclusive responsibility of the bank.

In the narrow legal sense, the government had no authority to direct the bank or to veto its action in the monetary field. However, in the broader constitutional sense, if a difference arose between the bank and the govern-ment which could not be resolved, the government inevitably had the ultimate responsibility.

The question of responsibility for monetary policy did not become a par-tisan issue until 1960. In 1958 and 1959 relations between Fleming and the bank were good, as Fleming has acknowledged in his memoirs. What criticism there was of the Bank of Canada in Parliament came largely from Liberals. I tried, in caucus and in private conversations, to restrain criticism by our members because I believed the monetary policy of the bank was sound. What was equally important, I could see no advantage to the Opposition in attacking Crown corporations or individual public servants. It was the government, not the public service, the Opposition wanted to discredit and defeat. My view was, and still is, that the government and individual ministers should be the only targets of a parliamentary Opposition.

I scrupulously refrained, for personal reasons, from taking any part in debates involving the Bank of Canada. James Coyne was my closest friend and J.R. Beattie, the senior deputy governor of the Bank was my brother-in-law. Once the government changed, I had ceased to discuss public affairs with either of them. I feared Coyne or Beattie might be accused of inspiring anything I might say about the bank.

By 1960, we in the Opposition believed, with good reason, that the cabinet was divided between ministers who supported sound money, of whom Fleming was the leader, and those who favoured soft money, lower interest rates, and a reduction in the exchange value of the Canadian dollar, whose main exponent was Alvin Hamilton.

Many MPs in all parties blamed every economic ill on the bank's so-called tight money. Pearson made the responsibility for monetary policy an issue in 1960. He asserted that the final responsibility rested with the government. To bolster his argument Pearson quoted statements to that effect by a former governor of the bank, Graham Towers, and a former minister of finance, D.C. Abbott. He was careful not to attack Coyne or the bank.

The same day Pearson spoke in the House, Coyne made a speech to the Canadian Club of Winnipeg, which was published as a pamphlet and widely circulated by the *Winnipeg Free Press*. Questions were raised about Coyne's speech by CCF members who alleged Coyne's speech contradicted a recent speech by George Hees. One member asked whether Coyne's speech was an expression of public policy. The Speaker correctly pointed out that Coyne's speech was not an expression of policy, but a comment on the Canadian economy. In his ruling, he had referred to Coyne as a civil servant. Fleming dodged the question by saying the governor of the bank was not, in any sense, a civil servant. Asked later if he did not agree that the position taken by the governor of the bank was diametrically opposed to his own position, Fleming replied that that observation was 'just plain nonsense.' He stated categorically that the Bank of Canada alone had control of the volume of currency in circulation. It was therefore clear, early in 1960, that Fleming accepted no responsibility either for monetary policy or for Coyne's speeches.

When a Tory member made a personal attack on Coyne, Paul Martin asked Fleming whether he intended 'to defend a public servant with whom he had ministerial contact of a very close kind.' Fleming replied that 'the Minister of Finance has no control over the Governor of the Bank of Canada.' Fleming obviously did not want to defend Coyne, but there was no sign that he disapproved of the monetary policy of the bank.

Later in the session, Martin said the one single voice giving leadership on economic issues was not the government of the day but the governor of the bank. Martin regarded this situation as a serious reflection on the government. He noted that while Coyne was making a series of important speeches in different parts of Canada, Fleming had also made speeches in Vancouver and Winnipeg. He felt the difference in tone and direction of Fleming's speeches indicated he did not fully share the point of view expressed by Coyne. Fleming made no reply to Martin. There was no further debate on Coyne and the Bank of Canada in the session of 1960.

Soon after the session of 1960–61 opened, a number of identical letters from academic economists addressed to Fleming appeared in the press before he received them. They were highly critical of the policy of the bank. The Opposition seized on this incident to revive the controversy over Coyne. Chevrier asked Fleming whether he intended to make a statement expressing confidence in the management of the bank. Fleming evaded the question. He said he had received a packet of letters by special delivery, after they had appeared in the press, adding that this was a free country where professors had the same right as anyone else to express their views.

The government was asked to refer the annual report of the Bank of Canada to the Banking and Commerce Committee of the House so the committee could hear witnesses, including Coyne. This request was obviously intended to apply to the report which had been presented in the spring of 1960. Fleming pretended the request applied to the report to be made in 1961, and said that question could be considered after the annual report was received, usually in March.

When the debate on the budget began in January 1961, Pearson raised the issue of monetary policy. He said there should be close, constant, and constructive co-operation between the government which has 'the ultimate responsibility in fiscal and monetary matters' and the Bank of Canada. He asserted the bank's policies must be acceptable to and in harmony with the policies of the government if the right kind of relationship was to exist. The apparent lack of complete understanding between the government and the governor, he said, made it difficult for the public to appreciate whether or not the governor was speaking for the government in his public appearances. If the governor was not speaking for the government, the House should be told. There was no reply from Fleming.

On 20 February 1961, Pearson, in a motion of want of confidence, condemned the government for failing to accept and discharge the proper responsibility of the government for monetary policy. He asserted that all ministers of finance, since the government had acquired full ownership of the Bank of Canada in 1936, had accepted ultimate responsibility for monetary policy. He cited statements from every minister to this effect. He dealt at length with the position taken by Walter Harris. Harris, Pearson pointed out, confirmed the traditional doctrine and did not try to deny government responsibility. Since Harris's position had been misinterpreted, Pearson quoted from a speech made by Harris on 11 August 1956 in which he said:

The government is satisfied, and I believe that the vast majority of informed observers are satisfied, that under the economic conditions of the past 12 months it was desirable to moderate the rate of monetary expansion ... I know of no responsible person who argues openly for inflation as a solution to the problem of excess demand.

I need hardly say that a condition of tight money performs a very important function in our kind of economic system in present circumstances. That is because it compels the borrowers and the lenders of money to review their plans and, if necessary, to revise them. This helps to ensure that the aggregate of all spending plans is consistent with the aggregate production that is physically possible.

It is right and proper that our fiscal system at this juncture should emphasize additional restraint in public spending wherever possible. It is equally appropriate that monetary policy should assist by exerting a moderating influence on the expansion of credit.

Pearson asked whether that was not the complete acceptance of responsibility for monetary policy by Harris, as it had been by Dunning, Ilsley, Abbott, Towers, and Mackenzie King, as well as by Macdonnell and Fleming when they were in Opposition. Pearson then quoted Fleming, speaking on 11 August 1956, as saying the minister of finance had 'a very direct responsibility because the action taken by the Bank of Canada in this respect surely has a direct influence on the whole field of responsibility of the government in relation to fiscal matters.' Fleming asserted 'that the government cannot shed its responsibility for full fiscal policy in the broadest sense of the word, and that must include the actions of the Bank of Canada – even when in a technical sense, those actions are taken by the governor of the Bank of Canada in the exercise of the powers conferred upon him by the Bank of Canada Act.'

Pearson contrasted Fleming's attitude in 1956 with his statement, as minister of finance in 1959, when he had said: 'In the matter of monetary policy this Parliament has placed the responsibility and power in the hands of the Bank of Canada. The government does not exercise any sway in the field of monetary policy.' Pearson pointed out that the minister of finance, contrary to what he had said while in Opposition, was now saying that the over-all responsibility had been assigned by Parliament to the Bank of Canada. 'We do not accept that interpretation of the Bank of Canada Act because, among other things, it would be completely incompatible with our system of responsible parliamentary government.'

Notwithstanding the evidence Pearson had produced that all previous ministers of finance had accepted ultimate responsibility for monetary policy, Fleming, in his reply to Pearson on 21 February, claimed once more that Parliament had given the exclusive authority over monetary policy to the Bank of Canada and no power to the government to interfere. He cited the Bank of Canada Act which placed on the bank the duty of regulating the money supply. He claimed that, when Pearson criticized monetary policy, he was not criticizing the government but the Bank of Canada.

Walter Harris himself replied to the charge that he had taken no responsibility for monetary policy in a speech to the Ontario Liberal Association. According to the *Toronto Star* of 15 April, Harris pointed out that the federal government must take responsibility for the policies adopted by the Bank of Canada or publicly disassociate itself from these policies. His statement, Harris said, was designed to make clear the difference between the attitude taken by the former Liberal government towards the Bank of Canada and the present attitude of the Diefenbaker government. He noted that the Ottawa government would not announce publicly whether it favoured these policies or not.

The *Star* cited Harris directly as saying: 'I've been quoted as having said I did not accept responsibility for the role of the Bank of Canada. I did not make any such statement.' Harris recalled that he was asked in Parliament in August 1956 about the increase in the Bank of Canada rate and he had replied: 'I said we had been advised before the announcement that the governor of the Bank of Canada intended to raise the rate. I was asked if the government had anything to do with the decision. I said no: this was the decision of the Bank of Canada governor on his responsibility alone. The purpose of the questions was to associate the government with the bank's decision. I did not accept this as a decision by the government alone.'

He had promised to make a statement the following day. In that statement, he said: 'I accepted the anti-inflationary policy as followed by the bank and defended that course. To say that I did not accept responsibility for the bank policy is a perversion of the truth.'

Despite this statement by Harris, Fleming continued to claim he was merely taking the same position about responsibility for monetary policy that Harris had taken. We believed, at the time, that Fleming did not want to defend or support the monetary policy Coyne was following because of divisions in the cabinet. There is no evidence in the proceedings in Parliament in 1961 that Fleming himself differed from the anti-inflationary monetary policy of the bank. Twenty-four years later in his memoirs he confirms the division in the cabinet where he states that Alvin Hamilton and George Hees 'had pressed for expansionist policies and had for a long time called for Coyne's head on a charger.'

Fleming's reluctance to support Coyne was no doubt all the greater because of Coyne's speeches. These speeches contained no criticism of the government and no reflection on its policies. It was clear, however, that they made Fleming uncomfortable, largely, as his memoirs disclose, because of criticism by his colleagues.

I was also uncomfortable about Coyne's speeches, not because of disagreement with their content, but because I did not think a public servant, however independent his position, should make speeches about controversial questions on subjects beyond the area of public policy for which he was responsible. In Coyne's case, I was sure his speeches, neutral though they were in tone, would sooner or later result in conflict with the government.

In his speech on Pearson's motion of want of confidence, Fleming confined his reference to Coyne's speeches to saying the government had 'no right of censorship over the speeches of the Governor.' Coyne did not show his speeches to the minister. Fleming asked: 'Why should he do so? This is a free country. He makes his own speeches and chooses his own themes.'

The debate went on for the usual two days provided by the rules. I was not present for the vote on the evening of the second day, having left for St John's to attend the funeral of my close friend, Senator Ray Petten. I was not sorry to be absent as I had grave doubts about the wisdom of the Opposition even appearing to oppose monetary policy designed to discourage inflation.

The subject of Coyne would not die. In a debate on 21 March, Paul Martin cited several suggestions by Coyne of ways to achieve higher employment and output. He asked whether the government agreed with the suggestions. There was no answer.

The annual report of the bank was tabled in March. Pearson at once repeated the request that Coyne be allowed to appear before a parliamentary committee, where he could be examined on the report. Paul Martin joined in the appeal. The government refused to agree.

On 22 March, Paul Martin said the minister of finance and the government could not allow a public official 'to parade from one end of this country to another enunciating publicly economic doctrines which he believes should form government policy.' It was making the goverment 'look silly and is putting it in a subservient position.'

Fleming diverted the question by asking whether Martin approved of such speech-making. Martin replied that he certainly did not believe it was right and proper for an official, in areas of authority not specifically given him by Parliament, to take a public position that put him in disagreement with the government of the day. Martin's statement was not really accurate, because the government had no position to disagree with.

On 27 and 28 April, Pearson and Martin again tried to get the report of the Bank of Canada referred to the Banking and Commerce Committee, but met with repeated blank refusals by Fleming and Diefenbaker. Martin, on 2 May proposed his own motion to refer the report to the committee. The Speaker ruled that a private member had no right to have priority given to such a motion. Martin's next effort was to raise, on 9 May as a grievance the refusal of the government to send the report to the committee. He argued that the government was preventing the House from doing its duty. In his reply, Fleming finally reached the point of saying that 'the government does not take the responsibility for the opinions of the Governor of the Bank of Canada as contained in the annual report.' This was the first time Fleming had publicly disagreed with the bank's policies. The issue was becoming hotter.

On 30 May, Pearson asked whether J.T. Bryden had resigned from the board of directors of the bank. Fleming replied that Bryden had resigned a month or six weeks earlier on the ground that he had too many other responsibilities. When Pearson suggested that was not the only reason, Fleming indignantly retorted it was the sole reason for the resignation.

The crisis was precipitated by a public statement Coyne made in Quebec City on 13 June 1961. The board of directors was meeting there, and Coyne told the board he had been asked by Fleming on 30 May to resign as governor. Coyne advised Fleming in a letter dated 9 June that he felt 'the whole situation must be brought before the full Board of Directors for their information and discussion' and that he could not give any further answer prior to the board meeting in June. Coyne gathered from informal discussion that the majority of the board members would support the minister's request for his resignation. He withdrew from the meeting on 13 June while the board considered other business, and issued a statement to the press. On his return he read the statement to the board and then presided while the board passed a resolution by a vote of 9 to 1 stating that it was in the best interests of the bank that the governor resign immediately.

Coyne's statement of 13 June 1961 reads as follows:

On Tuesday, May 30, the Minister of Finance on behalf of the Government requested that I resign at once as Governor of the Bank of Canada without waiting for the end of my present seven-year term of office which expires December 31 this year. To aid me in my consideration of this matter he said the Cabinet were upset by the fact that the Bank's Board of Directors had taken action in February 1960 to improve the conditions of the pension which according to the rules of the Bank's Pension Fund had always been provided immediately on the termination of service of a Governor or Deputy Governor. He said the Government were considering what action to take in the matter of the pension, had not yet come to a decision, and wanted my resignation before they came to a decision.

Mr. Fleming also said the Cabinet were of the view that I had failed to discharge the responsibility of my office in allowing the Board of Directors to take the action they did take unanimously and after thorough consideration in amending the pension fund rules, an action which the Department of Justice had said was entirely within the powers of the Board.

This slander upon my own integrity I cannot ignore or accept. It appears to be another element in a general campaign of injury and defamation directed against crown corporations, their chief executive officers and other public servants. I cannot and will not resign quietly under such circumstances.

For the sake of future Governors of the Bank, and in the interest of propriety and decency in the processes of Government and in the conduct of public affairs, I feel myself under an obligation to ensure that this matter is brought into the open in order that it may receive full consideration and discussion.

I may add that at no time has the Government expressed disagreement with the operations of the Bank of Canada under my management, either in the field of monetary policy, or in those fields in which we act solely as agents and under the instructions of the Minister of Finance, namely in debt management and in operation of the Exchange Fund. There has likewise never been any occasion on which the Bank of Canada has failed to cooperate, so far as it was concerned in the matter, in support of Government policy. In financial matters we have always loyally played our part in carrying out positive Government policies.

So long as I continue to hold the position of Governor, I will continue to perform the duties of that high office, as specifically prescribed by Parliament, in accordance with the dictates of honour and concern for the economic welfare of my country.

The Minister of Finance has suggested to me that another reason the Government wanted me out of the way was that they were preparing certain programmes which were apparently thought to be of such character that I would oppose them.

This mysterious and alarming suggestion has not been clarified. Clearly I would be betraying the duties of my office to resign under such circumstances. It is for the Government to disclose to the public what it is they are planning to do. I have never opposed Government policy, and do not wish to do so. It is conceivable that at some stage and in some circumstances it would be the duty of the Governor of the Bank to resign on an important question of principle or policy, or on the other hand to make a strong public stand against some Government proposal. The Governor should not, however, resign merely because he is asked to do so. I continue to hope, in the present circumstances, that the processes of thoughtful consideration and discussion will enable the Bank to continue as in the past to take appropriate action within its own field of activity in support of the financial requirements and economic policy of the Government of the day.

Shortly before the House opened on 13 June, the first report of Coyne's statement reached Ottawa. In the question period, Paul Martin at once asked Fleming whether he had asked for the resignation of the governor of the Bank of Canada. Fleming replied that he did not want to make any comment until he had examined Coyne's statement. At the opening of the House next day, Fleming made a lengthy statement about Coyne's action. He said it would not be appropriate to comment in detail on Coyne's published statement or on its defiant and provocative character. He said he must confine himself to the essential facts, 'virtually none of which appear' in Coyne's statement.

Fleming then proceeded, in his usual combative manner, to give what he called the essential facts. He said Coyne, by ill-considered action and a series of public declarations on public issues quite outside the realm of central banking, and by his rigid and doctrinaire expression of views, often and openly incompatible with government policy, had embroiled the bank in continuous controversy with strong political overtones.

Coyne's rigid attitude on the maintenance of high interest rates was one example. The government's policy was expansionist and the policies advocated by Coyne were restrictionist. The government had shown patience in the hope of avoiding further controversy pending the expiry of Coyne's term of office in December. Its hope had been frustrated by Coyne and it could no longer postpone decisive action.

At a time when co-operative action between the bank and the government was needed, Fleming argued it was impossible to expect such co-operation from Coyne. Coyne had lost the confidence of the board of directors and did not possess the confidence of the government. On 30 May, on instructions from the government, he had asked Coyne to tender his resignation to the board of directors before the regular meeting of the board on 12 and 13 June. He gave Coyne, he said, ample reasons for the government's request. The main reason was that the government was convinced that Coyne's continuation in office 'would stand in the way of a comprehensive, sound and responsible economic programme designed to raise the levels of employment and production.' He presumed Coyne's published statement was his reply to the government's request. He had hoped Coyne would have resigned and his successor have been appointed at the board meeting in Quebec and that 'the whole matter would have been handled with dignity and consideration.'

In this statement Fleming did not say that the government had ever suggested to Coyne that it objected to the bank's monetary policy or that he had raised the question when he asked for Coyne's resignation. The nearest he came to this question was his oblique reference to Coyne's rigid attitude on the maintenance of high interest rates, which he had apparently never discussed with Coyne.

Turning to Coyne's reference to the forthcoming budget, Fleming feared Coyne's phrase 'mysterious and alarming suggestion' might have 'left a certain false impression with the public.' Fleming said that Coyne had not been told of the contents of the forthcoming budget and, therefore, had no right whatsoever to express views about it. To Coyne's assertion that he had been given no indication of disagreement with his views on economic policy, Fleming gave the feeble reply that it was clear from his last two budgets and other public statements that there was a major difference of opinion with Coyne's expressed views.

Fleming contended that his earnest efforts to handle this unpleasant matter with dignity and consideration for Coyne had been frustrated by Coyne himself. Despite requests for Coyne's resignation by the board of directors and the government, Coyne had asserted his determination to remain in office for the remaining six and a half months of his seven-year term.

Fleming then turned to the pension question. He acknowledged that on 15 February 1960, the board of directors of the bank had, by a by-law, provided for a pension of $25,000 a year for the governor. He claimed that the government had not been notified of the by-law and the governor had not published it in the *Canada Gazette* when it was adopted. Coyne had only had it published shortly before making his statement. Fleming claimed the government learned of the pension by-law only in the spring of 1961. He had informed Coyne on 30 May that the government considered he was lacking in a sense of responsibility by accepting 'an additional benefit of $13,000 per annum for life without ensuring that the matter was brought to the attention of the government.'

Fleming asserted that the government had 'patiently borne misunderstanding and even abuse in the hope of shielding the bank' from becoming a centre of political controversy. He then informed the House that the government would 'shortly invite Parliament to take appropriate legislative action to meet the needs of the situation.'

Before any comment was made on Fleming's speech, the Speaker warned members that their remarks should be kept within the scope of the statement Fleming had made. He then recognized the leader of the Opposition.

Pearson began by saying that Fleming's statement was 'as controversial in fact and opinion' as any statement could be. Fleming's conduct had made it impossible to deal with the matter with 'dignity and consideration.' He had contradicted not only statements by Coyne but also his own earlier statements. Fleming had made the unprecedented decision to demand the resignation of the governor notwithstanding his earlier statements that the government had no intention of interfering with the Bank of Canada. The Opposition had repeatedly asserted that the government had the ultimate responsibility for monetary policy and Coyne had recently said the same thing.

Pearson said Fleming now claimed the issue had been developing for months, but he had never before indicated to the House that there was an issue between the government and Coyne. The issue and the demand for Coyne's resignation had been hidden from the House since 30 May. The Opposition had repeatedly asked the government to call the governor before the Banking and Commerce Committee, so the House might find out what was 'going on between the government and the bank' and the minister had refused to do that.

It was not easy for the House to find out what issue had led to the demand for Coyne's resignation. Fleming was now accusing Coyne of opposing the easy-money policy of the government. Pearson recalled Fleming's statement in February that Coyne did not refer his speeches to the minister and had asked: 'Why should he? This is a free country.' Pearson added: 'Well, if this "heads will roll" attitude becomes common on the part of the government we shall not be a free country for too long.'

Fleming had just stated that the governor had been in conflict with the financial and monetary policy of the government for some time. That statement had been completely contradicted by Coyne himself who said that at no time had the government expressed disagreement with the operation of the Bank of Canada. Pearson asked whether there ever was a clearer case for a committee of Parliament to inquire into the facts.

Turning to the pension issue, Pearson found it incredible that Fleming had learned of the change only in 1961. He found it strange that a government which denied responsibility for monetary policy should claim responsibility for bank pensions. If the minister was trying to force the governor out because of some pension difficulty, that was, to use Fleming's own words, very 'undignified.' Much stronger language than that could be used to describe the conduct of the government. If that was the reason, it was 'a shocking example of government interference with or injustice toward a man who has been a devoted public servant, whatever one might think of his policy or his words.'

As soon as the House rules permitted after his comment, Pearson proposed an urgent debate on 'the unprecedented request by the government for the immediate resignation of the Governor of the Bank of Canada and the circumstances related thereto.'

The Speaker accepted the proposal for an urgent debate. Pearson argued that the issue should be cleared up quickly and that the Banking and Commerce Committee meet at once for this purpose. He recalled that, in February Fleming had denied that the policies of the bank were restrictionist and argued that monetary policy had been expansionist. What happened between February 21 and June 13 to cause the minister to change his mind so completely? Whatever might be thought of the validity of some parts of Coyne's economic doctrine, he should not be 'persecuted or victimized or misrepresented for stating his views when the Minister of Finance says that the Governor has every right as a free Canadian so to do.'

If the government could establish, through a parliamentary inquiry, that Coyne had prevented the government from implementing its monetary and financial policies, the Opposition would support Coyne's removal. If the government could establish that its policies had been opposed by the governor, he should resign. No public servant should be in a position where he could prevent a democratic government from implementing its policies. But he insisted that Fleming had never at any time given Parliament any reason to believe this had been the situation. When the Opposition had suggested there was some difficulty between the government and the governor, Fleming had 'pooh-poohed that suggestion.' The Opposition, Pearson concluded, would not support the government in any attempt to use the governor as a scapegoat, and to use a phony issue to cover up their own mismanagement of the country's affairs.

Erhart Regier for the NDP made a powerful speech along the same lines. Paul Martin also made a vigorous attack on Fleming's conduct. Fleming's reply was not effective: he failed to tell the House he had received a letter from Coyne dated 9 June to say that Fleming's demand for his resignation must be reported to the board of directors. He had sought to give the impression that there had been no word from Coyne until he made his statement in Quebec City on 13 June, which Fleming described as presumably Coyne's reply to the government's request for his resignation.

Before making this reply on 14 June, Fleming had announced he would present his budget on 20 June. I could never understand why the government chose to present a budget before dealing with Coyne, unless Fleming felt the budget would distract attention from the issue.

The budget forecast an increase in the tariff protection for eviscerated chicken. In the question period on 22 June, I asked Fleming whether, in view of the character of the government, additional protection was needed for gutless chicken. Fleming took the question seriously and gave a reply about the importance of the proposal to farmers. He concluded his answer by suggesting that, at times, I might need protection. I commented that, in view of the entirely unwarranted personal attack, I should be allowed a word in my own defence. I suggested that what the minister needed most was some protection from home-grown Canadian humour.

There was not much humour in my speech on the budget later that day.

It was one of my rougher attacks on the government. There had been a good deal of advance publicity emanating from Tory public relations sources forecasting an expansionist budget that was to be a contrast to the alleged restrictionist policies of the governor of the Bank of Canada. I said I doubted if, in peacetime, there had ever been greater expectations raised about a budget. Instead of the promised contrast, the only difference was that Coyne had proposed a program for full employment, whereas the government had a program for the perpetuation of unemployment. Fleming's parliamentary secretary, R.A. Bell, asked, at that point, if I had adopted the governor's program. I replied: 'No, I do not adopt the Governor's programme. I am putting forward my own views. I am supporting the programme of the Liberal Party.' I added that, unlike the government, we had a program.

I was asked by a Tory MP: 'Tell us about it.' I replied that I was going to tell the House what the country thinks about the budget. After the great expectations aroused by Grosart's advance billing, the budget was bound to be an anti-climax. I attributed the publicity to Grosart, the Tory public relations director, because the style was succinct and catchy. Everyone knew Fleming had no such style. I believed that when misleading, inflated advertising preceded an empty package, the public felt let down.

I noted one remarkable aspect of the budget. It differed little from Coyne's own proposals of 15 February 1961 and, in most respects, was a pale reflection of them. I had, while listening to the budget speech, scribbled on the margin of my order paper 'Coyne and water, more water than Coyne.' By coincidence, a leading member of the press gallery (Arthur Blakely of the *Montreal Gazette*) had independently used the same phrase in his broadcast on the evening of the budget. I defied any fair-minded person to go through the budget proposals and find a single item, with one exception, that was not a pale reflection of the memorandum Coyne had sent the minister of finance on 16 February. Coyne had made this document public on 19 June, the day before the budget. Everything Fleming had proposed was in Coyne's memorandum, with the exception of the government's spending from the Exchange Fund.

Fleming interrupted to say that statement was silly. I claimed a friend had gone through *Hansard* to count the number of times Fleming had said 'nonsense,' 'silly,' and 'rubbish.' When the friend reached 5,000, he had said, 'I cannot take it any more.' That statistic, I said, was about as reliable as most of the statistics we got from the government.

I said of Fleming: 'This is the Minister who in 1957, in his first press release as Minister of Finance, said he was going to tackle the tight money situation and end it. Then a year later, when it was embarrassing, he had washed his hands, like Pontius Pilate, and said the government had no control over monetary policy. When interest rates started to fall again he said, "I did it with my own little hands," and then when interest rates went up again there was the Pontius Pilate act: "It was the Bank of Canada." '

We knew the minister was not a free agent any more. What we had was a one-man government with a lot of little boys running errands. None of them has been running more unpleasant errands than the minister of finance had had to run in the past few weeks.

The evening before my speech on the budget Diefenbaker had made a broadcast in which he had said: 'The case of the governor of the Bank of Canada is now out in the open where it can be thoroughly discussed and assessed in the light of the facts.' That same morning he had voted against two motions to provide the House of Commons with the facts out in the open. The prime minister had used his majority to keep those facts away from Parliament.

I charged there was one principle of this government – a 'head' every three months. Heads must roll. The head of the government has to have heads, one after another. I had just mentioned the commissioner of the Royal Canadian Mounted Police when my time expired.

If the budget was designed to take the heat off the Coyne affair it had been a miserable failure. The fate of Coyne was uppermost in the public mind.

A bill to remove Coyne

On 23 June, Fleming introduced a bill which contained only one clause which read: 'The office of the Governor of the Bank of Canada shall be deemed to have become vacant immediately upon the coming into force of this act.' Fleming offered to go ahead with second reading that day, if the House would give consent. There was not unanimous consent. The debate did not begin until 26 June. The same day Coyne made public a letter he had sent to Fleming. This letter was accompanied by another letter he had sent to Fleming on 9 June in which he had suggested that the Bank of Canada Act should be amended to make explicit the relative responsibilities of the government and the board of directors of the bank, making it clear the government had the ultimate responsibility for monetary policy.

Fleming, in his opening speech on the bill, quoted from a broadcast in which Pearson had said that, if there was a dispute between the governor of the Bank of Canada and the government, the governor should resign. Pearson replied immediately. He accused Fleming of failing to give his complete statement. In fact when Pearson was asked in the broadcast; 'Do you think he should resign now?' he had answered; 'I say his usefulness is over,' But, Pearson continued, 'Mr Coyne apparently is determined to defend himself against certain charges which he believes reflect on his integrity. And that is why surely Mr Coyne should have his day in court.' In Pearson's eyes, defending himself in the press when he was not permitted to appear before a parliamentary committee did not give Coyne his day in court.

Pearson agreed with Fleming that the situation should be dealt with as quickly as possible, but it should be dealt with in the right and proper way. The proper way was by an inquiry before a parliamentary committee where Coyne could appear. If Fleming would agree to the request that the bill be sent to a committee where evidence could be taken and witnesses heard, Pearson said that would end the second reading stage as far as the Liberal Opposition was concerned. Paul Martin interjected: 'Instead of hanging a man on the prejudiced statement of the Minister of Finance.' Pearson charged that justice was being denied by the authors of the Bill of Rights.

The issue, Pearson argued, was not Coyne's financial and monetary views which the Opposition had sometimes criticized in the past and which Fleming had defended. The issue was 'responsible government: the control of the elected representatives of the people over the Executive and the right of Parliament to scrutinize every act of the Executive.' The government was seeking to make the representatives of the people rubber stamps and to give the government a blank cheque to control the Bank of Canada. If harmony and co-operation between the government and the bank could not be maintained and if the governor did not resign voluntarily, a responsible government had a clear duty to bring the situation to the attention of Parliament and to propose suitable action which Parliament could take, but only after due and proper inquiry.

If the House meekly passed the bill in the form submitted to it, without the most searching debate and without any parliamentary inquiry, the effect would be, of course, to remove the governor of the bank. But a far more important effect would be to endanger the position of the governor of the bank in the future, and of the bank itself, and to place it in a position where it might be considered merely a creature of the government. Pearson predicted that the directors would appoint a governor agreeable to the government and that the new governor would know that, unless he toed the line, his fate would be an unpleasant one.

When Fleming protested that this argument was unfair, Pearson replied that the governor held office during good behaviour and that a proper procedure, such as that prescribed for removing judges, should be established for determining a breach of good behaviour. The question was whether a man in high office can be thrown out of that office by an act of Parliament which does not give him the opportunity to face his accusers. Without access to the facts except the version of the facts given by the government, Parliament was being asked to remove Coyne from office. This was an intolerable position. Even at this late date, the government should fall back on its own Bill of Rights. Pearson's position was strongly supported by Regier, the spokesman for the NDP.

In a powerful supporting speech, Paul Martin described the government's bill as a bill of attainder and a repudiation of the Bill of Rights. A bill of attainder was a Tudor device for condemning a specified person without a hearing. He opposed the bill because he believed in fair play and British justice. Was the House to make a decision on the mere say-so of a prejudiced minister of finance?

While I regretted that Pearson had said, in his broadcast, that Coyne's usefulness as governor had ended, I was satisfied with his speech attacking the bill and pleased with Paul Martin's powerful argument.

I had learned of the demand for Coyne's resignation from his press statement in Quebec on 13 June. It was only after that statement I felt free to participate in debate on the Bank of Canada. I did, however, see Coyne several times after this demand became public and to my certain knowledge he did not discuss the matter with any other active Liberal in Parliament or outside. I did not take part in the urgent debate on 14 June. I was satisfied with Pearson's position and did not think I could add anything useful until Fleming had disclosed what action the government proposed to ask Parliament to take. When I saw the bill, I was outraged. I decided to speak on the same day as Pearson and Martin. By doing so, I fell into a trap devised on the government benches.

A government supporter had argued that Coyne was claiming sovereignty for the bank as opposed to the government. I began my speech by stating that not one jot or tittle of evidence had been produced by Fleming or his two supporters to suggest that, in anything he did at any time, Coyne had sought to usurp the power of the government. On the contrary, there was abundant evidence that the government was seeking to usurp the rights of Parliament. The minister of finance over and over again had disclaimed responsibility which was his and which Coyne had urged him to assume. Instead, Fleming had dodged and shirked his responsibility and, when he got into a jam, had got orders from the prime minister to get rid of Coyne. The minister then sneaked behind the back of Parliament in an attempt to get the governor to leave, as he put it, with dignity and as quickly as possible. I accused Fleming of undermining Parliament by seeking to make a secret deal with Coyne about which Parliament would never have known if Coyne had agreed. Fleming did not succeed because, whatever else could be said about Coyne, it could not be said that he lacked courage. By refusing to permit a parliamentary inquiry, Fleming was trying to substitute himself for Parliament. His position was in sharp contrast to the claim he had made in 1955 that Parliament was the grand inquest which had the right to inquire into anything and everything. When he denied Parliament the opportunity to inquire in a committee into the Coyne affair, those words of 1955 convicted Fleming out of his own mouth. Diefenbaker had joined in this denial by saying in a broadcast that Coyne had made his case in the press.

Since Fleming and Coyne had appeared to be in agreement right up to the spring of 1961, what had led to Fleming's sudden difference with Coyne? The government evidently needed a victim to take attention away from their own difficulties. Maybe the decision was made by the minister? Maybe the prime minister ordered him to do it? I suspected the latter. Coyne must go quickly in order to conceal the facts from the people and Parliament. Did the government come to Parliament and make their case? Did they allow us to perform our functions as an Opposition? Did they allow Parliament to be sovereign? No; they said, 'we have a huge and servile majority; we will put a bill through this House to take away the rights of this man without letting him be heard.'

At this point, R.A. Bell, Fleming's parliamentary secretary, interrupted to say Coyne was in the headlines every day. I asked whether Bell, who was a lawyer, was suggesting that, if a man makes a statement in public outside the courts, he should be denied access to the courts? If that was the new doctrine of the Bill of Rights, it was not a doctrine any Liberal could espouse.

At this point Bell asked me if I would permit a question. I naively said, 'certainly.' Bell then asked me if I would indicate to the House whether I had been in communication with Coyne since the first of June. Too late, I knew that I had provided the government with the excuse for a badly needed diversion. Bell said that apparently I did not wish to answer his question to which I replied: 'It is a very well known fact that I have known Mr. Coyne for thirty years and that he is one of my personal friends. I live in a free country and, of course, I have not denied myself communication with my friends, even under this Tory despotism.'

Fleming interjected triumphantly: 'The bubble is pricked now; now we know.' I made no comment on this insinuation, but continued my speech by repeating Paul Martin's argument that we were faced with a bill of attainder – a procedure unknown to our practice and forbidden by the constitution of the United States. I then recalled that bills of attainder had been used in sixteenth-century England to punish many distinguished victims who could not have been charged with any offence under the existing laws. That was what the government was asking Parliament to do in this case.

Coyne had been appointed during good behaviour. Good behaviour meant that the government must not in any way seek to remove a person so appointed except by showing cause, and doing so openly in Parliament, not secretly behind closed doors. Passage of the bill could serve as a precedent for the executive to remove other public servants appointed during good behaviour. The governor of the bank was protected from the executive precisely because no free country, with a constitutional government, would give the executive the uncontrolled right to start the printing presses and thereby inflate its money.

I said the government had waited until the board of directors of the Bank were all its own appointees and then the minister of finance had instructed them to ask for the resignation of the governor. Fleming protested that was a false statement. I retorted: 'Let us see these directors and ask them questions.' The only person who now has any voice in Parliament is the accuser.

If the government got away with this arbitrary procedure in Coyne's case, it would not matter who was appointed in his place, the new governor was going to hesitate a long time before he failed to do whatever he was ordered to do by the minister of finance or the successor of the minister of finance. I predicted Fleming would not survive the debate very long, because he had made a mess of this business, and the prime minister would not forget it.

The fundamental reason the issue was so important was not Coyne at all, but the office of the governor and the necessary independence of that officer to protect the value of our money. If the government appointed its stooge, the Canadian dollar would fall in value, because the government was faced with an impossible deficit it was afraid to deal with in a proper fashion. It wanted some subservient person in office to start the printing presses.

I pointed out that, in one of his letters to Fleming, Coyne had proposed a method of resolving differences between the bank and the government. That method was to place the bank in the same position as the Bank of England. In England, the treasury had the legal authority to issue a public directive of policy to the bank. If the governor was not willing to accept the public directive and the difference could not be reconciled, the governor had no choice but to resign. That would have been a right and proper procedure carried out in public. 'But,' I said, 'Mr. Coyne should not resign and no governor should be expected to resign, merely because the minister does not like the colour of his hair or the amount of his pension or even some speech he has made.'

If Coyne had persisted in making speeches after the minister asked him not to make them, the minister would then have had a case. He could have come into the House and made his case, but he never protested at all. 'Neither the House nor the public had been given the slightest evidence that the governor of the Bank of Canada by any act, as opposed, perhaps, to some words which the minister did not like, has been in conflict with the present administration.'

Many of the operations of the bank had to be carried out without publicity and the governor had respected that requirement of confidentiality 'until the minister fired him, or tried to.' Coyne then felt he had a duty to Parliament and the people of Canada whose servant he was – 'not the servant of the Government, not the servant of the minister, but the servant of Parliament and the people of Canada' – to tell us that something was wrong and to give us a chance to find out what it was. That was the issue. 'If there is something wrong with the Governor, surely the Government would be delighted to give him a hearing and show he is wrong.'

Why was the government so frightened? Why did they not want an inquiry? The answer was that there was nothing substantial to inquire into. They 'want a scapegoat for the past – and what I suspect is a great deal more serious – they want a compliant tool in the office of the governor of the Bank of Canada to deal with their deficits in the future.'

I had probably spoken with more vehemence than usual because I felt such genuine indignation, but I realized from the moment I had answered Bell's question that I had provided an opening for the government. It was no surprise to me when David Walker, the number 1 hatchet man in the government, rose to reply to me.

Walker began by congratulating Fleming on his patience and wisdom in treating a person like Coyne, who had become almost an anarchist, with such sympathy and understanding. He then turned his attention to me. He found me 'in a semi-hysterical state of mind' but did not blame me for that, because I had been 'under great strain and stress.' He accused me of taking the place of the leader of the Opposition in conducting the business of the House and at the same time being 'the confidential adviser of the Governor of the Bank of Canada.' I interjected that I thought I had a question of privilege but 'would simply say that that libel answers itself.' Walker went on to say I had admitted I had been 'in constant touch with the Governor' and said, if I would deny it, he would withdraw his remarks. I replied that I had said, 'I had been in touch with him as a friend.'

Walker interrupted me to say: 'Well, out of his own mouth.' I said perhaps he would allow me to finish. I continued 'I said I had been in touch with him as a friend of many, many years' and 'I saw no reason, simply because of this action, to alter that friendship in any way whatsoever, nor do I think it is necessary to do so in a free country.'

Walker then said 'These letters, reams of which I have been reading today, have a strange familiarity' and he asked me whether I had assisted Coyne in drafting them, including the one of that day. I replied: 'The answer to that question is no.' Walker said he had to accept that answer, but went on to say that on my admission a governor 'who has been aloof from political turmoil' had been in touch with me and that he could only assume that the governor had been accepting my advice. Someone called 'shame' and Walker added it was a shame, a crying shame, that all these actions were not those of a person they had thought 'was a quiet dignified banker but are the actions of the semi-hysterical member for Bonavista-Twillingate.'

Walker then accused the Opposition of being in touch with Coyne to persuade him to resign so that we would not have to vote on second reading of the bill and that, as late as the previous night, the governor had refused to resign. Regier of the NDP interrupted Walker to say: 'I never knew how low one could sink.' Walker went on to predict that the members of the official Opposition would all vote in favour of the governor of the bank being discharged.

He referred next to what he called the proposal by the leader of the Opposition that the governor of the Bank of Canada should have another 'go' at this thing in a parliamentary committee. He said Coyne had 'explained his position in reams of well written letters in the Pickersgillian style' and had given press conferences in Quebec and Ottawa 'under some expert political coaching.'

Walker claimed he would like to act as counsel in a committee to cross-examine Coyne, but then asked: 'But why exacerbate the self-inflicted wounds of that poor man?' Walker said he was not going to say very much about the increase of the pension from $12,000. to $25,000. He said he did not know whether the pension had been negotiated with the advice of the member for Bonavista-Twillingate, but he asserted that, from the time the governor believed that, on retirement, he could feel secure with a pension of $25,000. with the hope of living thirty years at the cost to the taxpayers of three-quarter of a million dollars, Coyne had become bolder and bolder.

Walker professed to like me personally, but found me 'overwrought, distracted and somewhat hysterical.' When I came back to my normal thinking ways, he said, I would be terribly ashamed of the scene I had made in the House that night. Walker appealed to the House to 'bring down the curtain on this sad and unfortunate incident.' He accused Coyne of descending 'from the heights of Olympus to get into a political brawl' and of conducting himself 'not like the gentleman I always thought he was' but almost reaching the stage 'of being an anarchist.' He asked the House to pity Coyne, whose advice has been abominable. For that advice we can only blame members of the Opposition led by the person who would be leader of the Opposition, the member for Bonavista-Twillingate.

I was not ashamed of my speech, but I was not happy that night about the predictable reaction it would evoke. I realized its immediate effect would be to divert attention in the media from the clear case against the government made by Pearson. I knew this consequence would displease Pearson's staff and most of the members of our party in the House. I feared it might hurt Coyne, if the government could succeed in portraying him as an ally of the Liberal Opposition. Finally I was chagrined by my own lack of foresight.

I was completely right about the reaction of the media. The revelation that I had been in touch with Coyne eclipsed the accounts of the rest of the debate and I was not popular in our caucus for a few days. However, my fear that I might have hurt Coyne's case proved unwarranted. Almost no one believed Coyne was a Liberal partisan, much less that he had been trying to help the Opposition.

I was surprised that the government did not go on with the Coyne bill the next day, but reverted instead to the budget debate. I had assumed they would want to get their bill disposed of as quickly as possible. In fact the debate was not resumed until over a week later on 4 July, when Marcel Lambert resumed a speech which had been interrupted by the adjournment. He claimed he had discovered what he called 'parallels' between Coyne's letter of 26 June and my speech the same day. He charged 'that certain members of the Official Opposition have been consulting with and advising Mr Coyne in this deplorable affair.' The House, he declared, knew from my own admissions that I had had discussions with Coyne between 13 June and 26 June. He wondered whether there had been earlier consultation. If members of the Opposition had 'not been actively advising or consulting with the Governor, then certainly it is someone in the hierarchy of the Liberal Party, and the pipe line to honourable members opposite is short and direct.'

Lambert's speech later took another twist. Instead of sticking to the charge that Coyne was working with the Liberal Opposition, he said the Liberals after 30 May saw 'a wonderful opportunity ... a plan that Machiavelli might have admired.' This Liberal plan was to destroy Coyne and injure the government at the same time. 'Mr. Coyne would have to go through a political guillotine.' That did not worry the Liberals. They believed Coyne's policies had been one of the causes of their defeat in 1957 and wanted revenge. 'Retribution might be a little delayed but it was certain.'

I was puzzled by Lambert's speech. He was normally a tough, blunt, and direct debater. Subtlety and mystification was not his style. Luckily it was not effective in this case. After Lambert had concluded, there was little new to say on this second day of debate. Pearson's attempt to get a hearing for Coyne was rejected. Chevrier thereupon summed up the issue in the bill. What was to be decided was whether or not to remove from office a public servant who held office during good behaviour, without first establishing that there had not been good behaviour on the part of that public servant.

Dick Bell, Fleming's parliamentary secretary, argued that Parliament had the right to exercise its sovereignty in a case where there was an unbridgeable gap between the government and the governor. He accused the Opposition of supporting an attempted *coup d'état* by a public servant seeking to bring down the government and usurp the role of the House of Commons.

Rumours had already begun to circulate that the Senate might defeat the Bill. Bell accused the Opposition of seeking 'to go behind the backs of the elected representatives' and 'to have a few old men in another place serve their particular purpose.' Second reading of the bill passed that day, with every member of the Opposition present voting against it.

At the beginning of the final debate on 5 July, Pearson spoke briefly to summarize the issue in the bill as the Opposition saw it. The issue was not the policy or tactics of the governor of the bank, nor whether or not Coyne had co-operated with the government. The issue was 'the fundamental right of justice and fair play, the right of a Canadian to be heard before condemnation and to be heard before the body which is condemning him. It is a right enshrined in the Bill of Rights.' Without giving Coyne a hearing, passage of the bill 'would be an intolerable and indefensible violation of an elementary right of a free Canadian citizen.' That was why the Liberal Opposition would vote against it.

Two members of the NDP stated that before voting on the bill they would like to hear from the prime minister. This plea brought Diefenbaker into the debate for the first time. He made a very long speech in which he rarely mentioned the purpose of the bill. He dredged up incidents when Liberals had, according to him, disregarded human rights. Diefenbaker, as usual, seemed to feel his own sins could be justified by what he claimed were the sins of others. He said he had not intended to speak until he had listened to Pearson's speech so he would know what the position of the Opposition was. He accused us of ridiculing the Bill of Rights before it was introduced, claiming it was unnecessary and voting for it reluctantly. Now the Bill of Rights had become the cornerstone of our argument.

Instead of replying to Pearson's speech, Diefenbaker turned his attention to me. When he saw me, 'speaking of the rights of man, talking of bills of attainder and the dangers to individuals of the action being taken,' he thought 'what a transition had taken place in his thinking since he departed from the position of Clerk of the Privy Council.' He asked: 'Can he forget what he did to Mr. Pitt?'

This was a reference to a very painful episode in my life. I had accompanied Prime Minister St Laurent on a tour of western Canada in the fall of 1952. We had stayed in Winnipeg at the Canadian National hotel where Mr Pitt was then manager. St Laurent made a luncheon speech during the day at the Canadian Pacific hotel. Some time later in a conversation with Donald Gordon, the president of CN, I mentioned the contrast between service in the two hotels. Apparently my observations led to an investigation and Mr Pitt was transferred to another less important CN hotel. The Winnipeg *Tribune* published a story that Mr Pitt's demotion was the result of a complaint I had made. The Opposition took the matter up in Parliament. When the CN budget was before the House committee with Donald Gordon in attendance, he was questioned about Pitt. It was suggested CN had acted because of political pressure from me. At one point Gordon lost his temper and burst out that neither Jack Pickersgill nor anyone else could push him around. He insisted CN had acted on its own initiative.

As a public servant I had felt I had no right to say a word in public during the furore. Diefenbaker revived the subject at some length in campaign speeches in the election of 1953. By that time, I was in public life and free to reply. I wrote him a letter setting out the facts and received no reply. Diefenbaker had a long memory and apparently felt the Pitt incident had taken away any right I had to complain about the treatment of Coyne.

Having asked 'Can he forget what he did to Mr Pitt?' Diefenbaker continued: 'Was he given a trial? I ask the hon. gentleman: what trial did you give him?'

I rose on a question of privilege and said: 'the right honourable gentleman has chosen to revive an incident about which he made speeches in the election of 1953, and about which I wrote him a letter to which he never deigned to reply, in which I set out the facts about this matter.'

When the Speaker interrupted to ask what my question of privilege was I replied: 'The right honourable gentleman has made an accusation which affects my honour. There is absolutely no truth in his charge that I had anything whatever to do with any action which may have been taken by the head of the Canadian National Railways concerning Mr. Pitt. Those facts have been put on the record, and the right honourable gentleman was sent those facts in a letter to which he did not bother to reply.'

Diefenbaker blustered a little more about the incident and then turned to a charge that the Liberal government in 1945, 1946 and 1947 'destroyed the rights of individuals in this country by Order-in-Council.' This was a reference to a secret order-in-council under the War Measures Act which had been used to detain a number of persons mentioned in the Gouzenko revelations about Soviet espionage. From there he began to dredge up references to acts of the St Laurent government.

At this point Paul Hellyer raised a point of order as to the relevancy of this recital to the bill being debated. The Speaker ruled that the prime minister was evidently replying to references by the Opposition to the Bill of Rights, but warned that it was against the rules to enlarge the scope of the debate on third reading. Diefenbaker nevertheless continued his catalogue of charges against the previous government.

Late in the day, he finally mentioned Coyne. He said: 'I intend to particularly refer to Mr. Coyne's rights and obligations being interfered with when the Supreme Court of Parliament has before it his record' – at this point there were some interruptions while he completed the sentence with the words – 'his record as set forth in the letters which he has issued from time to time.' One can only guess what this sentence meant, but he was probably saying that, because Coyne had made his case public, he had no right to a hearing in Parliament.

He observed that in one of his letters, Coyne referred to a man 'in whom he places reliance.' Glaring across the aisle at me, Diefenbaker said: 'I look at that individual now and wonder whether I behold in fact the person who dictated certain portions of those letters.'

Pearson interjected: 'You do not see him.'

I rose again on a question of privilege. It was already six o'clock, the time of adjournment and the Speaker suggested I defer my statement until the debate could be resumed. Both Chevrier and Pearson exclaimed 'No.' Encouraged by their support, I said: 'Mr. Speaker, when one is defamed by the words of the Prime Minister, one should surely be given a second in which to reply.' The Speaker then asked if the House would give me unanimous consent to be heard. To my surprise, no one objected. I then said that the charge the prime minister has just made had already been made earlier in the debate, in the form of a question by the minister of public works (Walker). 'At that time, I gave a simple and direct answer which was No. My answer is still No. My reputation for telling the truth in this House, I stand on.' The House then adjourned, but not before Hellyer remarked: 'The Prime Minister plunged to new depths this afternoon.' (Later, in the Senate committee on the bill, where Coyne was allowed to appear, Coyne identified the person in whom he placed reliance as Graham Towers, his predecessor as governor of the bank.)

Rights to hearings

As Diefenbaker had not concluded his speech and as we assumed the debate would continue the next day, we raised no question when Churchill announced on adjournment: 'Government orders tomorrow, Mr. Speaker.' The Opposition was taken completely by surprise when, instead, the minister of finance proposed that the House should consider the amendment the Senate had made to a bill to amend the Customs Tariff Act which had already passed the House of Commons.

This bill had been forecast in the budget of December 1960 as an *urgent* method of reducing unemployment. In a speech on that budget I pointed out that the proposed amendment would give all power to the minister to decide the value of imported goods on which customs duties were levied and take away the existing right provided in the law for appeals to the Tariff Board or, on points of law, to the courts. I forecast vigorous opposition when the measure came before the House.

The legislation to amend the Customs Tariff Act first came before the House for debate on 1 February 1961. In the debate we concentrated exclusively on the proposed abolition of an existing right of appeal. We asked repeatedly what excuse there was to take from the taxpayer the right to appeal from the decisions of the minister who might determine the value of imported goods in one way for one person and in another way for another.

After three days of debate the government turned to other business and did not bring this *urgent* measure back for debate for ten days. At the end of one day, we showed no sign of letting the measure pass and the government put off the debate for another twelve days. Once more we attacked. The debate was adjourned at the end of the afternoon and resumed two days later. As the debate continued day after day, the issue of denying appeals resulted in a growing volume of editorial comment unfavourable to the government. Pearson had up to then left the debate to others, but he took part on the sixth day. He was particularly effective when he urged Nowlan to amend the measure to restore the right of appeal which would give the taxpayers a public hearing.

I thought Pearson realized the Opposition was making gains with the public. I was surprised, late that afternoon, to receive word from Pearson, who had left the chamber and gone to his office, that he thought the debate had lasted long enough, and that we should allow the first stage to be completed. We called off our opposition when the House resumed its sitting after dinner. I accepted Pearson's decision without question, but I was not happy about it. I felt we were winning the debate and making an impression on the press and, to some degree, on the public. There was a rumour that Nowlan was urging the cabinet to restore the right of appeal. That would have been a victory for the Opposition.

It was apparent the government no longer considered the measure urgent when further debate was delayed for another six weeks. We made two motions to amend the bill to provide for an appeal from the minister's decision and the NDP made a third. But we were not able to work up as much steam as we had in the earlier debate. The bill was passed without debate on the third day. Almost two more months passed before the bill was debated in the

Senate. The Senate amended the bill on 14 June to provide that the decisions of the minister should be subject to an appeal to the Tariff Board, as we had tried to do in the House.

We did not realize why the government was interrupting the final stage of the bill to remove Coyne until Fleming made an elaborate constitutional argument for disagreeing with the Senate amendment on the ground that it would infringe the sole and undoubted right of the Commons to impose taxation. Pearson replied that the amendment had nothing to do with the exclusive right of the Commons to impose taxes. All it would do was restore the right of appeal from a decision of a minister – a right which the Commons should never have tried to take away. He defended the right of the Senate to do so. Regier for the NDP supported the right of the Senate to act. I said that this was just another example of the attempt by the government to use a servile majority to establish a dictatorship and to remove from individual citizens those very rights the prime minister had boasted were safeguarded by the Bill of Rights.

The reference to the Bill of Rights led Diefenbaker into a lengthy digression on the secret order-in-council of 1945 and other alleged arbitrary actions by Liberal governments. Diefenbaker then recalled that Mackenzie King had promised to reform the Senate. He stated flatly that the government would not accept a Senate amendment to a tax bill. He questioned the constitutional right of the Senate to make such an amendment. Senate reform, he implied, was a question the Canadian people would have to decide sooner or later.

This outburst convinced us the government had interrupted the debate on the Coyne bill to try to intimidate the Senate before that bill came before it. Rumours were rife that the Senate might defeat the Coyne bill and Diefenbaker perhaps thought this menace of reform might prevent such a defeat. I cannot recall another threat to reform the Senate because it dared to frustrate the government until the Mulroney government said, in the spring of 1985, it would seek to limit the powers of the Senate because it delayed the passage of a bill to authorize borrowing by the government.

Far from intimidating the Senate, the refusal of the government to accept its amendment upholding the right of taxpayers to be given a hearing on appeal strengthened the resolve of many of the senators to give Coyne the hearing the House was denying him.

The following day (7 July) the debate on the Coyne bill was resumed and Diefenbaker went on with his speech. He claimed again that references to the Bill of Rights by the Opposition were mere lip-service. Diefenbaker then accused Coyne of trying to set up a rival government. He claimed that Coyne's published letters established beyond question that the attitude of the governor and responsible government were not compatible. There were irreconcilable differences on basic policies. The leader of the Opposition had said that

Coyne's usefulness was over. What would a committee achieve? It was inconceivable, he argued, that a hearing be held to advise the government and Parliament that its responsibility and supremacy should not be discharged. It was an exaggeration to talk about a bill of attainder. A bill of attainder provided for the death of the individual and the loss of his civil rights. He said: 'There was no pension involved in those days under a bill of attainder.'

Diefenbaker's personal resentment was betrayed when he contrasted the governor's pension with the lack of a pension for prime ministers. He thought Coyne should have disavowed the pension instead of publishing the by-law in the Canada *Gazette* to make sure it was legally established. Diefenbaker concluded with the statement: 'This government intends to govern and not to have its direction determined by one who follows a course which we cannot and shall not accept.' It was a feeble conclusion to an irrelevant and ineffective contribution to the debate.

Paul Martin and Walter Pitman both made excellent speeches replying to the prime minister, but the life had gone out of the debate. Douglas Fisher of the NDP made the last speech. He concluded by recommending a dissolution of Parliament and an election on the issue.

The bill amending the Bank of Canada Act was adopted by a vote of 129 to 37.

The Senate and the Coyne affair

Debate on the Coyne affair moved on to the Senate. There appeared to be a majority in that house reluctant to pass the bill and, in any case, determined to give Coyne a hearing. There was some doubt whether a majority of senators were ready to face a confrontation with the government unless they were assured that Coyne would not try to carry on as governor. This doubt was passed on to me and Coyne gave me permission to let certain key senators know that he intended to resign once his honour was vindicated.

The Senate gave Coyne a full hearing in its Banking and Commerce Committee. He gave a straightforward account of the difference with the government from his point of view and responded politely and respectfully to all questions.

Coyne's statement provides a marked contrast to the account Fleming gave in his memoirs a quarter of a century later. In retrospect Fleming has lost none of his bitterness. His language is extravagant and abusive. Coyne himself and everyone concerned with the affair, including Diefenbaker, is condemned. Fleming alone was the perfect gentle knight in shining armour. Coyne is accused of mishandling the record and mangling the facts to his own advantage in his presentation to the Senate committee. Fleming alleges, in apparent complaint, that he was not invited to appear before the committee. Statements made in the press at the time that the committee had invited him to appear before it were, according to Fleming, entirely false.

I have read the proceedings of the committee with care. It was made clear at the outset of the hearings that the chairman of the Senate committee, through the clerk of committees, had notices sent by special delivery to Coyne and Fleming that the bill had been referred to the committee and that the committee would be prepared to hear any representations they might wish to make. This may not technically have been an invitation, but it was perfectly clear Fleming was free to appear, if he so desired, to give his version of the affair. Fleming later discloses that he was free to do so when he admits that 'before the Committee had completed its hatchet work, I spoke to Dief and the Cabinet as to whether I should ask to appear before the Senate Committee and I offered to do so if they thought I should. They decided against it.'

In his final summing up Coyne told the committee he intended, once the bill was disposed of, to resign as governor. He appealed to the senators to find he had not been guilty of misbehaviour. As soon as the Senate had decided not to proceed with the bill, Coyne submitted his resignation to the deputy governor, 'typically,' according to Fleming, 'repeating his false accusations against the government once more.'

Fleming twenty-four years later accuses the Senate of taking satisfaction in pretending to reach a proper conclusion 'after excluding all the evidence except that of one man.' He concludes, with customary moderation: 'Truth had been crucified in the Senate of Canada.'

The fact, as Fleming himself admits, was that he and Diefenbaker, not the Senate committee, excluded his evidence. A quarter of a century later, he has still failed to reply to Coyne's presentation.

Fleming does admit 'the government handled the case badly' but he blames the cabinet not himself for 'every step taken or not taken.' He complains of some of his colleagues for 'placing the entire responsibility for the setback on me.' He states bitterly that 'Dief in his Memoirs has as usual decked himself in the robes of infallibility and excused himself from responsibility for the undoubted error.' Fleming quotes Diefenbaker: 'He [Coyne] made the correspondence public and demanded a public hearing before a Parliamentary committee. Mr. Fleming refused. My own view was that we should have agreed.' Fleming calls this statement a 'barefaced attempt to escape responsibility.' He adds that Diefenbaker 'earns neither thanks nor respect from me for this contemptible effort to shift his own responsibility onto my shoulders.'

Coyne resigned as a hero and, despite Fleming's belief that he got the blame for the fiasco, it is my opinion that, in the public mind, Diefenbaker was the villain. Many observers, at the time and since, have judged that the handling of the Coyne affair was the greatest single cause of the discrediting of the government and especially of Diefenbaker.

Peter Stursberg in his book *Diefenbaker: Leadership Gained* (1975) put to me the question as to how I felt the Coyne affair should have been handled. I replied: 'It shouldn't have been handled at all . . . Jim Coyne's term was nearly up, and if they couldn't get along with him a wise government would have just sat it out.' My statement continues: 'I can't be neutral about Jim Coyne. He is my closest personal friend. But I did not really approve of his campaign of speech-making. He took the view that he had this independent position, that he was *indispensable,* that the interests of the country were being sacrificed, and it was his duty to do these things.'

When I read Stursberg's book, I was sure I had not said that Coyne considered he was 'indispensable.' At my request, Stursberg had the tape of the interview checked and reported that I had said 'dispensable.' I knew that Coyne realized he was risking his career by acting as he had, but that he had felt that was his duty. With that one correction, I stand by every word in the interview with Stursberg and particularly the statement that 'if the government had made a real issue of those speeches, I would have been hard put to know what position to take. But instead of doing that, the idea of trying to suggest that Coyne was doing something improper and underhanded about his pension was so cheap and nasty and despicable that it just completely destroyed what case they had.' I said I thought the government's objection to Coyne's speeches was a debatable issue, but that dealing with Coyne by an attempt at blackmail was not.

Before the Senate committee, Coyne made a logical case for his speeches. He contended, as subsequent governors of the bank have done, that too much was expected of monetary policy and that monetary policy had to be supported by the right kind of fiscal and economic policies. He produced convincing evidence that the directors of the bank had approved of his speeches until the end of 1960, as had most of the press and much of the business community.

If the government had been able to formulate policies that made any kind of sense, it seems likely no conflict would have arisen. But the failure of the government to agree on any constructive policies created an appearance of conflict and embarrassment for the government. Coyne stopped making speeches when Fleming finally told him they were annoying the government. As a politician I no doubt perceived the probable effect of the speeches long before Coyne did, and I once expressed my disquiet to Beattie.

The Liberal Opposition was undoubtedly the political beneficiary of the Coyne affair, but it might easily not have happened that way. There were, in 1957, some Liberals who believed the so-called tight-money policy of the Bank of Canada was one of the causes of the defeat of the St Laurent government. As unemployment grew, there were members in the Liberal Opposition who attacked the bank, and Coyne in particular, for tight money.

Pearson and the prudent critics sought to pin the responsibility for monetary policy on the government rather than the bank. If Fleming had had a direct confrontation with Coyne over monetary policy, the Opposition would not have had an effective issue, and probably would not have tried to create one. Instead, the government chose to make the real issue the increase in Coyne's pension.

Until that attempt at blackmail, I had persisted in keeping aloof from any debates about the bank and, even afterwards, I made only that one speech which I did not feel had, on balance, been helpful. The charge that I or any other Liberal had planned Coyne's tactics or written his statements was so absurd that it gained no credence with the public. Anyone who knew Jim Coyne knew that he was too proud as well as too articulate to seek or accept that kind of help. That he was, in the slightest degree, politically partisan is simply not true. He did discuss his tactics with me on several occasions after he had made his public statement on 13 June 1961, but his conclusions and his statements were his own. I am not interested in replying to Fleming's abusive references to me in his memoirs and I am grateful to him for including our exchange of correspondence as an appendix thereto. His reflections on my character and motives are no worse than his reflections on others and no more credible.

It would have been better for the government's reputation, as Douglas Harkness pointed out, simply to have waited until Coyne's term expired in December 1961. But Diefenbaker himself obviously insisted on making the pension the main issue and on refusing to let Coyne appear before a parliamentary committee. The result was to make Coyne a martyr and to make the government look tyrannical and inept at the same time.

The courage of the Senate in refusing to approve the bill to remove Coyne was generally applauded. When the Senate persisted in its amendment to the customs tariff bill to safeguard the right of the taxpayers to a hearing, that bill also failed to pass. This fiasco, coupled with the aborting of the Coyne bill, made 1961 a vintage year for the Senate.

The treatment of
Donald Gordon

The treatment of Donald Gordon, who was president of the Canadian National Railways, proved almost as great an embarrassment to the government as Coyne. In 1958, many Tory back-benchers, especially French-speaking MPs from Quebec, had shown hostility to Gordon. One Toronto MP said his management of CN was so bad that his salary should be cut in half. When Gordon's appointment as chairman and a director of CN expired on 30 September 1960, the government took no action to replace or reappoint him.

By 22 May 1961, no action had been taken on the chairmanship, though Gordon was still president. That day the House debated a bill to increase the number of directors of Canadian National from seven to twelve. We decided at the committee stage, to give the government a hard time about Gordon. Chevrier opened by asking Leon Balcer, who had succeeded George Hees as minister of transport, if he intended to reply to attacks which had been made on Gordon and other officers of CN. Balcer declined to reply on the ground that the question had nothing to do with the bill. I asked Balcer whether Donald Gordon was in fact still a director of Canadian National. Balcer replied that his term had expired on 30 September 1960, but that the Canadian National Railways Act provided that a director whose term had expired remained a director until his successor was appointed. I then argued that we should not proceed with the bill until we were told whether the government intended to reappoint Gordon. In the light of the attacks made on him by all but one of the Tory members who had spoken, we were entitled to know whether the Bill was a device to get rid of Gordon. Never before in the history of Canada had the president of Canadian National or any other Crown corporation been kept on sufferance for months as Gordon had been. We should not vote money to be spent on additional directors before we were told what the government intended to do about Gordon.

After several speeches had been made, the chair ruled that a debate about Gordon was not in order on the bill. I then moved an amendment that one of the new directors should be 'the present President of the Canadian National Railways.' Though the amendment was ruled out of order, we got the debate back to Gordon. If the government wanted to keep Gordon as head of the railway, they should give him enough support to do the job properly instead of leaving him suspended between heaven and earth. There should not be five new directors when the government could not decide what to do with those whose terms had expired. The bill was debated all afternoon and finally we let it pass.

Another opportunity arose to raise the Gordon question on the annual CN financing bill on 8 July, the day after the bill to remove Coyne had been passed by the House of Commons. Chevrier and I shared in attacking the government for its disgraceful attitude to Gordon and the other directors who had been kept in suspense for nine months and eight days. The day before, I said, we had watched the leader of the government wield the axe against Coyne; now we were discussing a gentleman who had given long and great service to his country who had for nine months and eight days been kept under suspended sentence not knowing on what day the axe would fall. We did not question the legal right of the government to replace Donald Gordon whose term had expired; what Parliament had the right to know, before voting additional money to Canadian National, was who would be head of the company.

The session was adjourned on 13 July for a summer recess until 7 September. Chevrier raised the situation of Gordon again in a question to Diefenbaker on 18 September, almost a year after his term as chairman had expired. This time, the prime minister replied that the minister of transport would announce the appointment of directors in his estimates.

The transport estimates were the final item of business on the last day of the session. Balcer announced that Donald Gordon had been reappointed chairman of the board. He named all the other directors. Those whose terms had not yet expired were retained even though they had been Liberal appointees. We had not yet reached the constitutional heights of 1985 when all directors of Crown companies were fired and replaced by Tories, even when their terms had not expired.

No one doubted that Diefenbaker would have liked to please the critics in his caucus by getting rid of Gordon. Perhaps he hoped the humiliation of Gordon by the long delay would provoke him into resignation. By delaying his reappointment to the end of the session, Diefenbaker escaped outcries from his own back-benchers. But, after the Coyne fiasco, he evidently did not dare to wield the axe again.

Diefenbaker's problems
with his ministers

One minister who caused Diefenbaker repeated embarrassment was Henri Courtemanche MP for Labelle. He had been accused of being involved in land acquisition in his constituency by the government. He resigned suddenly from the House on the alleged ground of ill health and was appointed to the Senate in January 1960. The charges were not pursued further. On 16 June 1961, reports appeared in the press alleging that Senator Courtemanche had been involved in other financial irregularities. The next day, Pearson asked Diefenbaker if he had reason to believe there were irregularities when Courtemanche went to the Senate. Diefenbaker replied there had never been any such suggestion at any time. The allegations now appearing in the press had been made before a provincial royal commission dealing with the affairs of a hospital in Quebec. Diefenbaker said the Department of Justice had been asked to get an official copy of the transcript of evidence so it could be studied carefully. The matter came up again on 20, 23, 24, 26, 28, 30 June, and on 1, 4, and 6 July. Replies by the prime minister and the acting minister of national revenue were evasive delaying devices. In reply to a question from Chevrier on 7 September 1961, Diefenbaker said the government had received the transcript of evidence about Courtemanche from the royal commission, but felt no statement should be made until the royal commission reported. The report had not yet appeared when the session ended on 28 September. After the report was made public, Courtemanche, evidently under pressure, resigned from the Senate in December 1961. The Courtemanche affair damaged the reputation of the government.

The government was also hurt by the conduct of another French-speaking minister from Quebec, Noel Dorion, the secretary of state. Dorion had made a speech in the by-election held to elect a successor to Courtemanche. The press reported that he had accused the Liberals of trying to 'anglicize' French Canada by bringing over more immigrants from the British Isles than from any other European country. The Liberals, the report said, had tried to eliminate the French Canadians for the benefit of the English. Diefenbaker had promptly closed the door on this immigration and was trying to offset the Liberal 'anglicization' by fostering immigration from Italy.

On 18 January 1961, the day Parliament resumed after Christmas, I asked the prime minister if Dorion had been speaking for him. Before Diefenbaker could reply, Dorion intervened to say he had not been reported correctly. He, in fact, made no correction, but cited a speech by Walter Harris as the basis for his own statement. Diefenbaker did not answer my question.

I raised the matter again at the first opportunity. Unfortunately Dorion was not in the House that day. I was asked why I had brought the subject up again. I had done so, I replied, because I thought that kind of speech was a disgrace to this country. 'It is a disgrace for a Minister of the Crown to make this kind of cheap appeal and cheap misrepresentation calculated to promote disunity in other parts of Canada.'

Dorion later denied categorically that he had said Prime Minister Diefenbaker had promptly closed the door on English immigration and was trying to offset the Liberal anglicization by fostering immigration from Italy. He said this was 'absolutely and completely false.' Whereupon Azellus Denis interjected, 'I was there when he said it.' This led to a dispute as to which member was being truthful, in the course of which Denis said there were 'ten witnesses.' A group of Liberal MPs had been at the meeting.

Several days later Dorion was asked to table the copy of his speech in the Labelle by-election. When he relied on the rules and refused, saying his word must be taken, he was asked why the word of ten Liberal members would not be worth his word.

During the debate on the Immigration estimates, I quoted Dorion in a speech in a by-election in Ontario, in which he said Canada had been the victim of mass immigration in 1957 inherited from the Liberal government. He stated the immigration had been chopped down by the Progressive Conservative government. I pointed out that the mass immigration about which Dorion complained had included the Hungarian refugees. I added that in the election campaign in 1957 Diefenbaker had promised to triple the volume of immigration reached by the Liberal government and, instead, had restricted it.

It was not just French Canadian ministers who embarrassed the government. I was at the centre of a controversy over statements made by another Tory minister in 1961. The incident arose over the case of an unemployed man named Glen Exelby. Exelby had participated in a CBC program called 'Close-Up' on 7 March 1961 as an unemployed person. On 8 March one of the Tory back-benchers asked the minister of labour whether the National Employment Service was doing anything to find employment for him. This was obviously a planted question. Michael Starr, the minister of labour, said he had been given notice of the question and had made inquiries. In reply to the planted question, Starr used information obtained from the Hamilton office of the employment service about Exelby's record of employment. The information was that Exelby had been offered employment which he had not accepted.

The next day Dr McMillan, MP for Welland and one of our most effective back-benchers, at my suggestion, asked the minister of labour whether the minister, if he was asked to do so by a member of Parliament, could procure private information regarding the employment record of a person registered with the employment service. Starr replied that, since Exelby had disclosed his personal affairs of his own volition and created a false impression, it was quite proper to present certain facts on the same matter. I then asked Starr if he had read section 98 of the Unemployment Insurance Act, which stipulates that information about individuals must be kept in confidence. Was he aware that he had broken the law the previous day? When the Speaker objected to my question, I raised a question of privilege and charged that a minister had broken a law made by Parliament. I read section 98 of the Unemployment Insurance Act to support my argument.

The Speaker said I was correct in raising the point but not in arguing it and that the minister should be allowed to reply. Starr contended that the Hamilton office had a right and a duty to supply the minister with information which would reveal the true facts.

I felt genuine indignation about the invasion of privacy. As minister of immigration I had frequently been embarrassed when I had refused to disclose information received confidentially in the examination of immigrants. Even though the minister was not expressly forbidden to do so by the Immigration Act, I had consistently refused to use information which had been disclosed in confidence. The impropriety was even greater when such disclosures were contrary to the law. The estimates of the Department of Labour came up later that day. In a speech, I concentrated on the breach of the law by the minister and made an impassioned and, I felt, a highly effective speech.

Evidence appeared in the press next morning that some of the statements Starr had received from the Unemployment Insurance Commission were not correct and that the employment service had co-operated with the CBC in preparing its broadcast. During the question period, Chevrier and Martin made a good deal of these disclosures. Starr replied to my speech later that day. He claimed he had not broken the law because Exelby had disclosed the information and it was no longer confidential. I was not present, but Chevrier made the case that there had been a clear breach of the law.

The matter did not end there. A few days later I asked Starr if he had received a letter from Exelby. He said 'yes' and read extracts with comments. He later acceded to my request that he table the letter, which he produced the next day. I raised a question of privilege alleging that the letter showed the minister had misinformed and misled the House. I made a formal motion to have the minister's statement and Exelby's letter referred to the Committee on Privileges and Elections for appropriate action. The Speaker decided, after some argument and some interruptions, that there was not a *prima facie* question of privilege. I did not contest his ruling.

About ten days later I asked Starr if the employment service had yet found a job for Exelby. He said he had not been keeping track of the case of late. The next day I asked again and Starr said the employment service was continuing its efforts. I raised the question again several weeks later. Starr reported the efforts were continuing. The matter was not raised again. But never again were records of individual cases before the employment service used in the House. We might have pushed the charge that a minister had broken the law even harder, if anyone had believed Starr had done so knowingly, or if he had not been so well-liked on both sides of the House.

Serious moments

Since there was no Liberal member from Manitoba, I often spoke when controversial questions arose affecting that province. One of these questions was about the payments the government proposed to make to the wheat growers of the prairies for serious crop losses in 1960. These payments were to be shared jointly by the federal and provincial governments. Before the legislation was through Parliament, the provincial minister of agriculture had stated in the Manitoba Legislature that there was a verbal agreement with Ottawa to share these payments equally. Diefenbaker had already told Parliament that no action would be taken until the federal legislation was enacted. When I found the statement of the provincial minister in the Manitoba *Hansard,* I claimed that Parliament had been misled. Diefenbaker retorted there had been no misleading. Later the same day I asked Harkness, who was then minister of agriculture, whether there had been a verbal agreement. Harkness said assurances had been given to the prairie governments that action would be taken. I then asked Diefenbaker whether an assurance constituted a verbal agreement. His reply was that I did not understand the difference between an assurance and an agreement.

In an effort to discover the difference I asked the next day for the correspondence with the provincial governments on the acreage payments. Harkness said he would require the consent of the provincial governments. I realized Harkness feared the correspondence with Manitoba would contradict

Diefenbaker's statement, so I kept worrying away at the question, particularly after the minister of agriculture for Manitoba told the Legislature he did not have the slightest idea why the prime minister of Canada had said in the House of Commons that no commitment had been given by the federal government. I was asked what difference that made and I replied: 'What difference does it make, I ask, whether a government's word can be accepted . . . whether the word of the government of Canada means anything at all?'

After more than a month of harassing Harkness, I complained that his failure to produce the correspondence was a 'shocking example of contempt of Parliament.' My charge provoked a sharp exchange with Harkness, but we never did resolve the question as to whether there had been a verbal agreement with the government of Manitoba. Both Diefenbaker and Harkness looked bad in Parliament, but interest outside Parliament was understandably minimal.

Later in the session I had an exchange on the Northern Affairs estimates with Walter Dinsdale about the floodway which was being designed to divert part of the flow of the Red River around Winnipeg when that river flooded in the spring. The floodway had been proposed shortly after the disastrous flood of 1950. Diefenbaker had blamed the Liberals for doing nothing about it and had promised action in at least one speech in 1957. Negotiations had dragged on until 1961 when there were signs of impatience in Manitoba.

The Speech from the Throne in January 1962 announced that agreement had been reached with the government of Manitoba for division of costs of the floodway. I asked in April if the agreement had been signed and Dinsdale said 'No.' I expressed shock and Fleming admitted there was no firm, signed agreement, but one was expected soon. At that time dissolution of Parliament and an election were expected shortly. Roblin, the Manitoba premier, forecast there would be an agreement before Parliament was dissolved. On 16 April Dinsdale admitted there was still no signed agreement. Parliament was dissolved on 18 April and the agreement was finally signed only on 28 May. These examples of procrastination about matters affecting the friendly Tory government of Manitoba were of little importance, except to add to the growing impression of the incompetence and indecision of the Diefenbaker government. Luckily there had been no serious flooding since 1950, but the delay over the floodway illustrates how difficult it is for governments to deal with disasters, until they happen.

A serious question was raised in 1961 regarding Indians and Eskimoes in Labrador. At the time of the union, the Indians of the new province were not deemed to be Indians under the Indian Act since they had not had special status before the union but had been treated as ordinary citizens of the province. In the rest of Canada in 1949, Eskimoes had no recognized special status. Subsequent to the union with Newfoundland, the courts decided Eskimoes were juridically Indians. After that judgement, while Jean Lesage was minister of northern affairs considerable financial assistance was provided for the education and health of Eskimoes in the Northwest Territories, Manitoba, and Quebec, but not in Newfoundland-Labrador. I suggested to Charlie Granger, who was MP for Labrador, that Eskimoes there should receive similar treatment. Granger raised the question of treatment of Indians and Eskimoes in Labrador in 1961. I believe this was the first time the question had been raised in Parliament. Both the minister of northern affairs and the minister of citizenship and immigration replied that, under the Terms of Union, the responsibility rested with the province, but both agreed they would give consideration to proposals for federal assistance. No action was taken by the Diefenbaker government, but after the government changed, the native peoples of Labrador and Newfoundland, Indians as well as Inuit, have gradually been given treatment similar to what is provided elsewhere in Canada.

The Opposition continued in 1961 to commend any measure introduced by the government in which we found merit. There were not many, but one constructive initiative in 1961 was a bill to provide for the rehabilitation of agricultural lands and the development of rural areas in Canada. This came to be called ARDA. The measure was sponsored by Alvin Hamilton, the minister of agriculture, who was probably the most imaginative member of the government and the minister with the greatest public appeal.

The objective was to take marginal lands out of use for farming and to settle their occupants in areas which would not become rural slums. As I had spent ten years as a child in the interlake area of Manitoba where much of the land was marginal, I was given the task of stating the Liberal position on the ARDA bill. I began with an account of our experience from 1911 as a family on a homestead in an area where many of the homesteads had been abandoned after a few years. Based on that experience, I supported the objectives of the bill. I did raise a question about its timing since its immediate effect could be to throw poor farmers on to the labour market. ARDA could be really successful only in a dynamic growing society. We could not have effective rural rehabilitation while we had three-quarters of a million unemployed. I hoped Alvin Hamilton would not be blinded by his own vision and would realize that careful planning and timing would be needed if ARDA was to succeed.

The attitude of the Diefenbaker government to Britain's application to join the Common Market was something we could not commend. This became an issue between the government and the Liberal Opposition in 1961. A

Commonwealth ministers' meeting was held in September in Ghana, where Fleming and Hees represented Canada. Their speeches, as reported in the press, were highly critical of the British initiative. On 14 September, Diefenbaker was asked several questions, particularly about the report that Hees had said Britain had to choose between the Common Market and the Commonwealth. Diefenbaker claimed he had been unable to get texts of the speeches. Surely, I said, the government had decided on its position before the ministers left for Accra. There was no reply.

After Fleming and Hees returned to Ottawa, the Opposition accused the Canadian delegation to Ghana of trying to dictate to Britain. Fleming made a speech in their defence on the last day of the session, to which Chevrier, in Pearson's absence from the House, replied that, instead of opposing Britain's entry, Canada should try to have the Common Market expanded into an Atlantic Economic Community. The difference between parties over the question of Britain's application to enter the European Economic Community continued until Britain finally joined the Common Market.

Frivolous moments

I would not want to give the impression that I concentrated exclusively on the great controversial issues before Parliament or even other serious problems. I was fascinated by the day-to-day debates and often took part in proceedings which were not of great interest outside the House. Some of my interventions were frivolous.

For example, on 2 March 1961, I asked the minister of forestry (Hugh John Flemming, the former premier of New Brunswick) whether his department was making any progress in finding a means of arresting Dutch elm disease. The minister said he had no knowledge of the matter, but would take the question as notice. The Dutch elm disease was serious enough, but if I had really wanted information this would not have been the route to follow. When asked outside the House the reason for the question, I said I felt the minister, whose department had no real function, was being ignored, seemed lonely, and should get a little attention. The result of my question was that I kept receiving literature from the forestry department on the Dutch elm disease as long as I remained in Parliament.

On 16 March, David Walker, the minister of public works, returned to the House after several days absence. I asked him whether, during his absence, he had been able to meditate on the problem of finding a suitable site for the post office at Reserve Mines, Nova Scotia, which I knew had been vexing him for some time. (The Tory MP for Reserve Mines had once asked a question about the post office site.)

Walker said he did not realize who was behind the many, many letters, anonymous and otherwise, he had received. He thanked me for disclosing my hand and assured me the matter would receive just the same consideration it would have received if I had not asked the question. I rose at once on a question of privilege. The Speaker said he did not see how privilege could have arisen, but Walker asked that I be allowed to proceed. I said I had been accused of writing anonymous letters which was surely a shocking accusation for one member to make about another. I wanted to assure the minister that, unlike some of his correspondents, I had never been ashamed to sign my name to my letters. The Speaker agreed a question of privilege would have arisen if Walker's answer had been given serious construction, but that he did not take it in that vein. I said: 'Nor did I.'

The Diefenbaker government used partisan publicity far more extensively than any previous government. No other minister practised the art so blatantly as Alvin Hamilton after he became minister of agriculture. He turned some of the former information services of his department into organs of personal and party glorification to the point where this practice began to be described by Ottawa correspondents of more than one newspaper as Alvin Hamilton's political farming. One day I read three of these press reports, including one from the Russell, Manitoba, *Banner* which began: 'Surpluses would soon vanish if the federal minister of agriculture put as much effort into selling farm produce as he does in selling Mr. Hamilton to the public.' I supposed the *Banner* was not really suggesting that there was any reintroduction of slavery but was using the word 'selling' in the modern sense of Madison Avenue.

The *Banner* had also complained that about twenty-five mimeographed pages were received every week. Multiplying this figure by the number of weekly papers and radio stations made this a lot of paper. This, I added, perhaps explained the Minister's new policy (under ARDA) of planting trees, so that there would not be a shortage of spruce trees to supply paper for his press releases. My concern did nothing to reduce the flow of publicity.

I had a totally frivolous exchange during a Trade and Commerce debate with J. M. Macdonnell, who, for a short time, was a minister without portfolio in Diefenbaker's cabinet and who was my closest friend on the Tory benches. He had made a comprehensive and liberal speech on trade policy in which he had praised the efforts of the Mackenzie King government in the post-war period to aid, through loans, in the restoration of the economies and trade of Britain and our European allies. After Macdonnell had spoken, I congratulated him and said I was moved by 'what was a truly liberal speech.' I reminded him that in the days when he had been on our side of the House he had appealed for support to strengthen the Opposition. I assured him 'if he feels he can contribute to the strengthening of the Opposition there is always a light in the window for him on this side of the House.' I hoped his speech would fall 'on listening ears and not on deaf ears.' Macdonnell intervened 'to repudiate' my partisan suggestion that, whenever anyone said anything I considered sensible, 'it is a Liberal remark.'

One day when the Tory MP for Gaspé was boasting about the discovery of his riding by Jacques Cartier, I interrupted him to point out that before Cartier reached Gaspé, he had landed in Catalina harbour on the Bonavista peninsula of Newfoundland. He questioned my statement, but later when I showed him the source, he apologized handsomely in the House.

When one of the Tory members from Cape Breton claimed that John Cabot's landfall was really in Cape Breton, not Newfoundland, I repudiated this attack on the reputation of Bonavista. Jim McGrath, the Tory MP for St John's East, supported me and added that Bonavista had been a 'happy sight' for me as well as for Cabot.

When the appropriation for maintaining the Trent Canal came before the House in 1961, I noted the canal had always been useless for transportation. I said that every time a friend of mine crossed the bridge over the canal, he took off his hat as a recognition of the generosity of the Canadian taxpayers. 'I wondered whether the Minister had ever given any consideration to giving the Trent Canal to Mr. Frost in lieu of the $100 million he is not getting from the Prime Minister.' I made that suggestion in jest, but several years later, when I was minister of transport, I seriously considered the possibility of trying to persuade the government of Ontario to take over the Trent and Rideau canals as tourist attractions, since they had no value as transportation facilities.

Dick Bell, the parliamentary secretary to the minister of finance, was piloting the excise tax bill through the House. The bill proposed to exempt doors from the tax on the ground that they were building materials. Again, out of sheer mischief, I suggested practical problems might arise. I said I had bought a door and put it on two trestles to make a dining table for our house in Bonavista Bay. I asked whether that door would be taxable or not. My question provoked a protracted but frivolous discussion between Bell and me.

On another occasion, I asked Bell whether any part of the vote for the exhibitions branch of Trade and Commerce was to pay for the travels of the minister, George Hees, under the heading 'Exhibitions.'

For years in Opposition, Diefenbaker had attacked the Liberal governments of Mackenzie King and St Laurent for practising what he called 'government by order-in-council.' Since I knew the number of orders-in-council had increased since Diefenbaker became prime minister, I asked one day, out of sheer mischief, whether, as Diefenbaker had promised, the number had been reduced. My question was not answered, but Fleming pontificated that orders-in-council were made when necessary. I retorted: 'Of course, they were just made for fun when we were in office.'

One of the numerous Tories elected for the first time in 1958 had been an immigrant from Russia. His name was Reynold Rapp, the member for Humboldt-Melfort. In his maiden speech he recalled that the only previous time he had been in Ottawa was as a poor newcomer to a strange country. He spoke movingly of his pride in the opportunity Canada had given him, culminating in election to Parliament. I was touched and congratulated him, and we became friendly. In 1961, he introduced a private member's Bill to change the name of his constituency to Humboldt-Melfort-Tisdale. Unlike most private member's Bills, this one passed. I decided to make a brief speech to support the Bill. One reason I gave was that 'Tisdale' was a historic family name in Norfolk county where I was born, with a Dr Tisdale officiating at my birth. But my main reason was to remind Rapp that he had been fortunate to come to Canada in 1929 when there was a Liberal government to let him in, before the Tory government elected in 1930 stopped immigration.

These frivolous interventions were primarily designed to have a little fun, but I also persuaded myself that such pin-pricks did not help the government or the prime minister.

Outside Parliament

The House adjourned for the summer on 13 July 1961. Margaret had already left by train with the three younger children and our cocker spaniel, Ginger, for the Gaspé. Peter and a Newfoundland friend, Bill Baird, were leaving from there on a pulpwood boat for a trip to Italy. After seeing them off, Margaret, Alan, and Ruth went on by train. Walter Dinsdale and W.J. Browne were flying in a government plane to Newfoundland that day to preside at the official opening of Terra Nova national park. Dinsdale offered me a lift. I accepted at once. I then asked if they would mind stopping at Moncton to pick up my wife and two children. Dinsdale agreed, but without enthusiasm. My ministerial hosts were less than thrilled when they realized at Moncton there would also be a small dog in the cabin of the plane.

The plane landed at Gander and we went on at once to our house at Traytown. The next afternoon we attended the ceremony of the opening of the park. Dinsdale, as minister of northern affairs, presided and Browne was the main speaker. Premier Smallwood was a guest speaker. There was a large crowd, most of them my constituents. Margaret and I were seated in the audience. We were mildly embarrassed when Smallwood observed in his speech that he was not an expert in protocol, but he was surprised to see the founder of the park not on the platform, but sitting in the audience. Browne, like anyone else who had to speak after Smallwood, was an anti-climax. He was visibly disturbed and, intending to refer to Dinsdale who was a Salvationist, said Mr Pickersgill was the first member of the Salvation Army who had sat in the Canadian cabinet!

That summer part of Newfoundland was devastated by disastrously destructive forest fires from June till September. A pall of smoke covered most of the northern half of my constituency. At Traytown we scarcely saw the sun all summer. A friend provided us with a pump and hoses to fight the fire should it reach our settlement. A great deal of valuable timber was destroyed and with it the livelihood of hundreds of Newfoundlanders. The fire reached the boundaries of Gander airport and one day the airport had to be closed. The Trans-Canada highway for a stretch of several miles could only be travelled in convoy with police escorts.

In spite of the obvious need for all possible help, the provincial government was reluctant to ask the army to send firefighters because it was federal policy to require provincial governments to reimburse the federal treasury for the cost of such assistance. When our daughter, Jane, flew down from Quebec city in August for a short visit at a time when Gander was threatened, she was horrified that the army was not there. She persuaded me to telephone Smallwood and urge him to ask the federal government to send in the army. I advised him to ask for help, to give no undertaking to pay, and to sign nothing. Troops were sent promptly on request. The fires subsided soon afterwards.

When Parliament resumed sitting in September, I spoke about the fires; I praised the speed with which help had been sent from the navy and air force in late June, and later, when requested, from the army. I said people in Newfoundland were surprised to learn that federal assistance was not a national service in an emergency but that the government expected to be reimbursed from the provincial treasury. I appealed to have the help regarded as a national contribution to an emergency.

James McGrath, one of the Tory members for St John's asked if I knew why the government of Newfoundland had waited three months before asking for the army to help. I said the help might have been offered without waiting for a provincial request. The governments of Quebec and Ontario sent help without waiting to be asked. The overburdened taxpayers of New-foundland, I insisted, should not have this added burden placed upon them. The federal bill for the help was not paid while I was in Parliament and, I hope, has not been paid yet.

I was absent from Ottawa frequently in the fall of 1961. A federal election was expected some time in 1962. I was often in demand to speak at conventions to nominate Liberal candidates and at other party functions. One such convention was in Toronto-Rosedale. The candidate chosen was Donald Macdonald whom I had never met before. I was genuinely impressed and predicted he would have a great future in the party and, I hoped, in government. This politicking continued into the early weeks of 1962 even after the session began in January.

The most exacting engagement outside Parliament was a television debate with the leader of the NDP, the redoubtable Tommy Douglas, before a live audience in Ottawa. The subject of the debate was how political parties should finance election campaigns. Pearson was worried about my tackling so formidable an opponent. I was not entirely free of apprehension myself. I assumed, rightly, that Douglas would denounce the 'old parties' for raising their campaign funds from large corporations and becoming obligated to them. I felt I had a surprise for him. I agreed that campaign funds should not come from corporations or, I added, from *trade unions,* but that the legitimate costs of parties and candidates should be met by the Treasury. Such a system would, of course, require much more stringent restrictions on how much could be spent and for what purposes. I believe this was the first time a prominent politician had advocated this revolutionary policy, which I had favoured for many years. I felt the argument had gone well and I was reassured when a number of those in the audience and even more who had watched on television took the trouble to tell me they felt I had had the better of the encounter.

There were rumours late in the year of a sweeping revamping of the Diefenbaker cabinet. On 28 December the cabinet met in Quebec City where the governor general was in residence. There had been rumours in advance that Fleming would be moved out of Finance. This plan was allegedly thwarted by strong representations from financial circles in Toronto. By 27 December it was generally believed there would be no shuffle and merely the addition of Jacques Flynn, the deputy Speaker, as a minister in place of Paul Comtois who had become lieutenant-governor of Quebec.

28 December was a Saturday. I was the senior Liberal in Ottawa that day. The Canadian press invited me to the press gallery to listen to the report from Quebec. When asked for comment, I had a reply ready which I had rehearsed at the family breakfast table. My comment was that the prime minister had shuffled the pack and dealt himself the same old hand with an

extra joker. The comment was published everywhere in the same reports as the news from Quebec City and underlined the anti-climax.

Many Liberals were saddened at the reports in the new year in 1961 of the death of C.D. Howe. His death recalled many achievements of the great years in office. Senator Norman Paterson drove Douglas Abbott and me to Montreal for the funeral. Paterson entertained us by an endless flow of stories and a gourmet picnic lunch with champagne which we consumed in the comfort of his Rolls Royce. The most impressive tribute to Howe at the funeral was the presence of Jimmy Gardiner, who, like Howe, had served in the cabinet for the whole twenty-two Liberal years. At the age of 77, Gardiner had driven himself all the way from his farm in Saskatchewan; he turned round right after the church service and drove back home – a journey each way of nearly two thousand miles in the dead of winter. Just one year later in January 1962, Gardiner died. Pearson asked me to fly out to Saskatchewan to represent him and the Liberal caucus at the funeral, which was a moving tribute by a large assemblage of his life-time friends and supporters.

Early in 1962, a book entitled *The Liberal Party* was published by Mc-Clelland and Stewart, who also published *The New Party* by Stanley Knowles and *The Conservative Party* by Heath MacQuarrie. Pearson had been asked to write *The Liberal Party* but had persuaded me to do it, with an introduction by him.

An outside activity which gave me much pleasure was a visit to Quebec city on 1 February – Louis St Laurent's eightieth birthday. At a luncheon at the Reform Club I made a speech in French largely devoted to a eulogy of St Laurent. In the afternoon I shared in the family celebrations of his birthday.

Later in February Margaret and I were in Lennoxville for a panel discussion organized by Bishop's University. I spoke partly in French. The theme of the panel was the Canadian identity. In the quesiton period after my speech I made a reference to the language requirements for entrance to Canadian universities. The press reports resulted in angry letters to newspapers, protests to Pearson, and complaints in our Liberal caucus. I prepared a memorandum in reply to protests that had come to me and gave Pearson a copy to use in preparing replies to letters he had received. The memorandum reads:

The seminar was organized by the Quebec Branch of the National Federation of Canadian University Students for the purpose of discussing the Canadian identity. In the course of the question period following the presentation of speeches and discussions among the panelists I was asked by one of the students if I had any suggestion to make as to how a better understanding between English-speaking and French-speaking Canadians might be achieved. I replied that I had two specific suggestions as to how this understanding might be promoted. My first suggestion was that, over a five-year period, the English-language Universities in Canada might try to establish, as a condition of entrance, that all students should be able to read and understand the French language. I added that a parallel requirement on the part of the French-language Universities that matriculants should be able to read and understand English would be desirable, though it was less necessary, because practically all French-speaking students had, for economic reasons, to learn English anyway.

My second suggestion was that French-speaking Canadians elected to the Parliament of Canada should devote less of their energy to concern for the survival of the French language and culture and more to co-operating in the solution of the common problems of all Canadians. I added that survival of the French language and culture was completely assured today, and that what was in question now was the extent of the influence throughout Canada of French-speaking Canadians, and that would depend upon the extent to which they contributed to the solution of our common national problems. In this context I cited the excellent work done by the Hon. Jean Lesage when he was Minister of Northern Affairs.

Although I was exceedingly careful not to say that I thought students entering Universities should be expected to speak French, because I knew how difficult it was, in many parts of Canada, to learn to speak French, the Canadian Press report said the exact opposite. When I got back to Ottawa I found all my four children very indignant about what I was supposed to have said. However, when I explained what I really had said and pointed out that any intelligent student could easily learn to read French and, with the amount of French that is broadcast and the availability of records, it would not be difficult to learn to understand spoken French reasonably well, and when I added that every University in Europe and every good University in the United States insists on a knowledge of a second language as a pre-requisite to entrance, I found they took a different view, particularly when I reminded them that French was one of the official languages of our country.

I did not suggest, nor did I mean to suggest, that any external compulsion should be brought on the Universities to establish any such entrance requirement, since that would be entirely a matter for the Universities themselves. I can hardly imagine that any reasonable person would feel that an understanding of the French language by educated Canadians would not contribute to a better understanding between the two races. I hope this memorandum will convince those who made representations to you that what I said was not wholly unreasonable and that it was not illiberal.'

In the House a French-speaking Tory member from Quebec commented on the report from Lennoxville. He said I seemed to have become an advocate of bilingualism, and that it was the first time he and others had heard me speak about the subject. He thought I should have done so a long time ago. I could not let this comment pass without a reply. I did not go around boasting about my bilingualism, I said, but added that, from the day I came to work in Ottawa I had never, at any time, asked anyone to translate any document out of one of the official languages into the other for my benefit.

I had always taken the view that, if we were to make confederation work properly, we must seek in every possible and practical way to make it equally easy for Canadians to use either of the official languages in every part of the country. I was no new convert to these views. I added that it had not been too easy for me to learn French in the bush in northern Manitoba. If my critic was interested, I could tell him privately how I managed to get my foundation in French, but I would not waste the time of the House by doing so.

At that time, French or Latin was a requirement for entrance to the University of Manitoba. Until the final year of high school, I attended a one-roomed school at Ashern, Manitoba, where no French was taught. A former teacher from New Brunswick, an Acadian, lived in the village. We sold milk in the village from our nearby farm. My mother was worried that I might fail to get into the university if I did not make a start in French and she arranged to have this teacher give me lessons in French in exchange for free milk which I delivered in the evening. I had no problem with French in my last year of high school in Winnipeg and gaining admission to the university.

Many young people, especially in western Canada, complain about their alleged handicap caused by the lack of opportunities to learn French. From my experience in Manitoba when opportunities were much more limited than they are today, I know that where there is a will a way can be found. I have never ceased to be grateful that I found one.

The session of 1962

The fifth session of the 1958 Parliament opened in January 1962. Everyone expected dissolution and a general election some time before the end of the year.

The Speech from the Throne contained a good deal of election 'bait' but few proposals that were likely to raise contentious issues: nothing to equal the Coyne affair, the cancellation of the Avro Arrow, or the resignation of the commissioner of the RCMP.

When the session opened, the prime minister secured agreement to have the debate on the Speech from the Throne interrupted once the motion of the leader of the Opposition was disposed of. The government, he said, wanted to proceed with urgent measures to provide acreage payments to prairie farmers who had suffered from drought in 1961 and to make additional funds available for winter works.

There was no opposition to the acreage payments, but we Liberals made the debate the excuse to discuss a contract recently concluded by the Wheat Board to sell wheat to Communist China. Several Tory members had accused the Liberal party of opposing the sale of wheat to Red China. The charge was false but was widely believed on the prairies. We tried to set the record straight, without much success. Alvin Hamilton had visited Hong Kong before the sale was announced. He obviously intended to leave the impression that he had made the sale personally. We did our utmost to get the government to table the contract to show that it had been signed two days before Hamilton arrived in Hong Kong. We did not succeed. Hamilton and the Tory government continued to get credit on the prairies for the sale of wheat to China.

Once the acreage payment item for 42 million dollars was voted, debate began on an item for $300,000 for a special works program for fishing settlements in Newfoundland, where income of fishermen had declined drastically because of decreased catches. The members from Newfoundland, led by Chesley Carter and Herman Batten, argued that this was a miniscule program compared with the acreage payments to farmers on the prairies. They recommended an alternative plan that would have involved direct payments to fishermen through the machinery of the Unemployment Insurance Commission. Our proposal was ridiculed by some Tory members and rejected by the minister of fisheries, after I had spelled out precisely two methods by which payments could easily have been made to the fishermen, based on the similar acreage payment to the farmers. We had willingly voted the money for the farmers because they really needed it. But we claimed correctly that the fishermen needed income support just as much. It was hard to tell the fishermen the only way they could get help was to get jobs and sweat it out on work on the roads in the winter time for a total of $20 'when the western farmer gets a cheque for $200 from Alvin's cheque machine.' The niggardly appropriation was finally passed after a long debate. The Liberal stand in Parliament received, of course, favourable publicity in Newfoundland.

Once these two measures were passed we expected the House to complete the debate on the Speech from the Throne. Instead the government introduced a measure to increase the old age pension to $65.00 a month. Considering the depreciated purchasing power of the dollar, this ten-dollar increase was almost precisely equal to the six-dollar increase in 1957 which had been ridiculed by the Tories. Diefenbaker had repeatedly promised in 1958 to bring a United States-type contributory pension soon after the election. His contributory plan was to be in addition to the existing old age pensions. I pointed out that nothing had yet been done to implement this promise. The reason, I suggested, was that the government had no plan. A contributory pension, I recalled, was part of the Liberal program.

Comparable increases were also provided in the Old Age Assistance Act, the Blind Persons Act, and the Disabled Persons Act. The debates on these measures became increasingly partisan. In a speech on 8 February 1962 filled with factual inaccuracies in which he tried to claim credit for his government for action taken by previous Liberal governments, Diefenbaker ranged at large. He poured ridicule on the proceedings of the Liberal rally of January 1961 and the Kingston conference of 1960. At one point he quoted Tom Kent, whom he described as 'the leader of the Leader.' When Pearson, referring to John Fisher who was on Diefenbaker's staff, interjected 'Body by Fisher,' Diefenbaker retorted 'Body by Fisher is a great deal better than Brains by Kent.'

In his reply to Diefenbaker Pearson was almost constantly interrupted as the House became rowdier, especially after the prime minister left the Chamber. When I began to speak later in the evening I noted that the prime minister had introduced this totally irrelevant debate in which we in the Opposition had some satisfaction in taking part. I was interrupted even more frequently than Pearson had been when I began to correct several of Diefenbaker's inaccurate statements and misrepresentations. I suggested they might have been inadvertent because, after five years in office, the prime minister 'knows so little about government.' After more interruptions I added that 'any man who is absent from his office one day out of every two for three months cannot be doing his job and that is the Prime Minister's record in the last three months of 1961.' That figure was correct because, when I realized Diefenbaker was spending so much time politicking in preparation for a 1962 election, I had had someone count the absences.

My statement provoked a flood of angry interruptions from back-benchers protesting that everyone knew what a hard worker Diefenbaker was, that he was always in his office at 8 o'clock in the morning, and other similar retorts.

In the course of my speech, I stated that 90 per cent of the flights of ministers around the world could be eliminated without any loss to anybody. With equal lack of relevance I said one of my friends had asked me the other day: 'Under the Diefenbaker government has Canada any friend left in the world, except Castro?' I added: 'To the Minister of Trade and Commerce he is a good friend.' This reference to George Hees related to a visit of a Cuban trade mission to Canada in December 1960 when Hees had referred to the Cuban visitors 'as wonderful customers. You can't do business with better business men anywhere.' The exuberance of the minister of trade and commerce had somewhat embarrassed Diefenbaker and several of his colleagues at the time, and we made a point of not letting them forget their Cuban friends.

Earlier in the debates on the social security measures, I had listed Diefenbaker's unkept promises on the subject during the 1958 election campaign. My part in these unruly pre-election debates and in others during this period led Diefenbaker on at least one occasion to say while speaking outside Parliament: 'Whenever I need a laugh all I have to do is mention the name Pickersgill.' The result was one of Macpherson's finest cartoons in the *Toronto Star*.

In addition to the increases in the standard social security benefits, the government introduced another social security measure of particular interest to the members from Newfoundland. This measure provided for the payment of allowances, similar to those paid under the War Veterans Allowance Act, to merchant seamen who had served in theatres of war, to firefighters who had served in Britain, to veterans of the VAD, to overseas welfare workers, to civilian air crew of the Royal Air Force Transport Command, and to the Newfoundland overseas forestry unit which had served in the Second World War. All these groups were added to the very limited group covered by the Civilian War Pensions and Allowances Act already administered by the Department of Veterans Affairs.

Every year during the 1958 Parliament, we Liberal members of Parliament from Newfoundland had been urging that merchant seamen and Newfoundland foresters be classed as veterans and brought under the War Veterans Allowance Act. Financially the civilian allowance was precisely equal to the war veterans allowance. We all welcomed it, but we regretted that the Newfoundland foresters of the Second World War were denied the honour of being classed as veterans though the foresters of the First World War were so treated. The leader in advocating the claims of the foresters and merchant seamen had been Chesley Carter, but all of us had participated over the years. The Liberal Opposition rather than the government got the main credit for this measure.

Liberal spirits were raised early in 1962 by a Gallup poll which indicated 42 per cent of voters would vote Liberal compared with 38 per cent Conservative. Even more impressive, 42 per cent expected the Liberals to win an election and only 31 per cent the Conservatives.

We decided to continue to stress unemployment as the main issue in the country and to seize every opportunity to give publicity to the Liberal program for creating jobs. There was an enthusiastic meeting of the National Liberal Federation at the end of January. St Laurent was present to introduce

Pearson at the dinner – it was his first appearance at an important Liberal function since his retirement as party leader – and the whole meeting concentrated on the program for the coming election.

Having got through all the legislation likely to help the Tories in an election, the government returned to the debate on the Speech from the Throne on 19 February. The debate proceeded in an orderly fashion until 22 February. On that day Lucien Cardin made a bitter attack on Diefenbaker for his attitude to French Canadians which he described 'as a theatrical and grotesque show' to make them believe he attached 'great importance to the Ministers and Members from Quebec, whereas, in fact, they neither control nor decide anything.' He went on to accuse Diefenbaker of hostility to bilingualism and of distorting Pearson's statements about a national flag. At one point he said the prime minister must be reminded that 'in our democratic form of government the Prime Minister is not above the truth.' He said the office of prime minister was not above the law, nor above the rules of the House, nor above the standards of political decency, and certainly not above criticism.

Cardin was at this point interrupted by the government whip on an alleged point of order. At the request of the chairman, Cardin withdrew the phrase 'above the truth,' but he went on to say the prime minister's speeches 'degenerate into criminal court debating tactics filled with personal insinuations, half truths and sophistry' surpassing the records of any former prime minister of Canada.

Cardin continued in the same vein about other aspects of Diefenbaker's leadership. He was interrupted almost incessantly. The speech was resented by Diefenbaker who was not in the House when it was made, and that resentment was exhibited against Cardin as long as he remained in Parliament. On 26 February, George Hees accused me of writing part of Cardin's speech which he described as a vicious attack on the prime minister. I said the charge was unqualifiedly false. Hees retorted that 'whoever did write that vicious, guttersnipe, backalley speech should be thoroughly ashamed of himself.'

I spoke later the same day, amid frequent interruptions. David Walker replied to me in an abusive speech. The debate had clearly ceased to serve any purpose and it was fortunate that 22 February was the last day of the debate on the Speech from the Throne.

Argue quits the NDP

As early as 1958, the CCF had begun to be transformed into the New party and, later, the New Democratic party. Walter Pitman was elected in Peterborough as a New Democrat in October 1960 and the CCF in the House had adopted the new name. There was a contest for the New Democratic leadership between Tommy Douglas, the premier of Saskatchewan, and Hazen Argue who, since the election of 1958, had been leader of the CCF in the House of Commons. Douglas won the leadership in August 1961. Argue continued as House leader, though it was increasingly apparent he was not happy in the party. At the opening of the sitting on 21 February 1962, he announced that he had severed his connection with the New Democratic party and asked the Speaker to give him another seat. He stated that the NDP, in his opinion, was in the control of a small labour clique whose hold on the party was sure to continue and strengthen. He added that he desired to seek re-election in Assiniboia and that he expected shortly to make a further announcement about his political future.

Douglas Fisher, who had nominated Argue for the leadership of the NDP, attacked him in a bitter speech. Fisher said his colleagues in the House and particularly the three who, like him, had supported Argue for the leadership of the party, had asked him to comment for the party. Fisher's resentment was all the greater because Argue had first announced he was leaving the NDP on the previous Sunday, at a press conference in Regina attended by Ross Thatcher, an earlier renegade from the CCF. Fisher had no quarrel with a politician changing his political allegiance, but described the reason Argue had given for his change as 'cool, deliberate malignity.' At the Speaker's insistence, Fisher withdrew the word malignity, but not the bitterness of the charge. He recalled that the formation of the new party had started in April 1958 and that Argue had participated fully in the committee formed to set it up.

From the opening of the 1958 Parliament it had been a part of Liberal Opposition strategy to seek to co-ordinate action in Opposition and to avoid friction with the CCF wherever possible. Pearson had asked me to maintain liaison with Argue to this end. I got to know him well and our personal relations remained friendly even while the CCF in 1959 carried on an abusive campaign in support of the IWA in Newfoundland.

When he decided to leave the NDP, Argue talked to me about his political future. He made it clear he wanted to join the Liberal party. I reminded him that, when Thatcher had left the CCF, he had sat for some time as an Independent, before announcing he would join our party. I advised Argue to follow that course. Since he had often attacked the Liberal party quite sharply, I felt a period sitting as an Independent would make his conversion more credible. However, he preferred to become a Liberal at once. Argue contested his old constituency as a Liberal candidate in 1962 and won by a very small margin over the Tory candidate. In 1963 he was narrowly defeated by the Tory, thereby depriving the new Pearson government of an experienced parliamentary champion of the western wheat growers. After losing again in 1965, Argue was called to the Senate where he eventually became a spokesman for Saskatchewan in the cabinet of the Trudeau government after 1980.

Arizona Charlie's

Towards the end of the session of 1962, Dr W.H. McMillan, the MP for Welland, and I had some fun over the restoration as a historic site in Dawson City in the Yukon of the Palace Grand Theatre of gold rush days. McMillan was an old-fashioned Ontario Grit frequently concerned with ferreting out government extravagance. On the estimates for the National Parks Branch, he expressed the hope there was no extravagance. He said he had read something about a place in Dawson City which was to be restored, but he did not pretend to know whether it had been a dance hall or a theatre. Evidently, he reported, it was run during the gold rush by a wealthy American called Arizona Charlie who was in pursuit of more wealth by providing the boys with liquor, gambling, and other diversions for a price.

McMillan went on to quote from a book from the parliamentary library called *The Yukon* which said Arizona Charlie's Palace Grand was in competition with the Tivoli, Nigger Jim's Pavilion, and other places in providing select entertainment, liquor, gambling, etc. There were accounts of painted dancers and other ladies who were present as an adjunct to such an establishment. He said this dance hall or theatre, as the minister preferred to call it, has been declared a historic site, a shrine, or a monument, and he wanted to know why.

At this point, I interjected: 'A shrine?' McMillan wondered if it was to perpetuate the memory of Arizona Charlie, the ladies of the night, or those who spent their substance there. He thought the $138,000 could be better

THE TWILLINGATE TERROR

Reprinted with permission – *The Globe and Mail*, Toronto

spent on a memorial school or a small memorial hospital. He later asked whether the prime minister would attend the opening and dedication.

Douglas Fisher joined in the fun with a bright speech. The Tory whip, Eric Winkler, tried to change the subject. I raised an objection to Winkler's attempt and got on to Arizona Charlie's place and wondered whether this part of the northern vision was conceived before or after the person who conceived it had been at the bar in Arizona Charlie's. I assumed Arizona Charlie was white and wondered whether the restoration might raise a difficult problem for the prime minister, involving racial discrimination under the Bill of Rights against Nigger Jim unless we spent an equal amount on restoring his place.

Davie Fulton quite deservedly described my speech as fifteen minutes of nonsense. Walter Dinsdale, the minister – and a member of the Salvation Army – was somewhat embarrassed by the irony of having to defend Arizona Charlie's restoration and attempted to place most of the responsibility on the distinguished historians on the Historic Sites and Monuments Board who had recommended the project. I confess that I made no apology for helping McMillan and Fisher inject a touch of frivolity into the proceedings, particularly as the debate earned me a cartoon as Carrie Nation, the militant temperance advocate, taking her axe to a saloon.

Redistribution

After a debate on the Speech from the Throne was concluded, the atmosphere in the House became increasingly unpleasant. There was, however, a marked improvement in tone on 26 March. That day Diefenbaker moved to set up a select committee on possible changes in the procedures of the House. I replied to Diefenbaker on behalf of the Opposition. The debate was brief and non-partisan. Diefenbaker made a moderate and constructive speech. I replied for the Liberal Opposition and flattered Diefenbaker by recalling that 26 March 1962 was the twenty-second anniversary of his election to Parliament. I said: 'the Parliament of Canada would have been a very different place if the Rt. Hon. gentleman had not been elected 22 years ago.' I also congratulated him on the tone and temper of his speech.

Later on I reminded him he had promised in 1957 to abolish closure and said, in the light of experience, no government in its senses would ever use the existing closure rule again. I suggested we repeal the rule at once and pledged Liberal support to repeal it, if the prime minister would amend his motion. Regier for the NDP objected to my proposal. Diefenbaker, in concluding the debate, accepted Regier's advice not to act before the committee had considered closure. Despite our offer to abolish the existing closure rule out-of-hand, I believe Diefenbaker was prudent not to proceed.

As for amending the rules generally, I occasionally shocked my colleagues in Opposition by seeking to reduce or eliminate procedural devices which could be used to obstruct the business of government in the House. I took these positions because I expected to be a member of the government again and wanted changes in the rules which would make it easier to govern effectively.

The 1962 Speech from the Throne forecast legislation to establish an independent commission to carry out the redistribution of constituencies required by the constitution after each decennial census.

The results of the census of 1961 were available and it was clear that, unless prompt action was taken, redistribution could not take place before a general election. In February I asked the prime minister whether he could give the House an assurance that redistribution would be carried out before there was a general election. Diefenbaker replied that he thought it strange that those who have been calling every day for an election were now speaking about constitutional difficulties. I retorted that I was not 'those' and that I had taken no part in election speculation. Douglas Fisher then asked whether priority would be given to redistribution itself or to the establishment of a redistribution commission. Diefenbaker replied that legislation would be required and suggested it might come soon.

The subject did not come up again until Diefenbaker on 26 March introduced legislation to establish a redistribution commission. At that time everyone assumed there would be a single commission for the whole country. When debate began on 9 April, I stated, as spokesman for the Opposition, that the principle of redistribution by an independent commission was completely acceptable to the Opposition and was in accord with the resolution formally adopted by the national council of the Liberal party. The whole process of establishing a commission and then having the commission perform the redistribution would take a long time. There was no reason why the government should have waited until the census had been taken to have the commission established. If action had been taken in an earlier session, I pointed out, the commission would have been in place ready to start its work as soon as the census was completed. I had not finished my speech when the House rose for the day. When I resumed my speech next day I said we should either be assured there would be redistribution before an election or have this measure dropped since, if there was to be an early election, the time of Parliament was being taken wantonly and unnecessarily to deal hastily with legislation which should be left to a new Parliament with a fresh mandate.

A year earlier I had predicted that no action would be taken before 1962, that a commission would be mentioned in the Speech from the Throne and nothing more done for three months, by which time it would be too late to complete the redistribution before the next election even if the election was not until late in 1963.

In the course of my speech on redistribution, I said we should be spending our time doing the business of the country instead of having constant agitation about an election. 'What we have had for the last three months is the spectacle of the Prime Minister of this country like a little girl among the flowers in the meadow in the summer picking the petals from a flower and saying "He loves me, he loves me not – shall we have an election or shall we not?"'

Diefenbaker had evidently picked off the last petal by 17 April, because he announced that day the session would be ended and an election called the next day. He wanted the first stage of the redistribution legislation to be completed. I realized anything I might say would be anti-climatic, but I refused to let the motion pass without further debate. I pointed out that any commission set up would have a year or two of preparatory work to do, before it could start the actual redrawing of the boundaries of constituencies. We would not be satisfied to have such a commission appointed unless the names of the commissioners were included in the bill because these appointments should not be made by order-in-council, no matter what party was in office. Moreover, the commission should not consist exclusively of judges even if one was made chairman, because the commission was bound to be charged with unfairness, however unjustified, and judges should not be exposed to accusations of partisanship.

The government had blundered by delaying so long, but it was not their major blunder. There was a striking parallel between the past five years and the two years preceding the election of 1896 as described by Sir Joseph Pope in his memoirs. I felt I should share that description with the House. A Tory back-bencher said I was out of order, but Diefenbaker himself intervened to say the House should not be deprived of this 'gem' I had found. I recalled that Pope, who was assistant clerk of the Privy Council at the time Senator Mackenzie Bowell became prime minister in 1894, had described what happened in these words: 'Then followed days which I never recall without a blush, days of weak and incompetent administration by a cabinet presided over by a man whose sudden and unlooked for elevation had visibly turned his head, a ministry without unity or cohesion of any kind, a prey to internal dissensions until they became a spectacle to the world, to angels and to men.'

At that point, I interjected that this was before the Diefenbaker cabinet's pilgrimage to Quebec to shuffle the cabinet. I continued to quote Pope: 'At one period during the summer of 1896, I remember it was almost impossible to get public business transacted at Ottawa.' I commented that history seemed to repeat itself. The description by Pope seemed to epitomize the progress from blunder to blunder which had characterized the last five years.

Diefenbaker ignored my citations from Pope, and replied briefly to my argument about the delay in setting up a redistribution commission. We let the bill get first reading that day. That was the last of redistribution while Diefenbaker was prime minister. I did not expect I would be the one to introduce redistribution the next time.

During an earlier debate, when accused of obstruction, I had pointed out that government supporters were taking more time than the Opposition. My statement about the time taken up in debates by the government side was statistically accurate. There had in fact been no obstruction by the Opposition, despite repeated charges of ministers. Diefenbaker had evidently decided that June would be a propitious time and wanted some pretext to blame the early election on us. On 17 April, he said he had originally hoped there could be an election on 12 September, but, in the light of the delaying tactics of the Opposition, he had no alternative but to ask the governor general to dissolve Parliament at an early date. He proposed to do that, as soon as a few items of business he listed were completed by the House. If these matters were disposed of the government would ask on 18 April for interim supply for five months. He said the proposed date of the election was 18 June.

The announcement was welcomed by Pearson and Herridge, now acting leader of the NDP in the House. Pearson said the prime minister had admitted it was impossible for a government with 207 supporters to complete its legislative program unless the Opposition gave up its cherished rights to carry out its duties. He recalled the ditty sung by the queen in Gilbert and Sullivan's *Iolanthe* that:

Every bill and every measure
That may gratify his pleasure,
Though your fury it arouses,
Shall be passed by both your houses.

Pearson said the country would be pleased by the announcement of the election, but not as pleased as the Opposition. The few items specified by Diefenbaker were dealt with on 18 April; Parliament was dissolved that day and an election called for 18 June.

It was an untidy end to the Parliament. The main estimates for the year 1962–63 had been debated on 1 and 2 March and never brought forward again.

Not a single appropriation had been passed. There had been no debate on the budget. But most of the measures forecast in the Speech from the Throne which were calculated to get votes, including the abolition of tolls on the bridges across the St Lawrence at Montreal, had been adopted. The Opposition made the serious error of agreeing to vote interim supply to carry on the government for five months. Even though Diefenbaker failed to maintain a majority in the election on 18 June 1962, this vote of interim supply gave him an excuse for delaying the calling of the new Parliament until 27 September 1962.

The election of 1962

We Liberals embarked on an active election campaign. We expected to make substantial gains but did not believe we could overcome the huge Tory majority of 1958. In Newfoundland, the Conservatives were in no hurry to nominate a candidate to oppose me. I anticipated correctly that I would have an easy time. My opponent was Whitfield Bannister. I never met him in my life. He received about 25 per cent of the vote, as Winter had in 1958.

One reason I was so confident that there would be no effective opposition in my riding was the knowledge that the Diefenbaker government was discredited and unpopular everywhere in Newfoundland. It faced a serious threat from the Liberals even in St John's. No less important for me was the fact that, from the summer of 1959 on, the whole family had spent part of July and most of August at our summer place at Traytown. Margaret and all the children and our cocker spaniel had travelled with me all over the constituency. Each Christmas a card with a photograph of the whole family, often taken in Newfoundland, was sent to every household in the constituency. By 1962 we were well known throughout the riding.

I had only two periods of campaigning in Newfoundland, mainly in my own riding, visiting most of the settlements, but I had very few meetings as my opponent was not active and raised no issues. I did have one exciting day on Fogo Island where there was a widespread feeling of neglect, mainly directed at the provincial government and Premier Smallwood who had ignored requests to visit the island. We travelled from Gander to Fogo in a helicopter and stopped at most of the places on the island to advertise a meeting in Fogo Town. I picked up the Catholic priest and two Anglican parsons who also fancied a ride in the helicopter; all of them were at my meeting. Father McCarthy, an outspoken and lively Irishman who had been a pilot in the Royal Air Force during the war, was the chairman. Before introducing me, he denounced Smallwood for his indifference to Fogo and renewed the demand for a visit. He concluded, however, by a warm appeal for my re-election.

After the meeting we boarded the helicopter and I began to eat the sandwiches I had brought along as a lunch. We got up about 20 or 30 feet when the aircraft began to spin like a top. Almost miraculously, the pilot brought it down safely in the very constricted space where it had been parked. When we landed, I was the last person to leave the helicopter. As I emerged munching a sandwich, an observer said if only we had a camera I would not have to do any more campaigning. Father McCarthy, who had been sitting up front with the pilot, said he had been thinking that, if we had been killed, there would have been a state funeral and Joe Smallwood would have had to visit Fogo. The rear rotor had fallen off the helicopter and it could no longer fly. We had to send a message to Gander to have a float-plane pick us up at Seldom-Come-By. The rest of the campaign in Newfoundland was much less exciting. Because the campaign in my riding was so quiet, I was able to spend a good deal of time on the mainland supporting other Liberal candidates.

The greatest sensation of the election campaign was the devaluation of the dollar. In his budget speech on 10 April Fleming had said the International Monetary Fund wished to have Canada return to a fixed value for the dollar instead of allowing it to float, but was not pressing Canada into any hasty action which might be 'premature or impossible to sustain.' He said the government 'would wish the prospects of success to be more assured than they were when the Canadian government made its ill-starred attempts to maintain fixed rates during the years from 1946 to 1950.'

It was against this background that the public was shocked, after the Canadian dollar had been falling rapidly, to have a fixed rate set at 92.5 cents US on 2 May. Part of the Liberal publicity included the circulation of what was called the 'Diefenbuck' with $7^1/_2$ cents clipped off one corner. Like most such stunts, it is questionable if this one affected many votes. It was the weakness of the dollar and the lack of confidence which really hurt the government.

A second run on the dollar was precipitated when Alvin Hamilton stated that the cabinet had been divided between a 95 cent and 90 cent dollar and that they had split the difference at 92.5. Hamilton's statement had appeared in the press on a Saturday. Fleming's reaction was that, if it was not repudiated, Hamilton's statement would have created an enormous run on the dollar on Monday. He recalled years later that he tried, without success, to get Diefenbaker to repudiate Hamilton. Diefenbaker did agree that Fleming make a statement on Sunday evening in Montreal which he could say was made with the full concurrence of the prime minister.

We Liberals condemned the lack of cabinet solidarity, but probably our attacks did not have much effect. Speaking in retrospect years later, I said 'the greatest campaign against the dollar was put on by Alvin Hamilton who announced publicly that he wanted to devalue it even more than it was devalued and they split the difference in the cabinet. Then he was ordered by Donald Fleming to shut up and never mention the dollar again. We didn't need to campaign against he dollar; they did a terrific job.'

There was a milder sensation during the campaign in which I became involved. Fleming had been invited to St John's to speak to the Rotary Club early in June. The club received a grant each year from the provincial government. Smallwood told Rotary that the subvention would be cancelled if the club was used for a partisan purpose. The invitation to Fleming was then withdrawn. Smallwood's action was blown up in the press as a denial by the government of Newfoundland of freedom of speech. I was campaigning in Nova Scotia at the time, and Pearson appealed to me to try to do something to ease the situation. I telephoned Smallwood, explained how embarrassing Pearson and other Liberals found the incident, and persuaded him to send Fleming a telegram I dictated over the telephone. The telegram read:

I understand you are saying on the mainland that my refusal to extend provincial government hospitality to Rotary Club if the Club was used as a platform for a partisan speech by yourself was a denial to you of freedom of speech in this province, notwithstanding the complete freedom you enjoyed in this province to say anything you chose on platforms provided by your own political party. However, in order to remove any possible impression that you were denied freedom to speak in Newfoundland, I am authorized by the Newfoundland Liberal Association to say they are prepared to provide, at Liberal expense, the largest available hall in St. John's and travelling expenses if you and your Liberal opponent, Mr. Mitchell Sharp, can come to St. John's to debate the issue of devaluation of the Canadian dollar which would give you the opportunity to make the speech you intended to make in St. John's. Alternatively, if such a visit cannot be arranged our Liberal campaign committee is prepared to provide a hall in Toronto, at which you and Mr. Sharp can debate the issue of devaluation and to arrange for a filming of the debate which film we would undertake to have shown in St. John's at a public exhibition which would assure a far larger audience which would have the opportunity to hear both sides of the controversial question of devaluation. I hope, in the interests of freedom of speech, you and Mr. Sharp to whom I am communicating a copy of this message will be ready to accept one of these alternatives either of which would give the people of Newfoundland an opportunity to weigh the merits of this hot political issue, and without dragging the non-partisan Rotary Club into the controversy.

Fleming ignored the offer, but the telegram received enough publicity to prevent any Liberal from repudiating or attacking Smallwood.

As the campaign progressed, some of us began to hope we might actually win more seats than the government. Our hopes were frustrated by the results in Quebec where we had counted on sweeping victories. The cause was the sudden and unanticipated emergence of Social Credit as a substantial political force. Twenty-six Social Crediters were elected in the province; the Liberals won 35 seats, which was only ten more than we had kept in 1958. We were surprised that the Tories were able to hold on to fourteen of the fifty seats they had gained in the landslide.

We made almost no impression on the Prairies, but we did make gains in British Columbia, Ontario, and the Maritimes. The minister from Newfoundland, one of the two Tories, also lost his seat. The gains elsewhere did not compensate for the lack of anticipated recovery in Quebec. We had sixteen fewer members than the Tories. The result was, nevertheless, a remarkable success for the Liberal party. The Tories had gone down from 208 to 116, which was the greatest reduction of strength between elections any party had suffered since Confederation. We Liberals had won twice as many seats as we had in 1958; we now had one hundred. This was reduced by one when Richard Cashin's close election in St John's was nullified by the court. The survival of the government would depend on thirty Social Crediters and nineteen members of the NDP.

The loss of its absolute majority was only the greatest of the Tory misfortunes. A week after the election, on 24 June, Diefenbaker had to disclose that the country was facing a severe foreign exchange crisis. To meet the emergency the government adopted a series of austerity measures.

The austerity program was announced by Diefenbaker on the CBC. Pearson had already demanded that Parliament be called into session as soon as the law allowed. The austerity measures were all brought into force by order-in-council. They included changes in taxation which Parliament had not yet been called to approve. Pearson had already been briefed by Louis Rasminsky, the governor of the Bank of Canada, at Diefenbaker's request. He was restrained in his criticism, to avoid further danger to the Canadian dollar and the national economy. He called a meeting of the Liberal caucus, including the newly elected members, for 27 June, and the caucus agreed to co-operate in effective measures to protect the dollar. Pearson continued, at the same time, to urge the earliest possible summoning of Parliament.

Secure in the knowledge that the interim supply voted at the close of the previous Parliament would enable the government to finance expenditures until mid-October, Diefenbaker brushed aside Pearson's claim that the government had no right to carry on unless it could win a vote of confidence in

Parliament. The prime minister, without a majority, arrogantly stated that the situation should be allowed to cool off and deliberately delayed the opening of the session until September.

Once it was clear Parliament would not meet until the fall, our whole family went to Newfoundland at the beginning of July. We were there for nine weeks, our longest unbroken stay. Feeling sure there would be another election soon, I made several tours of the constituency and other parts of the province, including one visit to Labrador.

The new Parliament

The new Parliament finally met on 27 September. Roland Michener had been defeated in the election and a new Speaker had to be elected in the House of Commons. The choice of the government was Marcel Lambert, the member from Edmonton West. The nomination was seconded by Leon Balcer, the minister of transport and the senior French Canadian in the Cabinet. Usually the nomination of the Speaker was seconded by the leader of the Opposition. Balcer may have been chosen by Diefenbaker on this occasion because Lambert, though a French Canadian, was not from Quebec. In the previous Parliament, Lambert had been combative and partisan and there was some concern he might be less impartial than Michener. This apprehension was expressed by Lionel Chevrier in a speech supporting Lambert's appointment. It was, in my opinion, not justified by events. Lambert was less judicial in manner than Michener and often brusque, but I felt he was fair in his decisions.

The Speech from the Throne read like an election manifesto and was clearly intended to serve as a comprehensive program for the government in a forthcoming election. Very little of the legislation forecast was actually realized, much of it not even introduced.

Diefenbaker announced the changes in the cabinet which had been made on 9 August. Fleming had become minister of justice; Fulton, Public Works; Nowlan, Finance; Ellen Fairclough, Postmaster General; Hugh John Flemming, National Revenue as well as Forestry; Halpenny, Secretary of State; Martineau, Mines and Technical Surveys; R. A. Bell, Citizenship and Immigration; and the newly appointed senator, Wallace McCutcheon, a minister without portfolio.

The removal of Fleming was obviously designed to reduce confrontation

164

in the House. Diefenbaker detested Nowlan, but apparently realized he was much more apt to avoid friction with the Opposition. Fulton's removal to Public Works was clearly a demotion for a minister the prime minister was jealous of. The appointment of Dick Bell to the cabinet was long overdue; during his short time as a minister he performed well in a tricky portfolio. The appointment of McCutcheon was a concession to the Toronto business community, but, in fact, it added little to the strength of the government.

The Parliament of 1962 was very different in character from the Parliament of 1958. The government did not have a majority. It had lost its fighting spirit and even a little of its arrogance. The only outstanding new Tory was Gordon Fairweather from New Brunswick. On the other hand, the Opposition had gained a number of excellent debaters. Allan MacEachen was in Parliament again, as was Arthur Laing. We had effective additions to our strength in Walter Gordon, John Turner, Bud Drury, Edgar Benson, Larry Pennell, Maurice Sauvé, John Munro, Jack Nicholson, Jack Davis, Donald Macdonald, Lucien Lamoureux, and John Stewart.

And there was Richard Cashin from Newfoundland who had defeated Browne in St John's West. Cashin was the first Liberal to speak after Pearson on the Speech from the Throne. He did well, but this was his only speech, though he intervened frequently in the question period during the short time he was in the House. His election was contested in the courts on the ground that the number of electors who had voted illegally was greater than his small majority. The challenge was successful. His election was voided by the court on 25 October, and the decision reported to the House by the Speaker on 8 November. The seat remained vacant until the election of 1963 when Cashin won with a substantial majority.

Colin Cameron and Stanley Knowles were back for the NDP and that party had a good new member in Andrew Brewin – and an outstanding one in David Lewis. Social Credit was again in the House with three or four members who quickly became effective in debate. Probably no other Parliament had as many talented additions. With all the new talent in Opposition and a government which no longer had a majority, the short Parliament of 1962–63 became a lively place, though not likely to have a long life.

The first vote of confidence

In opening the debate on the Speech from the Throne, Pearson said it was the duty of the leader of the Opposition to move a vote of want of confidence since 63 per cent of the voters in the election had declared they had no confidence in the government, in its policies, and its leadership. If his motion was rejected by the House, he agreed that the government would have a mandate to introduce its legislative and other proposals. He promised the Liberal Opposition would consider those proposals on their merits exactly as if the government had a clear majority.

On the issue of confidence, he expressed surprise that the leader of the Social Credit party (Robert Thompson) had said, just before Parliament met, that a vote of non-confidence would be political and parliamentary irresponsibility. Pearson reminded the House that the co-leader of Social Credit (Réal Caouette) had said on 8 August he had fought against Diefenbaker outside Parliament and would not fight for him inside, that the country needed a stable government, and the quicker there was a new election, the quicker we would have such a government. Pearson said Caouette's were true words. He failed to understand Thompson's attitude. There could be no stability when the government could not, over a substantial period, command a majority in the House of Commons. Pearson recalled Diefenbaker's statements to the same effect in January of 1958 which he had given as his reason for advising the dissolution of Parliament.

Pearson underlined the magnitude of the government's losses in the election and attributed them in large part to the dollar crisis it had tried unsuccessfully to conceal and to Alvin Hamilton's preposterous statement that some members of the cabinet wanted a 90 cent dollar and some a 95 and they had compromised on 92.5. The Coyne affair, he said, had also contributed to the loss of confidence in the government. It was the beginning of the dollar problem.

Pearson also discussed the Commonwealth economic conference held in London after the election. The conference was primarily concerned with the British application to enter the European Economic Community. Pearson was highly critical of the government's negative attitude. He accused Diefenbaker of trying to get concessions for Canada which, if Britain had agreed to them, would have made sure the British application would not be accepted.

*"SHE'S AGONNA BE FAIR AND SQUARE, GANG . . . WE HEAR HIS
SIDE OF THE STORY FUST . . . THEN WE STRING HIM UP"*

He contrasted Diefenbaker's position with those of Australia and New Zealand and quoted the British secretary of state for Commonwealth relations who said that, where Australia and New Zealand were helpful in trying to find ways of improving Commonwealth market terms, Canadians were intransigent. Pearson went on to draw a sharper line than ever between Conservative and Liberal attitudes to Britain's application. Britain in the Common Market would help to shape a new Europe. Pearson said: 'Thank God it is being shaped.'

He ridiculed Diefenbaker's pre-election claim that there would be full employment in July and August of 1962. Unemployment was still the main problem. The reduction of unemployment would be a major Liberal effort. Pearson outlined other elements in the Liberal program and concluded by moving that the government did not possess the confidence of the House.

It was a long and effective speech lasting until ten minutes before the hour of adjournment, giving Diefenbaker little time to reply until the next day (2 October). His reply was neither long nor effective. Thompson then spoke for Social Credit: he decried partisanship and appealed for statesmanship. He moved a sub-amendment in which he added a long recital of Social Credit policies to justify voting lack of confidence in the government. He made it obvious that, if his sub-amendment was defeated, Social Credit would not vote for Pearson's straight want-of-confidence motion. When the vote came, only the Social Crediters voted for their motion.

T. C. Douglas, the leader of the NDP, had failed to win a seat in the general election. When Herridge spoke as acting leader, he gave no indication of where the party stood on the question of confidence. However, after the Social Credit sub-amendment was defeated, David Lewis was the next NDP speaker in the debate. He moved a sub-amendment condemning the government for 'having failed to propose a program of economic planning designed to bring about economic growth and full employment.'

In a speech later that same day, I dealt with the gross constitutional impropriety of the government carrying on without first seeking a vote of confidence as early as possible. About the dollar crisis, Fleming, I claimed, had anticipated trouble when he brought down the budget in April. The government wanted to get the election over before an exchange crisis developed. Alvin Hamilton's performance on 8 June as reported in the *Globe and Mail* the next morning, made a mockery of collective cabinet responsibility. He should have been out of the government on 9 June. The prime minister, I observed, had not mentioned Hamilton's performance in his speech. I felt mine was a good fighting speech, and I was flattered when David Lewis, himself a great debater, congratulated me enthusiastically.

Lewis's sub-amendment was defeated at the close of the day on 4 October. We voted with the NDP but the government was saved by Social Credit,

140 to 118. Pearson's amendment was then defeated by the same numbers with the NDP voting with us and Social Credit with the government.

The next day, Allan MacEachen, after a well-documented constitutional argument, moved another amendment which submitted that the failure of the government 'to place before the House at the earliest opportunity a measure to approve the collection of taxes which have been imposed by Order-in-Council, as part of the austerity program, denies to the House the exclusive constitutional right to approve the imposition of additional taxation which is the foundation of our system of responsible government.'

Fleming replied to MacEachen's argument by drawing a parallel with the action taken by Douglas Abbott in the dollar crisis of 1947 in taking similar emergency action to defend the value of the dollar. He used this precedent to support the opinion that the action taken by the government in its austerity program was legal and constitutional. He failed to point out that Abbott's emergency measures were later submitted to Parliament for approval, whereas the Diefenbaker government claimed they had a legal opinion from the deputy minister of justice to the effect that parliamentary approval was not necessary. The government, however, refused to table this legal opinion. MacEachen's amendment was also defeated and the government sustained with Social Credit once more voting with the government.

In the debate on the Speech from the Throne, the government had won the confidence of the House and was entitled to carry on the government as long as it avoided defeat in the House. We, in the official Opposition, who really wanted another election which we were confident we could win, kept seeking opportunities to challenge the government. Taxation without parliamentary approval continued to look like a good issue, and we made a determined effort to force the production of the legal opinion which the government claimed justified taxation by order-in-council. On 22 November, there was a debate on a motion for the tabling of this legal opinion. The defence of the government was led by Jed Baldwin, the parliamentary secretary to the prime minister, who was a good lawyer and an able debater. In the debate, Baldwin quoted a statement I had made, several years before, that the confidential character of communications between civil servants and ministers was an essential feature of responsible government.

I began my reply by saying that I had more regard for Baldwin as a lawyer than I had for anyone else on the other side of the House. I said my regard was not diminished when he quoted me as an authority in support of his very unconvincing argument. I said I took back nothing that I had said about the confidentiality of communication between civil servants and their ministers. I asserted that a legal opinion as to the validity of an order-in-council was not such a confidential communication. Such opinions had always been producible and sometimes were produced on the initiative of the government.

I admitted they were not usually produced, but this was not a normal case, since the government was seeking not merely to legislate but to tax by order-in-council. I argued this case was unique.

Such motions were debatable only for one hour at a time in private members time. This particular motion was filibustered by government supporters for five such hours, the last on 31 January 1963. We never did see the legal opinion.

Speaker Lambert and the House

The oral question period each day was getting longer and longer and the Speaker was growing more and more impatient about the difficulty of enforcing the rules of the House. On 16 October 1962, he made a long statement in an attempt to justify more rigorous enforcement.

The next day he attempted to apply his new discipline to a question asked by Paul Martin. The result was a lengthy series of points of order and questions of privilege culminating in an appeal by Martin against the Speaker's ruling that his question was out of order. The Speaker's ruling was sustained by a vote of 147 to 85. Only the Liberals voted against the decision of the Speaker.

John Turner gave his maiden speech on 18 October. In the course of his speech he was dealing with a question of procedure when the Speaker interrupted him 'to interject a little word of caution.' His caution was that ascribing motives to other members was not in keeping with the traditions of the House. He repeated it was merely a word of caution and that so far he had 'not heard anything that would infringe' but that on other occasions members had been 'extremely sensitive when motives have been attributed.'

Later in the debate Chevrier accused Nowlan of imputing motives and asked that he be called to order in the same manner as Turner had been. The Speaker replied that he had not called Turner to order and that Turner had been 'very careful and very proper.' Pearson asked: 'Then why caution him?' It was evident that challenges to the Speaker's rulings were becoming increasingly partisan, and that Lambert's efforts to enforce the rules strictly were bound to fail when the government lacked a majority.

The *Globe and Mail* for Thursday, 25 October 1962, contained on page seven a story from Ottawa entitled 'Three War-horses Curbed – New Voices for Liberals' by Walter Gray. It said: 'The other day Opposition Leader Lester Pearson summoned his three lieutenants, Paul Martin, Jack Pickersgill and Lionel Chevrier for a quiet but very firm chat. It is reported that he told the three war-horses that their captain was annoyed with their conduct in the House of Commons and they should govern themselves accordingly. The meeting took place as Speaker Marcel Lambert was being made to skip rope by the Opposition parties over his early decision to crack down on those Members of Parliament who have been trying to see how much they can get away with during the Commons question period.'

The story went on to say that Lambert often worked up quite a sweat when Martin, Pickersgill, and Chevrier held the ropes. Pearson emphasized he was dismayed and so were many back-benchers. The story suggested the new order was gently pushing the old aside and added it would take some pushing and Pearson would be lost without the old. It noted that Walter Gordon was getting some attention as were MacEachen, Turner, and Drury.

The story evidently related to what happened on 17 October when the Speaker's rulings were appealed twice, once by Martin and once by Fisher of the NDP. Pearson was in the House for both appeals and voted for them. I have no recollection of any such rebuke, which, if it happened, must have taken place that day or early the next day, as I left Ottawa on 18 October and was absent until late on 23 October. I have looked at the *Hansard* for every day from the opening of the session and it is clear that Chevrier, Martin, and I did not try to upstage the new members and, on the contrary, gave them every encouragement to participate actively both in question period and in the debates. I checked with Paul Martin and he has no recollection of any rebuke by Pearson. Some disgruntled Liberal back-bencher may have inspired the story. There is no evidence after 17 October that any of the three of us reduced his activities. This story in the *Globe* received no notice in Parliament except for a passing reference by Douglas Fisher.

After these incidents in mid-October I believe Lambert began to realize rigorous discipline would not work and more flexibility was desirable. For another reason, the atmosphere in the House became for a while less turbulent. On 22 October 1962, President Kennedy made his historic speech about the crisis over Soviet nuclear missiles in Cuba. Diefenbaker had the proceedings in the House interrupted so that he and the other party leaders could comment on Kennedy's speech. While there was some criticism outside the House about the government's reluctant support of the United States in the Cuban crisis, it was not reflected that day by the spokesmen of any of the parties.

On 25 October, the prime minister made a statement about Canada's support for the United States in the Cuban crisis. Pearson described the situation as grave. Thompson and Herridge also spoke. The prime minister made a further report on Monday 29 October stating that the Soviets were going to dismantle their missile sites in Cuba. The news was received with relief by Pearson, Patterson (for Social Credit), and Herridge. The Cuban missile crisis had, while it lasted, a sobering effect on Parliament.

The second vote of confidence

On 2 November 1962, the election of Tommy Douglas in a by-election in Burnaby-Coquitlam in British Columbia was reported to the House and Douglas took his seat. Diefenbaker made a brief speech welcoming him, as did Pearson and Thompson, and Douglas thanked the House for the welcome.

A supply motion on 5 November provided the occasion for another vote of confidence. Pearson moved that the emergency austerity program of tariff surcharges and tight money, introduced on 24 June, should be stopped at once. Thompson moved to add to Pearson's motion, the words: 'and replaced with a policy of debt-free money and constructive proposals to foster balanced domestic economy and balanced international trade.'

Thompson's motion posed a dilemma for the NDP. Should they vote with Social Credit and risk defeating the government or vote against it and be labelled as Diefenbaker's saviours. Douglas spoke immediately after Thompson without referring directly to the sub-amendment. He did say the NDP would not vote simply to defeat the government and bring on an election.

A special Liberal caucus was held next morning to decide what we, as a party, should do about the Social Credit sub-amendment. 'Debt-free money' was the Social Credit name for the kind of monetary system they advocated. Pearson, himself, was very reluctant to appear to vote for Social Credit funny money, but said he would accept the decision of the caucus. Like several other members, I argued strongly that we should vote for the sub-amendment after explaining clearly that we did not embrace 'debt-free money,' but that the total effect of the amendment and the sub-amendment was a vote of lack of confidence in the government and that we would not, as a party, vote confidence in the Tory government. We finally agreed to vote for the sub-amendment. Paul Martin was chosen to explain our position which he did on 6 November.

When Lewis spoke for the NDP and denounced the government, Paul Martin asked him whether he should not vote to take immediate steps to help in getting a new government that would put the country on the right road. Lewis replied that the NDP was prepared to take all honest steps to get rid of the government, but that voting for the Social Credit motion could not be an honest step; and, if the Liberals proposed to do so, it would merely indicate their insatiable desire for office and their willingness to make themselves look ridiculous by voting for debt-free money.

Walter Gordon spoke next and said he found Lewis's defence of the NDP intention to keep the government in office hard to follow. He said it appeared that, when Social Credit would not vote to save the government, the NDP would.

In his speech Paul Martin noted that both of the smaller parties claimed they wanted an election. Surely, he argued, all the Opposition parties should join together to defeat the government. Since Social Credit had merely added words to Pearson's motion, they had indicated approval of its content and should vote for it, even if their own sub-amendment was defeated. Martin argued that the term 'debt-free money' had many different definitions and the Liberal party did not accept the Social Credit definition. But the Liberals, he said, were not elected to oppose Social Credit or the NDP but to oppose the government. Martin then announced that the Liberals would vote for the sub-amendment, but, in doing so, they would not be voting for Social Credit principles, but voting against a government that must be removed in the interests of the nation. The vote was then taken on Thompson's sub-amendment which was defeated 113 to 121, the NDP voting with the government. The vote was taken immediately afterwards on Pearson's motion. The vote was 108 to 121.

By these votes, the NDP made it clear they would save the government, if Social Credit did not. Because of the obvious fear the NDP as well as Social Credit had of precipitating an election, we had no great hope of defeating the government unless we could find some issue which both of the small parties would not dare to oppose without entirely losing their credibility. We had little hope of raising such an issue over the government's austerity program, but lost no chance of opposing it on principle.

In one debate on taxation by order-in-council, I contrasted again the conduct of the Liberal government in 1947 in an earlier dollar crisis with the course being followed by Diefenbaker and Nowlan in 1962. (In 1947 Douglas Abbott had announced in a radio broadcast that the government, which had a majority in Parliament, intended to bring certain taxes into effect at once and to ask Parliament to approve them retroactively. When Parliament met, these measures were approved.) In June 1962, the Diefenbaker government, to defend the dollar, had imposed tax changes by order-in-council and claimed the orders were legal in themselves and no parliamentary approval was needed. Pearson, I recalled, had not opposed the emergency action taken in June 1962, but said Parliament should be called as soon as possible. That should have been done and the Opposition still wanted these austerity taxes submitted to Parliament. If they had been, in November or December, Parliament would not have approved them.

Breaches of responsible government

We would have fought this battle hard whether or not we hoped to win, because we felt the Tory claim that the government could impose taxation or increase taxes without the approval of Parliament was a fundamental breach of responsible government.

An equally fundamental breach of responsible government was the attitude of the Diefenbaker government to the expenditure of money which had not been voted by Parliament. This practice was not new. When Diefenbaker had Parliament dissolved in February 1958, only a few items of the estimates of expenditures for the fiscal year 1957–8 had been voted by the House of Commons. Most of the expenditures for that year were authorized by governor general's warrants which, constitutionally, are used only in an emergency. There was certainly no emergency when Parliament was dissolved in 1958 – ten days after the government had received a substantial vote of confidence.

In 1962, Diefenbaker had once more had Parliament dissolved – this time without a single item of the estimates having been voted. The Opposition had, rather weakly, agreed to vote interim supply for five months. Consequently Diefenbaker, despite losing his majority, had been able to delay the calling of Parliament until September, when the government once more had to ask for interim supply.

A prudent government would have concentrated on getting the estimates voted as quickly as possible. Instead, priority was given to other measures with the result that, in mid-December, the government had to ask for an interim grant of the tenth-twelfth of the estimated expenditure for the fiscal year. Pearson complained about the government's mismanagement of parliamentary business, starting with the delay in opening the new Parliament and continuing with the way government business had been brought forward. At this stage the government had boxed itself in and, for the first time in history, was asking for ten months' interim supply without a single item of the estimates having been voted. He blamed mismanagement for the delay and accused the government of contempt of Parliament. Pearson felt the Canadian people were entitled to something better than perpetual interim supply.

Pearson had made one of his most powerful speeches, but he made a mistake in concluding it two or three minutes before five o'clock when the debate had to be adjourned to make way for the private members hour. The Liberal Opposition applauded vigorously taking all the time until the clock reached five. Diefenbaker had risen to reply. At five o'clock, he asked for unanimous consent to speak. Though Pearson indicated he would agree, there was not unanimous consent. The next day, the press commented on the rude conduct of the Liberal back-benchers and gave little attention to the substance of Pearson's speech. The incident underlined Pearson's lack of attention to the details of Parliamentary procedure. It was also a classic example of Diefenbaker's capacity to make himself look like a martyr.

Diefenbaker's excuse for seeking to have the rules relaxed so he could reply to Pearson was that he was leaving the next day for Nassau to meet President Kennedy and Prime Minister Macmillan. The next day Hazen Argue remarked that Diefenbaker's departure had been delayed and wondered why he was not in the House to reply to Pearson, as he was so anxious to do the afternoon before. Later Knowles said he had agreed with everything Pearson had said the day before, but he condemned the conduct of the Liberals for behaving like an unruly mob. I made a mild disclaimer of this charge by Knowles. I had been distressed that Pearson had not strung out his speech until five o'clock. His failure had given Diefenbaker an opportunity to overshadow its effect.

The Atlantic
Development
Board

One constructive step taken by the government in the first part of the session of 1962–63 was the establishment of an Atlantic Development Board. The idea of such a board was borrowed from the Liberal program. It represented a formal recognition by Parliament that the four Atlantic provinces had less developed economies and a lower standard of living than the rest of Canada. The board was designed to find ways to give additional stimulus to their economic development through federal financial aid. The Liberal proposal envisaged a capital fund to be administered by the board, but the Tory measure provided for a board with no capital fund of its own and merely advisory functions. The sponsor of the bill was appropriately Hugh John Flemming, the former premier of New Brunswick. I was the first speaker for the Opposition. Our disappointment that the Atlantic Development Board was merely to be an advisory body and not an executive agency was the main theme. The areas the board should be concerned with, in our view, were: industrial centralization; the fishery; coal; transportation; the tourist industry; the export of pulpwood to Europe; trade with the Caribbean region. Our principal regret was that the board would not have a capital fund to administer.

Later in the debate, I complained about the lack of progress on the Prince Edward Island causeway. The prime minister, I recalled, had announced in May 1962 in Charlottetown that investigations had shown the causeway was feasible and that the government intended to proceed with it.

Before the debate ended, Allan MacEachen, after reiterating our discontent with the bill, moved to refer it back to committee to insert a requirement that the board prepare annually a program of capital projects to enlarge the basic economy of the Atlantic provinces. The amendment was ruled out of order and the Speaker's ruling appealed and sustained 113–90. The bill then passed. The Atlantic Development Board was set up promptly in January 1963. I welcomed the announcement and expressed the hope the board would start to work without delay.

A section of the Tory party and interests supporting it were always opposed to including fishermen within the scope of unemployment insurance. As early as 1961, the government had instituted an inquiry into the depletion of the unemployment insurance fund. The inquiry was known as the Gill commission, after the name of the chairman. Rumours spread early in 1962, that the commission would recommend the exclusion of fishermen. Once it was known the report was completed the Opposition repeatedly demanded its production in the House. Excuses offered for the delay, made it obvious the government did not want the report made public until the House rose for the Christmas recess. The report was published the day after Parliament adjourned. As forecast, the Gill commission recommended that self-employed fishermen be taken off unemployment insurance and given assistance in another plan. Because of my almost paternal interest I issued a statement the same day which read:

I am shocked by the recommendation of the Gill Report that self-employed fishermen should be excluded from the new unemployment insurance plan. I intend to oppose that recommendation with all the strength I have. The plan suggested in the Gill Report for assistance to fishermen is not satisfactory for two reasons. Many fishermen want to work in the off-season and they feel they should have the same right as other workers to build up benefits for future periods of unemployment. A separate plan of income support for fishermen would destroy the existing incentive to accept work in the off-season whenever there is work available. While there is plenty of room for improvement in the present system, the fishermen must not be cut off unemployment insurance and I intend to fight any attempt to do that.

The fishermen are still on unemployment insurance in 1986! Now that we have another Tory government, there are rumblings that fishermen will be excluded from the scope of unemployment insurance.

Bilingualism and Biculturalism

For many reasons, the most important moment in Parliament in 1962, was a landmark speech by Pearson on 17 December on relations between English- and French-speaking Canadians in which he committed the Liberal party to the establishment of a royal commission on bilingual and bicultural relations. There had, for some time, been a campaign centred in Montreal for such an inquiry. Diefenbaker had categorically refused to consider appointing a commission, thereby alienating an influential segment of the French Canadian community. Pearson's sympathetic response and the establishment of the commission by his government were the beginning of the process which led to the Official Languages Act and the constitutional recognition of the equality of the English and French languages.

The nuclear crisis

As 1962 closed, it was a time to take stock of what had happened since the election of 18 June. At the end of June the Diefenbaker government was reeling from the massive loss of seats which left it without a majority in Parliament. It had to face the public shock over the dollar crisis and the austerity program. Pearson had, in a responsible way, refused to exploit this crisis for short-term partisan advantage. He had, however, demanded that Parliament be called in late July or early August. No doubt we should have carried on a more vigorous and sustained demand for Parliament to meet, since Diefenbaker was carrying on the government as though he still had a majority, without first seeking a vote of confidence from the House of Commons.

Constitutionally Diefenbaker should have acted as Mackenzie King had done after the 1925 election when he had failed to win a majority. In that case, Mackenzie King had scrupulously avoided any action beyond what was required for day-to-day administration. He had refrained from making any appointments to offices. Diefenbaker, on the contrary, had attended a Commonwealth conference in London and made pronouncements about government policy. What was more serious the government had imposed taxes and taken other austerity measures by order-in-council. The government was able to do this because, since Parliament had given them five months interim supply before the election, they would not run out of money until mid-October.

Diefenbaker's conduct was the most prolonged disregard of a government's responsibility to Parliament since responsible government was recognized in 1848. During the session, we Liberals had done what we could to make an issue of this contempt of Parliament. It was clear that the Social Credit party, in order to avoid an election, was ready to keep the Diefenbaker government in office by supporting it on critical votes. We had supported the Social Credit vote of want of confidence which their members could not avoid voting for. We hoped that would defeat the government. On that occasion, the New Democratic party demonstrated an equal fear of an election by voting to save the government.

The government had refused to submit its austerity measures to Parliament, relying on a legal opinion they refused to disclose that taxation by order-in-council was legal. They had made no serious effort to get the estimates approved, so Parliament could vote the money to carry on the administration. Instead the government had relied on repeated votes of interim supply. The application for the tenth-twelfth in December led to a prolonged debate. We could probably have held up this grant indefinitely and forced the government to call an election at that time, but we feared that would be regarded as sheer obstruction which could be exploited by Diefenbaker. There would be an opportunity to hold up the next request for interim supply which the government would have to ask for when Parliament resumed its session in January.

However, a still clearer issue was developing at the end of the year 1962. On 19 June 1958, the NORAD agreement with the United States for the joint defence of North America had been approved by Parliament, almost unnoticed. The debate was brief. Only the CCF had opposed NORAD. No one guessed, in 1958, that controversy over NORAD would spark the Parliamentary explosion over nuclear weapons which destroyed the Diefenbaker government in 1963.

At the time NATO was formed in 1949, the allies recognized that a nuclear deterrent in the control of the United States was essential to the security of the West. The St Laurent government decided that Canada should not attempt to become a nuclear power and that Canadian forces committed to the alliance should not have nuclear weapons. When the Diefenbaker government, in 1957, concluded the North American Air Defence agreement with the United States, that agreement, called NORAD, provided for a joint air defence command.

Canada already had fighter aircraft to identify and intercept bombers over our territory. The government faced the question of putting these squadrons under NORAD command and replacing the aircraft with new and speedier fighters. There were also to be fixed sites for launching devices called Bomarcs. Both the fighter aircraft and the Bomarcs were capable of being armed with nuclear warheads. Two Bomarc bases were to be in Canada as well as squadrons of fighter aircraft. The minister of national defence, General Pearkes, had announced the program for the new aircraft and the Bomarcs on 2 July 1959. The question of arming them with nuclear warheads was debated inconclusively several times before 1962.

The Liberal policy on nuclear weapons was announced by Paul Hellyer and confirmed by Pearson on 4 August 1960. Essentially it was to get out of roles in joint defence either for this continent or in Europe which, to be effective, would require equipping Canadian forces with nuclear weapons. On 15 September 1961, Harkness stated that the Bomarcs and fighter squadrons could function with conventional arms, but they would be much more effective and destructive if armed with nuclear warheads. The decision as to whether nuclear warheads would be installed had, he said, not yet been taken. Pearson stated the Liberal position was not changed. Canada 'should not be engaged in continental defence . . . in a way which would necessitate Canada becoming a member of the nuclear club.'

By 1962, the government had agreed to equip the Canadian air division in Europe with new planes to fill a new role as a strike attack force. A debate on this new role developed on 20 March on the question as to whether the strike force could be effective unless the new planes were equipped with nuclear devices. Pearson and Hellyer both concentrated on trying to get Harkness to say whether they would be so equipped. Harkness insisted no decision had been reached and none was needed until the strike force was operative. Pearson ridiculed the indecisiveness of the government: if the US high command had known in 1959 that, by 1962, the Canadian government would not have made up its mind to permit the air division to perform effectively, he was sure the US itself would have undertaken the task. He was unable to get Harkness to answer the question: was the NATO command satisfied that the strike attack role accepted by Canada could be carried out with conventional weapons?

Pearson recalled that Pearkes had said in 1959 that an agreement would be required with the United States to permit the Canadian planes to carry nuclear weapons and that agreement had almost been concluded. Yet, no decision had yet been reached as to whether the RCAF would be equipped to do the job it was set to do in NATO.

In this relatively brief debate Pearson made it clear that the strike attack role required the nuclear warheads. He said Canada would be in a humiliating position if the allies could not count on us to keep our commitment. He concentrated on trying to smoke out the government. He limited his statement of the Liberal position to recalling that the Opposition had objected to the strike attack role when it was proposed. At that time Hellyer had said this was the wrong kind of job for the RCAF because it would require nuclear warheads. The government, against the advice of the Opposition, had decided to purchase the planes for that role and now refused to tell the House which kind of equipment would be given to the RCAF to discharge this dangerous role.

The public became more than usually interested in defence in late 1962 because of the Cuban missile crisis. Many Canadians had been disturbed because the government was so tardy in supporting the United States in the early days of the crisis. While there was no support for an independent nuclear role for Canada, there was general support for our participation in the North Atlantic alliance and in joint continental defence.

The question of arming the Bomarcs in Canada and the five squadrons for continental defence was urgent, but the question of the air division in Europe was going to reach a crisis once the planes were delivered in late 1962. The question would have to be faced when Parliament met again in 1963. The cabinet was divided on the issue of arming the RCAF strike force with nuclear weapons. But there was also a serious risk that the Liberal Opposition would be divided on the issue. The Liberal party had been formally on record since August 1960 as opposed to arming any of the Canadian forces with nuclear weapons. Instead, the party advocated negotiating the withdrawal of any implied commitment to our allies. Paul Hellyer, who was the defence critic for the Opposition, visited the Canadian forces in Europe late in 1962. He was convinced their morale was suffering from the reluctance to discharge our obligations to NATO by arming our forces in Europe with nuclear weapons, as the government had agreed to do in 1959. He reported that to the Liberal caucus on 22 November, but Pearson was dubious about changing Liberal policy.

I had not been following defence policy closely, since Pearson, Hellyer, and Drury were all active in this field. At the end of the year, Pearson asked me to read a paper prepared for him by a leading expert on military questions. I read the paper on 2 January 1963, and wrote the following note about it for him. My handwritten note read:

I have no reason to doubt that this paper contains very good advice to a government in office, but I am sure that any detailed statement of future plans from a politician without the power to carry them out and, presumably, without the secret strategic information on which some of these judgements could alone be made with validity, would simply provide a target for opponents of all kinds.

But what is far more *serious,* most of these proposals would be misunderstood by servicemen and would lose votes which may well be decisive in the next election. Moreover I cannot believe any detailed policy that we can possibly formulate can get us any additional support anywhere. Surely we should confine ourselves to taking positions on questions that have to be settled *now* or should have been settled already, plus *general* principles *only* for the future.

Above all we should avoid suggesting that we are going to try to talk ourselves out of existing commitments (however desirable that might be if we were in office). If we do that we will be back in another morass almost as bad as the one we are trying to get out of. The average person just cannot grasp subtle and constantly qualified positions and the average MP or candidate can't explain them either. Despite its inherent complexity, surely our position can be explained simply and clearly and positively.

I believe a speech along the lines of this paper would be an irretrievable political disaster for us. Sorry to have had to scribble observations in this way.

The following morning I wrote a further note to Pearson on the subject in which I said:

Before leaving Ottawa this morning I thought I should try to be more constructive and ask myself what I thought the Leader of an Opposition expecting soon to be a Prime Minister should and/or could say on defence; also what he *should not say*.

There is only one defence question that enters the realm of *practical politics,* viz. nuclear weapons. On that the public condemns the government for vacillation, but those who notice us say we are just as bad. You have already decided what our position must be on existing commitments and there was no dissent in caucus. But let it be said simply and decisively and without any qualifications about trying to get out of it. That I regard as vital. I think it almost as important to put this nuclear weapon issue in the perspective of our total *political* defence commitment and to make it clear that Canada is not and will not *ever* become a nuclear power on its own; that our commitment relates exclusively to our position in an alliance for the defence of the continent and of the free world and that our position in the alliance, which we had a large part in forming, depends upon the confidence of the allies, particularly the US, in our *loyalty* and our *reliability*.

I am almost equally concerned *as a practical politician* about retaining the support of the armed forces without which we cannot win an election. For (with dependents) close to a quarter of a million voters are involved and, like other voters, most of them are primarily concerned with their livelihood, and that quarter-million voters in places like Chatham, N.B., North Bay, etc. not to mention larger places like Halifax are highly sensitive to the attitude of political parties to the forces. Then there are veterans with pride in the three services.

A Prime Minister has a duty to take political risks and responsibility for reorganizing the armed forces and keeping them up to date. The Leader of the Opposition has neither the duty nor should he be expected to have the detailed strategic and technical information to plan such reforms. His duty ends when he has set out the objectives of defence policy and gives his assurances that a government he leads will pursue those objectives resolutely.

To envisage distant and hypothetical ends before one has the means of achieving them will, in the field of defence, be almost sure to upset and disturb thousands of voters without the slightest compensating political (or other) advantages that I can envisage.

It is because I believe this is the one subject on which a wrong course could sink our prospects without a trace that I have written so emphatically.

Yours in great haste,
J.W.P.

I had had to prepare these documents so hastily, because Margaret and I were leaving that day (3 January) for visits to Paris and London from which we did not return to Ottawa until 14 January. I then left on 15 January for a week in Newfoundland and was therefore not back in Ottawa until 21 January, the day the session of Parliament resumed. Therefore, I was not aware of what was going on from day to day about defence policy after I sent my notes to Pearson. I have since consulted Paul Hellyer about the sequence of events. He confirms that the subject of honouring our existing commitments about arming the Bomarcs and the aircraft in Europe with nuclear warheads had been discussed at a Liberal caucus, presumably before or just after Parliament adjourned. At the caucus there seems to have been general agreement that Canada should live up to its commitments. Hellyer is clear that Pearson took no position at the caucus. He has told me that neither he nor Walter Gordon learned of Pearson's change of view until Pearson made his speech at Scarborough on 12 January. My notes to Pearson on January 2 and 3 make it apparent that Pearson had already indicated to me that he had decided what our position must be on the existing commitments. I was, therefore, not trying to change his mind, but merely to get him to express his position clearly and without qualification. I have also consulted Richard O'Hagan, who was press secretary and adviser to Pearson. On my return to Ottawa, he gave me a copy of a memo he had sent to Pearson on 7 January in which he said in part:

Without presumption, I hope, may I say how impressed I was with the points made by Jack Pickersgill in his memorandum to you of January 3 respecting defence policy. It is obvious of course that in elementary political terms the whole question revolves on nuclear weapons, simply and starkly. Will we accept them, and on what basis?

I agree entirely with Jack that the answer you give the country must be a model of simplicity and decisiveness, even – and I say this advisedly – at the risk of some over-simplification. We will be hailed or censured not on the subsidiary refinements, however important they may be, but on the central position we adopt, or at least what that position appears to be.

In defining that position, I hope you will not hesitate to ring a few patriotic bells – not irresponsibly, of course, nor in the chauvinistic sense. Do it rather, as I am sure you will, in a way and as a means of reminding people of what we, as a nation, must do if we are to honourably and adequately serve the cause of freedom.

Pearson decided to make his announcement on 12 January at Scarborough, without informing Hellyer who was in Antigua or, as I learned from Hellyer,

Walter Gordon. As I was still in Europe I did not know about the speech until after it was made. In his speech Pearson said a Liberal government would carry out the commitment of the Canadian government to arm the weapons with nuclear warheads.

Pearson's Scarborough speech altered the political landscape and created an issue between the Liberal Opposition and the government which was the dominant theme of the rest of that Parliament.

When the session resumed in January 1963, the government agreed to set aside 24 and 25 January for a debate on the estimates of the Department of External Affairs. The debate was to deal with defence as well as external affairs. Pearson was the first speaker on 25 January. In his speech he explained the change in the Liberal position on nuclear weapons. The government, he stated, had adopted fighter aircraft and fixed rocket-launching installations for joint continental defence which would be fully effective only when armed with nuclear warheads. The government had subsequently agreed to transform the Canadian air division in Europe into a strike attack force which also required nuclear warheads to be effective. These commitments had been made to our allies in spite of earlier Liberal objections to a defence role which would require nuclear warheads to be fully effective. After making these commitments to our allies, the government now refused to say whether it would make the necessary decision to ensure that our forces had the most effective means to discharge their obligations.

He recalled that, in the election campaign of 1962, the Liberal program had stated that, on the basis of what was known at that time, a new Liberal government would not require Canada to become a nuclear power by the manufacture, acquisition, or use of nuclear weapons under Canadian or American control. That program also stated that a Liberal government would examine each situation in the light of the over riding responsibility for the security of the Canadian people.

Pearson pointed out that the Liberal program of 1962 had not totally excluded the possibility that the Canadian forces in Europe might be armed with tactical and defensive nuclear warheads. Having restated the Liberal program of 1962, Pearson set out the new Liberal position on the arming of the Canadian forces with nuclear warheads.

He said that, as long as there was sufficient time for Canada to change its commitments in negotiations with its allies, the Liberal Opposition had advocated that change. But the government, despite Liberal arguments, had maintained those commitments and the time had come when the new weapon systems were being installed, and pledges must be implemented as long as they continued to exist. 'A Liberal government,' Pearson declared, 'would honour those pledges made by its predecessor for Canada in agreement with our allies as long as they exist, until they were changed.' We would put Canada's armed services in a position to do the job entrusted to them.

'As I see it,' he stated, 'that would be the only honourable course for the new government representing the Canadian people. Any other course would betray our trust, weaken Canadian reputation for living up to its word, and deceive our own people with regard to pledges we had undertaken . . .' He added that 'while keeping our pledges, we would seek a better and more effective defence role for Canada in the alliance.' The speech was delivered, almost without interruption, to a very attentive House. It was one of Pearson's finest performances in Parliament. The government was damaged by the contrast between his decisiveness and their indecision.

Diefenbaker seemed to realize how critical the situation was. He replied at great length and with moderation and, for him, coherence. Most of the speech was devoted to a review of Pearson's statements on defence policy from 1958 on. He concluded with a brief justification of the governments' refusal to make hasty decisions. This argument was based on the agreements made at Nassau by President Kennedy and Prime Minister Macmillan which, Diefenbaker alleged, had contemplated changes in NATO strategy. He said: 'We have never and will never consent to Canada breaking any of her pledged words or undertakings,' but added that NATO defence policies would all be reviewed at the NATO meeting to be held in Ottawa in May. Meanwhile the government would negotiate with the United States so that, in case of need, nuclear warheads would be made readily available. His closing words were: 'I would rather be right, Mr. Chairman, so that those who come after may say: "He refused to be stampeded. He refused to act on the impulse of the moment. He and his colleagues together, with the support of the Canadian Parliament, brought about a policy, in co-operation with their allies and by influence over their allies, that led to the achievement of peace."'

Diefenbaker was followed by Caouette for Social Credit and Brewin for the NDP. When a Tory back-bencher rose, I interrupted to ask whether the minister of national defence intended to participate in the debate. Harkness replied that after the nearly two-hour speech by the prime minister there was not much to be served by his going into the debate at the moment. The debate concluded that day.

On Monday 28 January, Harkness astonished the House and the country by issuing a press release interpreting the prime minister's speech of 25 January. He represented that Diefenbaker's speech had set forth a definite policy for the acquisition of nuclear arms. Tommy Douglas asked Diefenbaker if this was a correct interpretation. Diefenbaker dodged the question by asserting that his own speech was very clear, very direct, and very comprehensive and did not require any interpretation. Supplementary questions obviously embarrassed the government.

Despite this disagreement between Diefenbaker and Harkness, we had little hope of defeating the government on the nuclear issue. On a straight note in favour of arming our NATO and NORAD forces with nuclear warheads, we knew the vote of the NDP would be negative. Caouette made it clear the Social Credit members from Quebec would continue to oppose nuclear arms. Our best hope of making the position of the government impossible was to delay the appropriation by Parliament of the money required to carry on the administration. The tenth-twelfths of interim supply would expire on 31 January and the government would have no money to pay public servants or other costs of government by 15 February. I could not believe the government would not either seek to have some of the annual estimates approved or ask for interim supply as soon as the debate on external affairs was concluded. Instead the government decided to have the debate on a proposal for a national economic development board continued on Monday 28 January. This bill had no urgency whatever. At the end of that day, Churchill announced that the same debate would continue the next day. I asked for an assurance that the External Affairs estimates would be brought up again during the week, so the House could debate the repudiation of the prime minister by the minister of national defence. I got no answer.

On 29 January, Pearson asked the prime minister whether he wished to make a statement on the reported differences between himself and Harkness. This query precipitated a series of supplementary questions to which there were no clear answers. The debate on the economic development board dragged on that day.

There was further questioning about nuclear weapons which became very heated on 30 January. That day the government brought on the estimates of the Department of Labour for debate and proposed to have estimates debated for the rest of the week. The plans of the government were abruptly changed by a statement issued that evening by the Department of State of the United States.

The statement began by saying the department had received inquiries about the disclosure in the Canadian House of Commons of negotiations over recent months between the United States and Canadian governments relating to nuclear weapons for the Canadian forces. The state department declared that, shortly after the Cuban crisis in October 1962, the Canadian government proposed confidential discussions concerning the circumstances in which nuclear weapons might be provided for Canadian forces. It stated these discussions were exploratory as 'the Canadian government has not as yet proposed any arrangement sufficiently practical to contribute effectively to North American defence.'

The statement recalled that in 1958 the Canadian government decided to adopt the Bomarc-B weapon system and that two Bomarc-B squadrons were deployed in Canada to protect Montreal and Toronto as a part of the US deterrent force. The matter of making available a nuclear warhead for the Bomarc and other weapons systems, the statement continued, 'has been the subject of inconclusive discussions' since the Bomarcs were installed in 1962. It added that a similar problem existed with respect to the supersonic jet interceptors provided for the RCAF, since these aircraft 'operate at far less than their full potential effectiveness' without nuclear warheads.

The discussions, the statement continued, also concerned possible arrangements for the provision of nuclear weapons for Canadian NATO forces in Europe, similar to those made with other NATO allies of the United States. The statement dealt with the references made in the House of Commons to the discussions at Nassau between President Kennedy and Prime Minister Macmillan in which Diefenbaker had had a small part. Diefenbaker claimed Nassau had changed the situation regarding the strategy in Europe. The statement noted that the agreements made at Nassau had been fully published and asserted 'they raise no question of the appropriateness of nuclear weapons for Canadian forces in fulfilling their NATO or NORAD obligations.'

The state department press release was a direct contradiction of Diefenbaker's statement in the House of Commons on 25 January of what Kennedy and Macmillan had agreed to at the Nassau meeting. The state department asserted that 'a flexible and balanced defence requires increased conventional forces, but conventional forces are not an alternative to effective NATO and NORAD defence arrangements using nuclear capable weapons systems.'

The last two paragraphs of the US state department press release explained that NORAD was designed to defend North America against air attacks and asserted the Soviet bomber fleet remained a significant element in the Soviet strike force. Effective defence against this threat was necessary. The provision of nuclear weapons to the Canadian forces would not expand the 'nuclear club.' The statement pointed out: 'As in the case of other allies, custody of U.S. nuclear weapons would remain with the U.S. Joint control fully consistent with national sovereignty can be worked out to cover the use of such weapons by Canadian forces.'

As soon as he received a copy of the US press release that evening, Pearson issued a public statement, saying it was surprising that the United States government considered it necessary to issue a statement about the prime minister's speech and public declarations by the minister of national defence. He said questions of Canadian policy should be left entirely for discussion and decision by Canadians.

Diefenbaker saw in the ham-handed US intervention the opportunity to divert attention away from the indecision of his government by representing Pearson as an American stooge. At the opening of the sitting of the House on 31 January, Diefenbaker made a statement protesting the unprecedented and unwarranted intrusion by the United States into Canadian affairs. He said that, as he read the document, it bore a striking resemblance to Pearson's speech in the House on 25 January. When Pearson rose to comment on Diefenbaker's statement a Tory member called out: 'Go ahead, Yankee.'

Pearson denied the allegation that his speech on defence had been worked out in consultation with the United States government and that some of the words in the United States press statement bore a striking resemblance to words in his speech of 24 January. He said it was unworthy of the Prime Minister: 'a cheap and false insinuation.' He reminded the House he had objected to the interference by the United States as soon as he learned of it the previous evening.

In his comment, Pearson said the prime minister's speech, Harkness's clarification, and the state department statement all related to joint arrangements for common defence. In the light of the contradictions, Pearson declared that the real issue for Canadians was: what are the facts and what is the truth? Harkness had contradicted certain of the prime minister's statements whereupon Harkness interjected: 'I did not.' The United States government, Pearson added, contradicted other statements by the prime minister. He felt 'it was inappropriate for them to have done so.' He appealed for the facts 'without any further shilly-shallying or delay.' At this point, Diefenbaker interjected: 'When are you going back for further instructions?'

Pearson deplored divisions within the free world. He said any political leader in either country who for partisan purposes stirred up or enlarged a difference between the two countries would be putting his party ahead of his country. This would be seeking immediate political advantage above the mutual interest in peace and prosperity which the two countries share. He was interrupted by Tory members who suggested that was what Pearson was doing.

Thompson and Douglas then commented on Diefenbaker's statement. As soon as the party leaders' comments were concluded, Pearson made a motion for an urgent debate on the statement by the US state department. Such urgent debates are only permitted if there is no other appropriate opportunity for an early debate. Under the rules, the Speaker was the sole judge of urgency. After permitting a substantial debate on the question of urgency, the Speaker decided a debate was not urgent. He pointed out there was no appeal against his ruling. Paul Martin appealed the Speaker's ruling that there was no appeal. The House supported Martin's appeal 122 to 104.

Having secured the right for a debate, Pearson made a long speech on the US statement which extended into the evening. He examined in detail the contradictions between the US press release and Diefenbaker's speech of 25 January and also the contradictions between Diefenbaker's speech and Harkness's public interpretation.

After the leaders of the other parties had spoken in the urgent debate Harkness replied to Pearson. He denied that he had contradicted the prime minister and defied anyone to find anything in his interpretation which was not contained in the prime minister's speech.

A day or two later, I made a regular broadcast to Newfoundland. This broadcast, being contemporary, provides a better reflection of the atmosphere at the end of January 1963 than any later account I could give. I called the broadcast 'The Crisis That Evaporated' and this is what I said.:

Until Wednesday of this week, one MP was at the centre of the Ottawa stage. He had kept the centre of the stage by refusing to speak. That man was Douglas Harkness, the minister of national defence. On Thursday and Friday of last week there had been a combined debate on external affairs and defence arranged by the prime minister, so that, in his words: 'there would be an opportunity for the Opposition to give the House the benefit of its views . . . It was something new, in my twenty-five years in Ottawa, for a prime minister to propose a debate on the views and policies of the Opposition. In that debate, the minister of national defence had declined to speak . . .

If the minister had nothing to say in Parliament, it was different outside the House where he began at once to explain away the prime minister's speech. On Saturday he made his first 'interpretation' of what the prime minister had said. On Monday he issued a second written 'interpretation.' This second Harkness statement was a contradiction of Mr Diefenbaker's words in Parliament. Old Ottawa hands can remember occasions when open disputes between ministers in the same cabinet had to be patched up by the prime minister; no one can recall a case where a minister corrected a prime minister and stayed in the cabinet.

During the question period in Parliament on Monday [28 January], Mr Diefenbaker, visibly shaken, declared his words needed no interpretation. He admitted he had not been consulted about the Harkness interpretation and had not seen it before it was issued. Gossip had it that the 'interpretation' was a compromise worked out by Gordon Churchill to prevent a resignation [by Harkness]. Mr Harkness declined to explain his extraordinary action. In Britain, or in Canada before Diefenbaker, a minister who publicly corrected a prime minister would have resigned or been asked to leave the cabinet.

Until Wednesday night, the Opposition parties had had no opportunity to debate this apparent split in the cabinet, though many questions had been asked about it. The question everyone was asking was: would Harkness buckle under or resign? It was hard not to feel sorry for Mr Harknesss. He is a simple, straightforward person, obviously devoted to the men in uniform whose fortunes he shared in war and whose feelings he probably still shares. He has repeatedly expressed his conviction that Canada's forces should be armed with the most modern and effective weapons. Everybody in Ottawa knows that Douglas Harkness believes in his heart there is only one right and honourable course for Canada.

The hard choice facing Doug Harkness was the same choice that faced one of his colleagues over three years ago. When Davie Fulton returned from British Columbia to make his farewells to Ottawa on Tuesday, all of us recalled the fateful week-end when his downfall started. He, too, had believed Canada had only one right and honourable course. After several hours of agony of spirit, he had submitted to his chief and stayed in the cabinet. After that submission, Davie Fulton never recovered his old spirit. A week ago he took on the task of reviving the Conservative party in British Columbia. Despite the almost hopeless prospect of success, Davie Fulton looks and acts like a man who has been liberated. The tragic example of Davie Fulton was in everyone's mind as we waited to see whether Douglas Harkness, too, would submit to his chief. That was the situation on Thursday morning after the US state department had dropped its verbal bombshell.

When the combined Opposition forced a second debate on defence over the stubborn resistance of the government and the ruling of the Speaker, everyone expected the prime minister to reply to the Opposition leaders and to state Canada's position in the light of the new situation; to give Parliament the facts and the truth Mr Pearson had demanded. Instead Mr Harkness replied. His reply was the greatest parliamentary anti-climax in living memory. A debate on the subject of human survival was brought down to the level of a barber-shop discussion. The intervention of the state department of the United States, which all parties had deplored, was barely mentioned by Mr Harkness. He spent all his time asserting, and trying vainly to prove against the evidence, that his words and the prime minister's meant the same thing; that there was no difference between them. One impression emerged clearly; Douglas Harkness had submitted to his chief and the crisis had evaporated. Davie Fulton's submission three years ago was a tragedy; unhappily Douglas Harkness turned his submission into a farce.

I was clearly wrong about the crisis having evaporated. When the House met on Monday 4 February Harkness rose to announce his resignation as minister of national defence. In his statement Harkness said he had believed, when he spoke on 31 January, that the position he had outlined in his press release on 28 January was in conformity with the speech by Diefenbaker on 24 January, but that subsequently it became apparent to him that the prime minister's views on nuclear arms and his own were irreconcilable. He explained he had remained in the cabinet in the hope of getting the nuclear arms question definitely settled. He concluded by saying he had resigned on a matter of principle, when the point was finally reached that he considered his honour and integrity required that he take that step.

The government falls

The government had already announced a supply motion would be made that Monday (4 February). The Opposition normally moves an amendment to a supply motion expressing lack of confidence in the government. Pearson made a motion which read: 'this government, because of lack of leadership, the break-down of unity in the cabinet, and confusion and indecision in dealing with national and international problems, does not have the confidence of the Canadian people.'

Pearson had phrased the motion in general terms in the hope of securing the support of the smaller parties, support which would not have been given to a motion dealing exclusively with nuclear arms.

Thompson followed Pearson. During the afternoon he seemed to be wavering between two alternatives. Just before the dinner recess, he gave the impression Social Credit might vote to save the government from possible defeat. When the House resumed sitting after dinner, Thompson announced that Social Credit had reluctantly come to the conclusion an election would be preferable to prolonging the life of the government. He moved a sub-amendment which condemned the government for failing to give a clear statement of defence policy, failing to organize House business so the 1963–4 estimates and budget could be introduced, and failing to outline a positive program of follow-up action respecting many things which Parliament had already authorized.

Thompson was followed by David Lewis for the New Democratic party who sounded throughout his speech as though the NDP would rescue the government, since he could find no difference between the government and the Liberal Opposition on the nuclear issue or any other. He accused the Liberals and Social Credit of presenting vague and general motions instead of a specific issue.

Gordon Churchill was the first speaker for the government. He defended the record of the government in organizing the business of the House. He said nothing about the defence question, except to criticize Pearson for failing to make it the sole issue.

Hellyer then spoke on his visit to the Canadian troops in Europe. It was a very effective speech, listened to with close attention. Hellyer replied to Lewis's charge that Pearson had said we would fulfil our commitments and then negotiate our way out of them immediately. He said, with Pearson's concurrence, that we would carry out the existing commitments but not make new ones when the existing weapons became obsolete.

When the supply debate resumed on 5 February, Hellyer continued his speech and defined the Liberal position precisely. He announced that the Liberals would support the sub-amendment moved by Thompson of Social Credit which 'expresses in somewhat different words the same lack of confidence' in the government. By agreeing to support the Social Credit motion, the Liberal Opposition made sure Social Credit could not change its mind. Hellyer welcomed the opportunity to repeat the Liberal policy on defence stated by Pearson when he had said 'the government should re-examine at once the whole basis of Canadian defence. However, until the present role is changed, a new Liberal government would put Canada's armed forces in the position to discharge fully commitments undertaken for Canada by its predecessors.'

Diefenbaker followed Hellyer with a long and rambling speech filled with irrelevancies and disparaging references to Pearson. Throughout the rest of the debate the uncertainty about what position the NDP would take increased the tension in the House. We wondered whether that party would save the government. Tommy Douglas was the last speaker. He expressed equal lack of confidence in the Conservative government and the Liberal Opposition. He then stated that Parliament had been 'reduced to a state of such impotence that the only answer now is to give the people of Canada an opportunity to go to the polls.' The suspense was over. The government was defeated 142 to 111.

The election of 1963

A government had been defeated in Parliament for only the second time since Confederation. The ministry was in disarray. There was no minister of national defence and two of the leading members of the government, Fulton and Fleming, were about to retire from Parliament. Parliament was dissolved the next day and an election called for 8 April 1963.

I was not much involved in the Liberal strategy, though I campaigned a good deal outside Newfoundland. I had to devote much more time to my own riding in 1963 than I had in 1962. My Tory opponents in 1962 and 1963 had no substantial following and were not a threat. However, in 1963, I was challenged also by another candidate, Walter H. Davis, who described himself as a true Liberal and a genuine Newfoundlander. He had two aims: to rid Newfoundland of this mainlander and to have a CBC television station established in Newfoundland. Davis was striking in appearance with a commanding presence and a capacity to speak impressively.

At the outset I did not take Davis seriously and was surprised to learn that Premier Smallwood was worried about his potential appeal. Smallwood arranged, without consulting me, to have statements repudiating Davis and supporting me delivered to every household in the town of Bonavista where the electorate was the least stable in the riding. I was concerned that the second statement might attract more support for Davis than opposition to him. I did not suggest, and Smallwood did not offer, that he speak on my behalf. I wanted to win on my own. I soon realized that I must have meetings throughout the riding as I had done in 1958.

On several occasions, Davis tried to disrupt my meetings. The most amusing was at Salvage where I was speaking in the Orange Hall. The audience refused to let Davis into the hall; he had a loud speaker on top of his car which he placed under a window; he made his speech outside while I was speaking inside the hall. Davis made a spectacular appearance at my meeting in Bonavista striding down from the back of the hall after the meeting had started. I insisted he come up on the platform and make a speech before I made mine. The confrontation at Bonavista was shortly before the close of the campaign. I reached the conclusion that Davis was providing a degree of excitement for audiences, but gaining no substantial support.

The appeal Davis was making for a CBC television station in St John's had no appeal in Bonavista-Twillingate where existing TV reception was very poor. What my constituents wanted was a clear picture in their own area, not two stations for the people of St John's. I had not altered the view I had taken, when television was started in Canada, that alternate service should not be permitted so long as private stations were affiliates of the CBC and broadcast most of its programs. I realized, however, that, if we won the election, a Liberal government would have to face the question of a CBC station in St John's, the application for which had been approved by the BBG a few days before the election.

Don Jamieson was one of the owners of the private station, CJON-TV. I have never ceased to be grateful for his disinterested advice that the political pressure could not be resisted for long and that I should not commit myself too strongly against a CBC TV station. I valued this advice all the more because an alternate station would be harmful financially to CJON-TV and to Jamieson personally. By following his advice, I saved myself possible embarrassment after the Pearson government was formed and I became spokesman for broadcasting in the House of Commons.

I had one exciting adventure in my own district. I had arranged for a small plane on skis to take me to Twillingate for an evening meeting. The sea was frozen between the mainland and New World and Twillingate islands and we anticipated no difficulty in landing on the ice. As we approached New World Island which we had to cross to reach Twillingate, snow began to fall and the pilot wanted to turn back to Gander. My friend, Edgar Baird of Gander, a veteran pilot of the RAF and an experienced pilot of small planes, was with me. I suggested the pilot land us first on the ice in front of Summerford. When the pilot asked me where Summerford was, and I had to show him on a small road map, Edgar could hardly wait to get out of the plane.

We landed safely, managed to get lunch in the settlement and found someone to drive us to Hillgrade, which was the nearest point on the tickle between New World and Twillingate islands. At Hillgrade we were able to get a horse and sled to take us across on the ice. The sled carried our luggage and we walked behind in the track it made in the light cover of snow. I had had no experience of sea ice and did not realize how rubbery it was. I don't suppose there was any chance of plunging through, but I was glad when the mile was completed and we set foot on Twillingate island.

By that time it was snowing hard and we had to wait an hour or two before the snow plough arrived. We hitched a lift to Twillingate town on the plough. Wind and snow had made the road around Twillingate harbour impassible and it was useless to try to have a meeting. The next morning the sun was shining and the whole place was sparkling. But there was no time to organize a meeting. We got word to Gander and a small plane was sent out to fly us back. At least, I had been to Twillingate. Davis never went there at all.

The winter was mild and I had little difficulty getting around to the main places. I concentrated most of my efforts in the southern part of the riding, especially the Bonavista peninsula where Davis spent most of his time. Despite his noisy efforts, Davis received about 500 fewer votes than the Tory candidate. I had over 250 more votes than I had received in 1962, about 75 per cent of the total in each election.

While I was active in my own riding, I took little part in the campaign elsewhere in Newfoundland. None of our members was in any danger of defeat; Cashin was almost certain to win in St John's West, where Browne was no longer a candidate. Liberal prospects were good as well in St John's East. McGrath, the sitting member, had been passed over by Diefenbaker, and Newfoundland had had no minister since the 1962 election. Diefenbaker himself was as unpopular as ever in the province.

I devoted about half my time to campaigning on the mainland. I criss-crossed Ontario and the Maritimes and got as far west as Edmonton. The French version of my book, *The Liberal Party*, called *Le Parti Libéral* was published in Montreal on 5 March with considerable publicity.

At the beginning of the campaign Liberals expected to win a substantial majority. Most Conservatives I talked to felt they were facing a crushing defeat. In fact they lost only twenty-one seats, of which more than a third were in Ontario. The Prairies were virtually as solidly Tory as before. The Liberals lost Argue's seat in Saskatchewan, but won Calgary South in Alberta and Winnipeg South in Manitoba. Neither the New Democratic party nor Social Credit gained anything in the prairies. It was clear that Alvin Hamilton and Diefenbaker himself had a strong hold on the western farmers. Surprisingly, the Tories held eight of the fourteen seats they had kept in Quebec in 1962. They lost four seats in the Maritimes and their last seat in Newfoundland, where the Liberals had a clean sweep. They lost only two in British Columbia. It was a defeat but far from a disaster for the Tory party. The greatest single factor in turning potential disaster into a mere defeat was the amazing campaign conducted by Diefenbaker himself. His was the last old-fashioned campaign by train with whistle stops and impassioned appeals directed to those who saw him and not to the media. What denied the Liberals a majority was the continued support for Social Credit members in Quebec. Social Credit lost only four of the twenty-four seats they had won in 1962. We emerged from the election with 129 seats out of a total of 265, four short of a clear majority.

A Liberal government again

I was back in Ottawa to vote on 8 April and spent the evening at the Chateau Laurier in Pearson's suite listening to the returns. We were disappointed when the final returns left us four seats short. For a short time after the election there was uncertainty as to whether Diefenbaker would resign as prime minister or stay on to meet the new House of Commons and ask for a vote of confidence as he had done in 1962. When six Social Credit MPs from Quebec announced their intention to support Pearson, Diefenbaker decided to resign. Pearson was at once invited by the governor general to form a government. The process took more than a week.

The Pearson administration was sworn in on 22 April, one day before Pearson's sixty-sixth birthday. He was almost the same age as St Laurent had been when he became prime minister in 1948. Pearson told me he had already chosen ministers for three portfolios, Justice, External Affairs, and Finance, which were to go to Chevrier, Martin, and Walter Gordon. He said I could have whichever of the other departments I preferred, and added he thought I might wish to take Transport. I said I would be embarrassed to be minister of transport until several transport problems of special concern to Newfoundland were dealt with. I astonished him by saying my first choice would be to become secretary of state. His reaction was that it was a minor portfolio without prestige and that I deserved something better. He asked why I had suggested so modest a post.

I reminded him that two elections had been held in which the constitutional obligation for redistribution had been ignored. It would be scandalous not to tackle it immediately. Since we did not have a majority, we could not count on four or five years before another election became necessary. Not only was it our duty to comply with the requirements of the constitution without delay, but the Liberal party had undertaken to remove the process of redistribution from the House of Commons and have it performed by an independent and non-partisan process. It would take substantial time to set up the appropriate machinery before the redistribution itself could begin. The legislation would be complicated and controversial. I doubted if any other member of Parliament was as familiar with the subject and its problems as I was, since I had been involved while I was in the Prime Minister's Office with the two previous redistributions. I did not believe there would be any competition in the party for this thankless task, which I undertook later in the year.

We Liberals were also committed to specific and controversial changes in the broadcasting legislation enacted while the Diefenbaker government was in office. Apart from Pearson himself, I had been the main Liberal critic of broadcasting policy in Opposition. I could probably pilot the necessary legislation through Parliament more easily than anyone else available, if I was given the ministerial responsibility. I said that I would not have offered to become secretary of state if I had not believed Pearson would be willing to give me as well the ministerial responsibility for the National Film Board, the National Gallery, the Public Archives, and the National Library. As minister of citizenship in the St Laurent government I had had ministerial responsibility for all those agencies. I assumed I would also, as the only privy councillor from the Atlantic provinces, be given responsibility for the Atlantic Development Board.

Pearson had no hesitation about accepting all of these suggestions and agreed that, even if the portfolio itself had little prestige or importance, I would have no lack of responsibility. When I added that I would also like to be the leader of the government in the House of Commons, Pearson was shocked. He asked me whether I did not feel my combative attitude in Opposition would make it difficult for me to secure the necessary co-operation from the Oppositon in arranging parliamentary business. I said I hoped he did not think my attitude and tactics in office would be the same as they had been in Opposition. I believed my knowledge of parliamentary rules and procedures was the equal of any other of our members. Chevrier had been our house leader in Opposition. As his assistant, I had shared in the negotiations behind the curtains since 1958 and had experience of the indispensible requirements to make Parliament work.

Since we lacked a majority of our own party members, a majority would have to be created to ensure the passage of every controversial measure. We would have to make sure, as well, that our own members were always available for votes. This task would require the almost constant presence of the government leader in the House. This would be easier for me since my portfolio would involve few administrative duties. I assured Pearson that appointment as government leader was not a condition of my acceptance of the office of secretary of state. I would not take offence if he decided he would prefer someone else as leader, even though I believed I could do the job.

I suggested that we regard the rest as settled and that he make no immediate decision about the house leadership. The situation remained that way for a day or two, but he eventually told me he had decided to let me undertake the task for the first session of the new Parliament and see how it worked out. I was pleased and relieved. But it was also desirable to have a French-speaking member associated with the management of the House. I recommended that Guy Favreau should act for me when I was absent from the House and assist me at all times. I had formed a high opinion of Favreau, mostly at second hand. Pearson readily agreed to this suggestion.

The original members of the Pearson cabinet in order of precedence were:

1. L.B. Pearson, prime minister
2. Lionel Chevrier, minister of justice
3. Paul Martin, secretary of state for external affairs
4. W. Ross Macdonald, leader of the government in the Senate
5. J.W. Pickersgill, secretary of state of Canada and leader of the government in the House of Commons

6. Paul T. Hellyer, minister of national defence
7. Walter L. Gordon, minister of finance
8. Mitchell Sharp, minister of trade and commerce
9. Azellus Denis, postmaster general
10. George J. McIlraith, minister of transport
11. William Benidickson, minister of mines and technical surveys
12. Arthur Laing, minister of northern affairs and national resources
13. Maurice Lamontagne, president of the privy council
14. J.R. Garland, minister of national revenue
15. Lucien Cardin, associate minister of national defence
16. Allan J. MacEachen, minister of labour
17. Jean-Paul Deschatelets, minister of public works
18. Hédard Robichaud, minister of fisheries
19. J. Watson MacNaught, solicitor general
20. Roger Teillet, minister of veterans affairs
21. Judy LaMarsh, minister of national health and welfare
22. C.M. Drury, minister of defence production
23. Guy Favreau, minister of citizenship and immigration
24. J.R. Nicholson, minister of forestry
25. Harry Hays, minister of agriculture
26. René Tremblay, minister without portfolio.

During the election campaign, Pearson had accepted an unwise suggestion from the party organization that, if he became prime minister, the government would be committed to 'sixty days of decision' once Parliament met. The original suggestion was 'a hundred days,' but Pearson rejected that because of Napoleon's hundred days between his return from Elba and Waterloo. Sixty days was, in practice, even worse. The Speech from the Throne opening the session contained an impressive but scarcely realizable program of legislation. Legislation was forecast for the establishment of a department of industry with an area development agency; the recasting of the Atlantic Development Board; the creation of a municipal development and loan board; amendments to the National Housing Act; the creation of a Canada development corporation; the establishment of an economic council of Canada; amendment of the Department of Agriculture Act to provide for a second minister from eastern Canada; provision of additional federal assistance to complete the Trans-Canada highway; comprehensive contributory retirement pensions; amendments to the Unemployment Insurance Act; redistribution of representation in the House of Commons; amendment of the Citizenship Act to give naturalized citizens equal status with natural-born citizens; the continuation of subsidies to the railways pending new railway legislation; and several other lesser measures.

In addition there were bound to be debates on the establishment of the Royal Commission on Bilingualism and Biculturalism; the Columbia River treaty; the establishment of a twelve-mile fishery zone and federal-provincial relations.

The session of the new Parliament began in a thoroughly conventional fashion on 16 May. Alan Macnaughton, a fully bilingual Montreal lawyer, who had been the chairman of the Public Accounts Committee while Diefenbaker was prime minister, was elected Speaker. Macnaughton proved to be less firm than Lambert and less learned and judicious than Michener. He was inclined to be intimidated by Diefenbaker, and too often permitted his rulings to be discussed after they had been made. He was faced with far too many appeals from his decision in the first session. I became increasingly resolved to do my best to have appeals from the Speaker's rulings abolished – fortunately for me a goal I had already set publicly when in Opposition.

Lucien Lamoureux was chosen as Deputy Speaker. He quickly proved himself a splendidly articulate and utterly impartial presiding officer and was later to become one of the really great Speakers. Herman Batten, a Newfoundlander, became deputy chairman of committees. Batten was a firm and imperturbable presiding officer who, in due course, was to become Deputy Speaker and who always retained the respect of the House.

The debate on the address in reply to the Speech from the Throne was begun by Diefenbaker, as leader of the Opposition, on Monday 20 May in a rambling speech, which concluded with a vague motion of want of confidence which caused us no concern, as we were convinced no party in Opposition wanted another election. If we made sure our members were present for votes, we were not likely to be defeated, even though we lacked a majority. The first serious threat came on 21 May on a sub-amendment moved by Douglas for the New Democratic party, regretting that the government had indicated its intention to acquire nuclear arms for Canadian forces. We knew that the Social Credit MPs from Quebec would support Douglas in condemning nuclear arms. We were greatly relieved to learn that the four Social Crediters from the West would vote with the government, thereby assuring us a bare majority. We knew that Harkness would not vote against the acquisition of nuclear weapons and we hoped some other Tories would abstain. The actual vote was 124 to 113. This was the only division about which we had any real concern in the first half of the session, except for votes on appeals from the Speaker's rulings.

The Gordon budget

The session proceeded without difficulty until Walter Gordon presented the budget on 13 June. We had been granted interim supply, but had not yet completed any legislation at that point. The budget and the method of its preparation aroused a storm in Parliament which has been described from many points of view. The measures proposed by Gordon also encountered serious opposition outside the House and some of them had finally to be abandoned. What concerned me more, as House leader, was the controversy over the way the budget had been prepared. Gordon had retained the services of three consultants from outside the public service to advise him.

The budget debate was not to begin until Wednesday 19 June, but on the day after the budget was delivered (14 June) Douglas Fisher asked Gordon for an assurance that he and his officials 'alone prepared the budget speech without assistance of outside consultants or ghost writers from Toronto.' The Speaker ruled Fisher's question out of order, but Knowles phrased the question in a different way and Gordon replied that he took 'full and sole responsibility for everything which was contained in the budget.' Diefenbaker intervened to say the question involved the privileges of the House and it required to be answered by an unequivocal 'no.' Fisher insisted it was the British and Canadian tradition that because of the importance of changes in taxation the whole matter of budget preparation 'should be kept in secrecy.' Reports that the minister had brought people outside the government from Toronto to help prepare it deserve a denial or an explanaiton. Churchill asked whether the outside consultants had taken an oath of secrecy. Gordon replied that everyone who assisted in its preparation had taken the oath of secrecy. To a question whether there were persons with knowledge of the budget contents who had left Gordon's office at six o'clock the day before he delivered the budget, Gordon replied that he had left his office before six o'clock the previous day and that he was 'fully familiar with the budget.'

Several members tried to get further information from Gordon about outside consultants, including their identity. Knowles finally asked whether the minister would, either that day or at the next sitting, give the names of persons outside the government who had taken the oath of secrecy.

The questioning was ended by the Speaker at this point, but later in the day, Gordon got unanimous consent to make a statement about the consultants. He gave the names: M.P. O'Connell, G.R. Conway, and D.C.H.

Stanley whose appointment had been authorized by Treasury Board on 2 May and who had taken the oath of allegiance and the oath of office and secrecy. Diefenbaker rebuked Gordon for his surreptitious manner earlier in the day when he had cut a sorry figure and hoped it would be a salutary lesson to him and other like-minded ministers.

Douglas was not satisfied and felt there should be further debate particularly about the continuing relationship of the consultants with the investment companies which employed them. When other members tried to intervene, I asked the House to give unanimous consent to permit any reasonable additional questions. Consent was given. Later when Douglas began to speak a second time I objected that he was going beyond what the House had agreed to. I said a later occasion might be set aside for debating the subject. My objection was supported by George Nowlan who agreed that a debate would be desirable on another occasion.

The next sitting day was Monday 17 June. At the opening of the House, Douglas Harkness raised a question of privilege about a report from Calgary that a memorandum respecting the tax changes had been received in a law office there by 9:30 a.m. the morning after the budget was delivered. The memorandum was from Gordon's former partners: Clarkson, Gordon and Company. Harkness wanted to be assured budget secrets had not been leaked in advance. Gordon finally read a telegram from the senior partner in the firm which explained how information received in Toronto after the delivery of the budget had been able to reach Calgary at 8:30 the next morning. The explanation was accepted in the House, but the misleading insinuation that Gordon's firm had been favoured had been harmful.

Diefenbaker later moved to have an urgent debate on 'the admission by the Minister of Finance . . . of facts relating to the preparation of the budget, which facts constitute a flagrant departure from constitutional budgetary practice, imperil the tradition and essential secrecy of the budget, and which have had an unsettling effect on this House and on the country.'

The Speaker asked for comments on the question of urgency. As House leader, I said the government was ready to have the matter debated as early as the House desired. The budget debate was set to begin on Wednesday, but the government was prepared to bring it on at once, so the matter raised by Diefenbaker which related entirely to the budget could be debated.

Strong objection was taken to my proposal. It was argued that the outside consultants constituted a separate subject which required urgent debate. Pearson intervened to suggest that the Speaker give his ruling and added that, if the Speaker's ruling was adverse on the question of urgency, as he felt it should be, the government, to avoid delay, would go on with the budget debate that day. The Speaker ruled Diefenbaker's motion did not require urgent debate. His ruling was appealed even though he had pointed out that, under the rules, the Speaker's decision was final. Thanks to the votes of the Social Crediters the Speaker's ruling was sustained.

During the daily question period which followed, Knowles raised a question about whether the consultants had been legally appointed, which led to a number of further questions. Gordon promised an answer next day. Though that was the end of questions for that day on the outside consultants, the House was in an unruly mood and the daily question period went on into the evening. Only a short time was left for government business.

When the House met the next day (18 June) Knowles raised a question of privilege alleging Gordon had misled the House about the way in which his outside consultants had been appointed. He alleged that they had not been appointed in the manner required by law. Gordon replied that he had not intended to mislead the House and did not think he did, but apologized if he had. He went on to explain the method of appointment in detail. Knowles and Churchill still insisted that Gordon had misled the House. Pearson intervened to say that, if any doubt existed about the legality of their appointment, the Department of Justice be asked for an opinion. Shortly afterwards Diefenbaker asked the prime minister in order to get the facts 'connected with the extraordinary and dubious transaction' to have a preliminary investigation by the Standing Committee on Privileges and Elections. Pearson promised to consider the suggestion. When questions continued, Pearson offered to bring on the budget debate that day. The offer was not acceptable to the Opposition.

Before the budget debate began on 19 June, Gordon withdrew one of his proposed tax changes. Diefenbaker asked if he had informed Eric Kierans, the president of the Montreal stock exchange, in advance of his announcement to the House. A number of other questions were asked about possible budget leaks. It was not a happy prelude to the budget debate.

Despite the fact that the budget debate was to continue on 20 June, the minister of finance faced a barrage of questions, including one relating to a rumour that Gordon might resign. The harrassment of Gordon continued on 21 June and on Monday, 24 June. Gordon spoke that day. He dealt with the employment of the consultants, the withdrawal of the withholding tax, and questions raised about other items in the budget. At the conclusion he commented that some members in the House and some people outside had made it plain they would like to see him leave public life. He said he had made mistakes and might make some more if he stayed in the House. As long as he remained a member of the House he would strive to do those things he believed to be in the best interests of the great majority of the people of this country. He spoke modestly and in a conciliatory fashion, which improved the attitude of the House.

Gordon had, in fact, offered his resignation. There had been a cabinet meeting at Harrington Lake to discuss the whole situation. I did not feel Gordon's resignation should be accepted, believing it would be a sign of weakness to sacrifice a minister who was under fire. Gordon had been accused of no wrong doing, but merely an alleged technical breach of parliamentary tradition. I did not regard this technicality as of the slightest practical importance or the least harm to the public interest. I was relieved when Pearson decided the resignation should not be accepted and we should fight back.

It has often been alleged that Gordon received no support in Parliament from any of his cabinet colleagues. That is not true. In his maiden speech on 24 June, Mitchell Sharp made an unequivocal and effective defence of Gordon's action in securing expert assistance from outside the public services in preparing the budget.

The vote was taken on the Tory amendment expressing lack of confidence in the government over the budget. Douglas spoke just before the vote. He said the NDP would not vote confidence in the government. On the other hand, the party did not believe the people of this country wanted an election which would be the third in fifteen months. The NDP believed the people wanted Parliament to get on with the job of governing Canada. For that reason, their members would abstain from voting. The vote was 73 to 113. The Social Credit members also abstained.

There were a few questions on the budget on 25 June, but the atmosphere was less tense. 26 June was the final day of debate. The budget was not referred to in the question period. As Wednesday was the short day, when the House did not sit in the evening, there was time left for only two speakers in the budget debate before the vote had to be taken. Both Social Credit and the NDP abstained and the budget was approved 119 to 74.

The difficulties over the budget had reduced the prestige of the government and had been a humiliation for the minister of finance. But the crisis had petered out, the government had survived and continued to function.

There had been a minor crisis on the last day of the budget debate on 26 June when Leon Balcer tried to interrupt the regular business to have an urgent debate on the alleged ground that the Municipal Development and Loan Board bill was an invasion of provincial jurisdiction. The Speaker rejected the motion and his decision was appealed. For the first time in 1963 all members of the Opposition parties voted together. The Speaker's ruling was upheld by a vote of 108 to 106. The vote would have been tied had not Dr Marcoux, who had withdrawn from the Social Credit caucus and was sitting as an independent, voted to sustain the Speaker. Technically, the rejection of a Speaker's ruling is not a defeat of the government. However, when the government cannot muster enough votes to sustain the Speaker, its prestige suffers. This vote had been too close for comfort.

I was more determined than ever to do everything possible to have the rules changed so the decisions of the Speaker would be final and not subject to appeal in any circumstances.

Though I had not spoken in the budget debate, I was pleased to have a chance to support Gordon in debate on his first supply motion after the budget debate ended. Diefenbaker had moved an amendment expressing want of confidence in almost the same words as the Tory amendment on the budget. I raised a point of order that this was an attempt to revive the budget debate and that it was against the rules to revive, in the same session, a question on which the House had made a decision. After considerable debate the Speaker agreed that the motions were very similar, but he found one phrase which was different. He therefore ruled Diefenbaker's motion in order but hoped the debate would stick to this one phrase. It did not. The debate lasted only one day. I was the final speaker. For the only time in the session, my speech was combative, contrasting in the rather extravagant terms the irresponsible financial policies of the Diefenbaker government with the prudent and responsible attitude to public expenditure of the new minister of finance. Despite almost constant Tory interruptions, my speech was greeted with rousing enthusiasm on our side of the House. Once more the smaller parties abstained and Diefenbaker's amendment was defeated 115 to 75.

Adjusting the Atlantic Development Board

One of the few measures in my name in the session of 1963 was a bill to amend the Atlantic Development Board act. The Atlantic board amendments were the third item of government business on the day after Gordon delivered his budget speech. I did not expect it to be reached that day. When the second government measure was called, which was the first stage of the bill to establish a municipal loan and development board, I expected the debate on the board to last for the rest of the day. I went off to the washroom. I have since suspected that the Opposition, knowing the item in my name came next, cut off the debate on the board while I was out of the House, so the government would be embarrassed when I was not there to move my own motion on the amendments to the Atlantic Development Board. Gordon moved it on my behalf. Just as the Speaker began to read the motion, I walked back into the House to the applause of our side. The embarrassment ended.

The Atlantic Development Board had been established in the dying days of the Diefenbaker government. We Liberals had welcomed the establishment of the board, but had criticized the Diefenbaker bill because the board was to have only an advisory capacity. We undertook, when back in office, to reconstitute the board and endow it with a capital fund which could be devoted to specific projects. While its projects would require the final approval of the Treasury Board, we argued that a veto was unlikely to be exercised unless the board recommended something outrageous. In fact, no project was rejected so long as I was minister.

During the debate, I announced that the board would have a capital sum of one hundred million dollars to contribute to specific development projects. We intended to ask all the members of the board appointed by the Tory government to continue to serve. Parliament was asked to increase the membership of the board to make it more representative of the main economic activities of the Atlantic region.

All the existing members agreed to remain on the board. I was able to persuade Brigadier Michael Wardell of Fredericton, the publisher of the *Atlantic Advocate* and the *Fredericton Gleaner,* to resign as chairman, but to stay on the board. Wardell, an Englishman and long-time associate of Lord Beaverbrook in England before coming to New Brunswick, had been an active and highly partisan Tory propagandist. Despite the objection of more partisan colleagues, I believed the board would work more effectively if Wardell remained a member and was, in consequence, unlikely to be critical of its activities. Wardell did not serve his full term but his remaining for some time made the board virtually immune from Tory criticism.

On the day before the House rose for the summer recess (2 August), I announced the appointment of the six new members of the Atlantic Development Board and stated that all the members of the board already appointed by the previous government had agreed to serve out their full terms and would be eligible for reappointment. I also announced that Ian MacKeigan, QC, of Halifax would be the new chairman of the board. A meeting of the board would be held in Halifax on 6 August 1963 at which I hoped to be present. At that meeting in Halifax I spoke about the objectives of the government in strengthening the board.

The previous government had appointed a full-time director of the board and I was content to leave him in place. This director was Ernest Weeks, a native of Prince Edward Island, who had been economic adviser in the Department of Public Works when the St Laurent government was in office. I did not know him well then, but I quickly developed growing admiration for him. Weeks tackled the job with enthusiasm. He enlisted the warm co-operation of all four Atlantic provincial governments. I took an active interest in the work of the board and Weeks always had ready access to me, as did Slim Monture, the retired director of the federal mines branch who was one of the most distinguished Canadian Indians. Monture had been helpful to me when I was minister for Indians affairs in the St Laurent government, during the period I was piloting amendments to the Indian Act through Parliament in 1956. While we were in Opposition I once met him at Dorval airport in Montreal; he was at that time one of the mining experts retained by the United Nations Development Agency. When I asked him where he was going, Monture replied: 'to Indonesia where this descendant of generations of North American savages is supposed to give technical advice to the members of one of the world's most ancient civilizations.' Monture with his wonderful sense of humour proved invaluable as an economic and technical adviser to Weeks and the Atlantic Development Board.

Diefenbaker repudiates his party

One piece of legislation I was closely involved with was the proposal to increase the indemnities paid to members of Parliament. In order to induce several potential candidates to accept Liberal nominations, Pearson had undertaken privately to have the indemnities for members of Parliament increased in the first session of the new Parliament. Such legislation would be in the name of the prime minister. Pearson told me he would not introduce the legislation unless I could get undertakings from all Opposition parties that it would not be opposed. I had no trouble with the Social Credit party; most of their members were poor and needed more money. I anticipated difficulty with the New Democratic party since some members of the old CCF had opposed every increase in the past. To my surprise, Stanley Knowles, their House leader, assured me they would all go along. I accepted his word without question, as I always did. I knew the majority of the Tories felt increases were overdue. Some of the Tories had resented Diefenbaker's unwillingness to increase indemnities while he was prime minister. I told Gordon Churchill that Pearson would not act if there was going to be any opposition in the House. Churchill said the question would have to be considered in the Tory caucus. After the caucus, Churchill sent me a note of assurance which read: 'Jack: If you place on Votes and Proceedings the appropriate notices re Indemnity and the other matters so that the normal 48 hours notice is given we are prepared to pass all stages on Monday.'

The discussions with the other parties and our own deliberations were not completed until late July. Pearson promptly gave notice of the proposed resolution and it was debated on Monday 29 July. The legislation was to increase the indemnity of MPs from $10,000 to $18,000 per year. It was also to provide additional allowances for leaders of parties (other than the prime minister and the leader of the opposition) having twelve members or more and for the chief government whip and the chief opposition whip. No change was to be made in the salaries of ministers or of the leader of the opposition. There were to be no special pensions for ministers other than what they would receive as MPs, but a prime minister for four years or more and his widow would be provided with a larger pension.

Pearson, in his speech, stated that he understood the proposed measure had the support of all parties in the House. To the consternation of the occupants of the Tory benches, Diefenbaker announced that he would vote against the increase and, if it was approved, refuse to accept the increase in indemnity for himself. During Diefenbaker's speech Churchill never took his eyes off me. Several times I put my hand in my pocket as though I was going to take out his note and read it. The temptation to do so was strong. It would have been an immediate parliamentary triumph. But I realized that, if the statement was read, I could never hope for decent working relations with Churchill, relations which were almost essential to effective management of House business. I refrained.

Diefenbaker's defection along with six other Tories was regarded as treachery by most of the rest of the party. Their attitude was expressed with great courage and sincerity by a Tory back-bencher from western Ontario, W.H.A. Thomas, a loyal and reliable member who rarely spoke. When Diefenbaker concluded his speech, Thomas raised a question of privilege in which he said that normally in the House each party worked as a party and its leader spoke for the party, but on this occasion Diefenbaker was not speaking for the party.

Diefenbaker and the six were joined in the vote by Réal Caouette and two other Social Crediters. Caouette said he was not opposed to the pay increase but felt we should increase family allowances first. In his speech Diefenbaker had argued that the proposed indemnities were being increased excessively, and he had taken particular objection to providing a salary for the leader of any party with twelve or more members in the House.

Pearson felt he had been double-crossed by Diefenbaker, but it was Diefenbaker who was the real loser. It was then, and has been since, my judgement that his action dealt a fatal blow to his leadership of his own party. There was no open revolt, but his followers never fully trusted him again. His effectiveness as leader of the Opposition was, by that repudiation of a caucus decision, permanently impaired.

The fact that I had not used Churchill's note in debate helped me in my relations with him. Although the note was never mentioned, our relations in arranging business outside the House were more friendly. I often wanted to consult him by himself, as opposition House leader, about procedural problems and House business generally. In such cases, I invariably went to see him instead of asking him to come to see me.

My working relationship with Eric Winkler, the chief opposition whip, was excellent. While we were in opposition, I knew Winkler only slightly. After the session started, he approached me to discuss the management of House business. I was pleased by his approach. I said I would be perfectly frank with him and tell him whatever I could about our plans, except where the government had decided to keep some of them to itself. I would try never to mislead him, and hoped his attitude would be the same. I said it was always my disposition to accept the word of anyone I was dealing with, but I did my best never to be deceived twice. In the rest of my years in Parliament, I found Winkler to be thoroughly dependable, while completely loyal to his own party. Our co-operation behind the curtains helped to facilitate business in what was to become a contentious session.

Despite the delay over the budget debate, Parliament accomplished a good deal by the time we adjourned for a summer recess on August 2. All but two of the budget bills had been passed. The Department of Industry, the Economic Council of Canada, and the Municipal Development and Loan Board had been established. The Atlantic Development Board had been reconstituted and 90 per cent of the cost of completing the Trans-Canada highway in the four Atlantic provinces was already being paid by the federal government. Pearson's announcement on 4 June that the government intended to establish an exclusive twelve-mile fishing zone was well received in the Atlantic region.

Divorces settled

Just before the summer recess began, the procedure in Parliament for granting divorces was drastically changed. There were no divorce courts in Quebec and Newfoundland: the only way residents of those provinces could secure divorces was by private acts of Parliament. For many years, these divorce bills were introduced in the Senate and the grounds for divorce were considered carefully by a special Senate committee. This examination was at least as thorough as that in the law courts in the other eight provinces. When the bills reached the House of Commons these bills were, for years, normally passed in all stages without debate. No House time was wasted.

The procedure changed after two CCF members, Frank Howard and Arnold Peters, were elected to Parliament. In 1958 Howard and Peters started a campaign to give the Exchequer Court (now the Federal Court) the power to hear divorce cases from Quebec and Newfoundland. The Diefenbaker government was not willing to permit legislation in Parliament to give a federal court power to deal with divorces in cases where the provincial legislatures would not give any law court jurisdiction within the province. Such legislation would have been opposed by almost every Catholic MP.

Howard and Peters conducted their campaign to get divorce out of Parliament by debating each individual divorce bill when it came from the Senate. Divorce bills could be considered only in one private members' hour a week. From 1961 onwards these two members succeeded in preventing any divorce bills from passing. Meanwhile the growing backlog of petitions for divorce was causing irritation and, in some cases, real hardship. Favreau and I decided to try to find a device which would remove this irritation. The Pearson government was no more prepared to sponsor legislation to give jurisdiction to the Exchequer Court than the Diefenbaker government had been. But our government was willing to look for a compromise.

The compromise we worked out was to have the jurisdiction to grant divorces and annulments conferred on the Senate. A commissioner was to be appointed who would have the status of an additional judge of the Exchequer Court. This commissioner was to examine the petitions for divorce in the Senate divorce committee, which would then decide whether the divorce should be granted. The drafting of the bill to authorize the Senate to dissolve or annul marriages was done by Favreau. He did much of the negotiating to secure its acceptance by our own back-benchers and shared with me the discussions outside the House with the Opposition parties.

We decided the bill to give jurisdiction to the Senate should not be a government measure, but a private member's bill. If the bill was sponsored by a private member, no political party would incur the blame for encouraging divorce. We arranged to have Nicholas Manziuk, a Tory MP, introduce the bill. Manziuk was chosen because he had been the chairman of the committee which dealt with divorces while Diefenbaker was prime minister. The details of the bill were not debated in the House of Commons and it passed all stages in a few minutes on 1 August after Arnold Peters and spokesmen for all parties had made congratulatory speeches. I uttered one sentence and

Favreau said nothing. But everyone knew the main credit was his. Favreau's skill in this matter won him the respect of the whole House and a reputation for negotiation and conciliation which was thoroughly deserved. Peters then agreed to let all the divorce bills before the House pass without debate. I was pleased that this recurrent parliamentary nightmare had been ended in Pearson's first year in office and while I was House leader.

The Social Credit schism

Once the session adjourned for the rest of the summer, I went to Newfoundland to join the family at Traytown. I was very tired and did almost no travelling until after the family returned to Ottawa at Labour Day. I stayed on for another couple of weeks to tour my constituency and to visit St John's. If I had found the leadership in the House strenuous before the summer recess, I realized, when I returned to Ottawa, that a greater test was still to come.

Early in September there had been a schism in the Social Credit party over its leadership. Caouette and twelve other MPs from Quebec had withdrawn from the Social Credit caucus and formed a separate group which they called the Ralliement des Créditistes. The Social Credit caucus under Robert Thompson was left with only eleven members.

In the election of 1962 the Social Credit party had won more seats than the New Democratic party. On numerical grounds, the Social Credit party claimed the right to sit next to the official Opposition and closer to the Speaker than the New Democratic party. This claim had been discussed with Speaker Lambert. The New Democratic party had reluctantly acceded to the Social Credit demand.

There was a procedural advantage to being recognized as the senior third party in the House. The NDP agreed the precedent of 1962 should be followed when the new Parliament met in 1963, because the Social Credit party still had more members than the NDP. Once the schism occurred, the NDP had more members than either of the Social Credit groups and claimed seniority. The Social Crediters all recognized this was a valid claim, but there was a bitter dispute as to the priority between Caouette's group with thirteen members or Thompson's with eleven. There was also a dispute as to whether Caouette's group was really a party or merely a number of independent members.

These disputes almost paralysed the work of Parliament before they were settled. In September 1963, after the schism but before the session resumed, all three groups had been in touch with the Speaker, expecting him to decide among their claims. At first Speaker Macnaughton had given the impression their precedence in seating should be determined by their numerical strength. It was a natural reaction because of the precedents of 1962 and 1963. But, in September 1963, the situation was complicated by two other factors. One was the question as to whether a group should be recognized as a new party when its members had not been elected under that party label: the other was that the law which increased the indemnities of MPs and senators had also provided allowances for the leaders of recognized parties with twelve or more members in the House. If the Ralliement was recognized as a party, its leader, since the group contained thirteen members, would be entitled to a salary, while the leader of the original Social Credit party would lose his salary since the group was left with fewer than twelve members.

After considering the representations he had received, the Speaker wisely concluded he did not have the authority to settle their differences and that the decision should be made by the House. At the opening of the sitting on 30 September, the seating was unchanged from what it had been on 2 August with the continuing Social Crediters and the members of the Ralliement intermingled and the New Democratic party at the far end of the chamber. Macnaughton made a lengthy and well-argued speech in which he concluded by suggesting that the problem should be referred to the proper committee of the House for consideration and report.

Stanley Knowles then made an excellent speech reporting on the way the problem had been handled in 1962, claiming that the New Democratic party was entitled to precedence because it was now the largest of the smaller parties, accepting the suggestion of the Speaker, and moving that the Speaker's statement and the whole matter be referred to the committee on privileges and elections.

Diefenbaker at once tried to fish in the troubled waters by insinuating that the split in the Social Credit party was merely a struggle for the salary of a party leader and reminding the House that he had voted against the legislation to provide these salaries. Pearson said we would support Knowles' motion.

Both Thompson for Social Credit and Gregoire for the Ralliement spoke briefly and agreed to support Knowles' motion. It was adopted without a dissenting voice. I was greatly relieved and briefly hopeful that the House might proceed with other business rapidly while the committee was deliberating. My relief did not last long.

Constitutional argument with the government of Quebec prevented us from going ahead in 1963 with legislation for contributory old age pensions. We wanted, meanwhile, to increase the universal old age pension from $65 to $75 a month and to include the increase in the October cheques. To do so, we had to introduce legislation at once. We hoped it would pass quickly, but the debate dragged on into a second day, when Diefenbaker introduced an amendment to our proposal to start the increase retroactively to April. The Speaker ruled this mischievous motion out of order, as Diefenbaker knew it was. He appealed the Speaker's ruling, which was sustained by a vote of 111 to 90. The vote would have been very close if Thompson's group had not voted with us. This was just the first of several appeals from rulings of the Speaker. The debate continued for a third day when we finally got the old age pension bill introduced.

We could not go on with the debate on old age pensions the next day (3 October) because we had to ask for interim supply so we could pay the public servants and other costs of government. The prospects for getting an early grant of interim supply were poor because of the growing tension over the dispute about precedence for the smaller parties.

There were other obstacles to overcome. We faced parliamentary embarrassment over nuclear weapons. Diefenbaker, on 2 October, forced a vote on a motion calling for the tabling of the secret agreement with the United States on nuclear weapons. The government defeated the motion only with the help of the four Social Credit MPs from western Canada. The issue over nuclear weapons threatened to hold up interim supply when Tommy Douglas raised the nuclear issue as a grievance which was debated most of the day on 3 October.

The next day, Diefenbaker took all morning and most of the afternoon with a speech about labour disputes to which Allan MacEachen as minister of labour was obliged to reply. I was seriously concerned about getting interim supply voted in time to pay the government's bills. In the late afternoon I appealed to the House to grant interim supply quickly and promised to bring on a regular supply motion on Monday. Such supply motions were the normal opportunity for votes of want of confidence in the government and the airing of grievances.

In response to this appeal, one of Caouette's supporters made it clear their group intended to hold up interim supply until they were recognized as a party. To meet this threat of a filibuster, I gave notice of a motion which proposed that the House should not adjourn until interim supply was disposed of and that all proceedings should be dealt with at a single sitting of the House. Since the House might, if such a motion was adopted, have to sit continuously for two or three days, this was closure with a vengeance.

When the motion came up for debate on Monday 7 October, I said it was being proposed with the greatest reluctance. I reviewed the various developments of the previous Friday, including the agreement of spokesmen for all parties, except Caouette's, to grant supply at the end of the day. My statement was based on Gregoire's declaration that interim supply would not be voted until the committee on Privileges and Elections had remedied the situation of the smaller parties. Gregoire had said it rested with certain members of the government to see that a decision was taken as soon as possible, since it was absolutely illogical and utterly ridiculous not to recognize a group of thirteen members.

The dispute was not a matter for the government, I replied, but for the House which had accepted the Knowles motion to send the matter to the committee. The House could not act until the committee reported. I explained in detail what salaries and other payments the government could not make if the interim supply bill had not passed both Houses and received royal assent by the following evening. Unless I could receive assurances that supply would be granted by 10 o'clock that day, it would be my duty to have the motion voted on.

In reply, Gordon Churchill described my action as the most amazing development in his twelve years in the House. He spoke at length about mismanagement by the government and about our record when in Opposition in delaying interim supply. He proposed an amendment which would have suspended proceedings in the House and ordered the Committee on Privileges and Elections to meet with instructions to report within forty-eight hours. The Speaker ruled the amendment out of order. Churchill appealed his ruling, which was sustained on a vote of 101 to 88. The only Opposition MPs who voted with us were the Social Crediters supporting Thompson.

Thompson then spoke in support of my motion, attacking Churchill, deploring the fact that, if the old age security amendment was not passed, the pensioners would not receive the increase in their October cheques and begging the Créditistes to give up their filibuster.

Alexis Caron, the chairman of the Committee on Privileges and Elections, followed Thompson and announced that he had called a meeting of its steering committee for that afternoon. He offered to have the whole committee sit all evening while the House was sitting. A committee could not sit while the House was sitting without the permission of the House. One of the Tory members suggested Caron's proposal offered a way out of the impasse. I then got permission to intervene again in the debate to suggest the steering committee meet at five o'clock and the full committee at six to seek permission to sit while the House was sitting. Gregoire followed to say his group did not want to hold up proceedings, but merely to be recognized as a separate party in the House. After further debate, a Tory member suggested that the House could give the necessary permission to the committee to sit without waiting for a request from the committee. I jumped at this sensible suggestion and said that, if someone would move the adjournment of the debate, the

House could at once adopt a motion to empower the committee to sit while the House was sitting. This was done. The crisis was over for that day. The question period dragged on until early evening, but the interim supply was then granted. It had been a close call for the government.

At ten o'clock I announced we would go ahead the next day with the old age pension bill, unless some other urgent matter should arise. That bill was passed the following day.

We had managed to get interim supply and the old age pension bill passed. And we had also got the dispute over the status and precedence of the smaller parties put aside while the committee on privileges and elections prepared its report. But our troubles were still far from over.

Crisis over Hal Banks

While Parliament was almost paralysed by the Social Credit schism, a crisis erupted over the conduct of Hal Banks, the head in Canada of the Seafarers' International Union (SIU). In 1962, in response to charges outside Parliament about the violent way Banks was running the union, the Diefenbaker government had appointed Mr Justice Norris of British Columbia to investigate these charges of violence and intimidation against Banks. The Norris report fell into the lap of the Pearson government and the accusations of serious criminal offences by Banks and other officers of the SIU and four other related maritime unions could not be ignored.

The charges against Banks and his associates went back a long way. In the 1940s most of the seamen on Canadian ships belonged to the Canadian Seamen's Union headed by Pat Sullivan, a known communist. The CSU repeatedly interrupted service on the Great Lakes and in the small Canadian deep-sea merchant fleet. Prolonged strikes in the late 1940s by a communist-led union were particularly disturbing as the cold war developed.

The SIU was the strongest union of seamen in the United States and on the American lake ships. It had a small branch in Canada which was not militant. Some of the Canadian shipowners encouraged the international headquarters of the SIU in San Francisco to appoint a more aggressive leader for the Canadian union with the objective of wresting control of seamen in Canada from Sullivan's CSU and restoring peace on the waterfront. Banks was chosen for the task. It did not take him long, after he came to Canada in 1949, to gain virtual control for the SIU of employment on Canadian ships. This take-over was looked on benevolently by the Canadian authorities directly concerned.

In its early stages, the activities of the SIU attracted little public attention. The only early mention I have found in Parliament was on 8 April 1949 when M.J. Coldwell, the leader of the CCF, asked the minister of transport about a reported riot at Halifax involving CN ships. Lionel Chevrier, the minister, replied that he had been informed that 176 men had boarded the ships at 3 a.m. that day with little or no opposition from the pickets. There had been an exchange with water hoses between the men on the ships and the strikers on the wharf, until the ships were able to move out into the harbour. Missiles had been thrown and one or two shots fired. There were no serious injuries.

This incident was evidently at the beginning of the SIU take over, but curiously it was not followed up in Parliament. The first significant reference to Hal Banks I have found in *Hansard* was in 1954. On 22 February, Ellen Fairclough, the labour critic in the Tory opposition, asked the minister of labour, Milton Gregg, why the government had appointed Banks, a citizen of the United States with a record of court convictions in Canada and the United States, as a Canadian representative to a meeting at the International Labour Organizaton at Geneva. Gregg explained that the representatives of labour organizations were nominated by the national body and it had been the usual custom to pass on such nominations almost automatically to the ILO. In this case the minister had concurred with and transmitted the recommendation. That was the only sense in which this was an appointment by the government.

George Drew, the leader of the Opposition, then intervened and asked whether the minister did not express his own judgement on the choice or make any inquiry. Gregg said the minister had the right to inquire and did inquire and confirmed the desire of the national organization that Banks should be the nominee. Drew asked whether the minister had considered representations as to the unsuitability of the nominee and whether he had sought information from the Department of Justice as to his record. Gregg replied that he had not conferred with the minister of justice. Drew asked whether the minister of labour exercised his judgement and Gregg replied 'Yes.'

Further questions about Banks on 23 February resulted in a procedural wrangle which led nowhere, though William Hamilton, the MP for Notre Dame de Grace, Montreal, asked the minister of citizenship and immigration whether Banks, with his record of convictions, would be permitted to enter Canada when he returned from Geneva. Walter Harris, the minister, said he would answer when he had informed himself of the case.

As a result, the question of Banks was raised in cabinet on 25 February. The minutes of the meeting show that Gregg proposed to reply in the House that Banks did not represent the government at Geneva, but his own union, and that his expenses were not paid by the government. The question was not, however, raised again in the House at the time.

At the same cabinet meeting, Harris gave notice that it would at some time be necessary to decide whether Banks, as a US citizen with a police record, should be deported. Harris stated that the police record was not known when Banks was landed as an immigrant in 1952. He reported that the question of setting up a board of inquiry had been considered some months earlier, but it was decided at the time it was not necessary. Public attention, since Banks had gone to Geneva, made it advisable to decide whether a special inquiry should be held. It was stated that, despite the US police record and a conviction in Canada respecting the smuggling of cigarettes, there had been no labour difficulties with lake shipping since Banks took over the union. In discussion it was noted that a dispute between shipowners and the SIU was then under way over a proposed welfare fund. It would be undesirable to take action which might lead to deportation while negotiations were under way. It was left to Harris to decide whether and when to take any action.

In a written answer to a series of questions by Fairclough on 12 April 1954, Harris stated that Banks had signed the usual landing card when he was admitted as an immigrant and that his police record was not known to the department at that time. Banks had already returned from Geneva and there had up to that time not been a board of inquiry. When Fairclough asked Harris on 11 May 1954 whether a board of inquiry would be set up, Harris replied that the matter was under consideration.

Prompted, it was later learned, by an officer of another union, George Drew made attacks on the conduct of Banks on 9 June and again on 26 June. Drew asserted that Banks had been landed as an immigrant on 8 May 1952 shortly after he had been convicted under the Customs Act for the possession of 36,000 smuggled cigarettes and fined $200. Drew also referred to convictions in the United States and to the appointment to the ILO. He asked why there had been no official inquiry. Harris replied on 26 June that an inquiry was being held in Montreal from which there was an appeal to him as minister. He felt he should not express any opinion until the report of the inquiry was received.

Harris had received the report of the special inquiry officer by 30 June, which was his last day as minister of citizenship and immigration. He raised the question of deportation in cabinet that day. According to the minutes, he reminded the meeting that Banks had originally come to Canada for the purpose of clearing up a difficult labour situation in Great Lakes shipping where the majority of seamen belonged to the communist-dominated Canadian Seamen's Union. Banks had remained as head of the SIU in Canada and had been granted landing as an immigrant in 1952. There had recently been many representations that he should be deported because he had a criminal record and was otherwise undesirable. A special inquiry officer had recommended deportation. As minister he would have to decide whether to accept the recommendation or quash the order and allow Banks to remain in Canada.

Harris noted that Banks was constantly attracting trouble, but that his alleged criminal record was for minor matters. Since he had been given permanent landing, he felt Banks should be allowed to remain in Canada. Several charges both in the United States and Canada had been dismissed or dropped. There were only two convictions: when twenty years old, Banks had been convicted of issuing worthless cheques, one for $17 and one for $19 for which he had served over three years; and for minor damages to his landlady's property for which he was fined $20. He had been convicted in Canada of possessing cigarettes which had apparently been smuggled. (Banks had received a full pardon for his offences in the United States from Governor Warren of California who has since become Chief Justice of the United States.) He had been of real service in ending labour troubles on the Great Lakes. Since his divorce he was alleged to have married a Canadian woman.

In the cabinet discussion it was agreed that since Banks had been a landed immigrant for over two years, there did not seem to be sufficient grounds for deportation.

Cabinet noted with approval that Harris proposed to allow the appeal, notwithstanding the adverse report of the special inquiry officer. Harris subsequently quashed the deportation order and recommended that an order-in-council be adopted confirming the status of Banks as a landed immigrant. Before taking his decision to quash the deportation order, Harris had discussed the case with me since I was to succeed him as minister and I concurred in his decision. The order-in-council was not made until 6 July 1954 when I was minister, a circumstance which was to occasion some confusion in 1963.

Banks achieved some degree of notoriety as a result of an article by Peter Newman in the *Financial Post* of 16 October 1954 and a more comprehensive article by Sidney Katz in *Maclean's* of 15 February 1955. This article reported that Banks had applied for landing as an immigrant on 8 May 1952 and stated the mystery was why the application had been approved. Katz asserted that Banks had filled out form 1000 which included a question 17 which read: 'Have you ever been convicted of a criminal offence?' The article went on to point out that the government did not learn Banks had a criminal record until about a year later.

This mystery was cleared up by questions and answers in the House. The form had never contained the question about criminal convictions until it was revised some time after Banks was landed; the new form contained the question cited in *Maclean's*.

Considering the sensational character of the articles by Newman and Katz, it was surprising the Opposition did not make an issue of the Banks affair, though on 21 July 1955 Bill Hamilton and H.W. Herridge of the CCF did make speeches attacking Banks and his fellow officers of the SIU for violence and intimidation. The speeches also referred to his criminal record and his failure to permit union elections. There was no follow-up to these charges, and almost no later reference in Parliament to Banks and the SIU while the St Laurent government was in office.

George Nowlan did ask me on 12 June 1956 if Banks was yet a naturalized citizen. I replied that, as he had been landed as an immigrant at the time I became minister in July 1954, he would not have been in Canada as an immigrant for the required five years. Nowlan then stated that Harris had informed the House that Banks had been landed earlier than 1954 and asked me to check the files. Instead of agreeing to check I repeated my assertion that he had not been landed until the end of June or early July 1954. If I had checked I would have found that I had told the House in answer to a written question in February 1955 that Banks had been landed on 8 May 1952. To this day I cannot understand why I failed to remember that answer and continued to believe the order-in-council of 6 July 1954 had given Banks immigrant status. Nor do I know why, since Banks had been landed as an immigrant in 1952, a second order-in-council was considered necessary in July 1954.

The subject of Banks and the SIU was rarely raised in Parliament in the years Diefenbaker was in office. The one notable reference was on 19 June 1959 when Herridge stated that the application by Banks for citizenship had been denied by the citizenship court as he was considered undesirable. Herridge asked if the government would not deport him. Ellen Fairclough, then minister of citizenship and immigration, stated Banks had Canadian domicile and there were no provisions or regulations to permit deportation. When Herridge urged her to speak up for Canada, Fairclough said it was her duty to observe the law.

The Norris commission was not appointed because of any agitation in Parliament. Its report makes it clear that it was set up in response to a letter dated 23 May 1962 to the prime minister by Claude Jodoin, the president of the Canadian Labour Congress. The CLC had expelled the SIU and was then supporting a rival union. The letter demanded an investigation into what Jodoin described as the 'reign of terror' Banks and the SIU had created on the waterfront. After further correspondence, the minister of labour on 17 July 1962 appointed Mr Justice Norris of the British Columbia Court of Appeal as an industrial inquiry commision to inquire into and report on:

1. The circumstances leading to the disruption of shipping in the Great Lakes System including interference with the operation of the works and facilities of the St. Lawrence Seaway Authority.

2. The denial of the use of port or other works and facilities to vessels calling at Canadian and United States ports on the Great Lakes System.

3. The activities and internal operations of organizations of employees acting on behalf of employees engaged in shipping and work affecting shipping operations in the Great Lakes System including without restricting the generality of the foregoing the Seafarers' International Union of Canada.

4. The relationship and any conflict that may exist between employers or employers' organizations, and employees or organizations of employees, in the shipping industry in the Great Lakes System.

5. Any matters incidental or relating to any of the foregoing matters.

The report of the Norris commission was presented to Allan MacEachen as minister of labour on 6 July 1963. Norris had charged Hal Banks and other officers of the SIU and four other related maritime unions with serious criminal offences. The report recommended, in addition to prosecutions, that the five unions should be placed under a trusteeship to manage their affairs.

The Pearson government tried to arrange a privately organized trusteeship for the unions in question. Because the SIU was an international union, the organization of a private trusteeship was discussed with the secretary of labor of the United States and the SIU headquarters in that country, as well as the Canadian Congress of Labour. On 30 September Allan MacEachen told the House, that unless a private trusteeship over the maritime unions could be worked out during the weekend as a result of these discussions, the government proposed, as recommended by the Norris commission, to proceed with legislation to establish a public trusteeship.

On 4 October, without waiting for legislation by the government, Diefenbaker found an excuse for a long speech dealing with the revelations in the Norris report of the conduct of Hal Banks. He tried to place on me the responsibility for the continued presence of Banks in Canada, because I had been the minister of citizenship and immigration when the order-in-council was passed giving Banks status as a landed immigrant. (Neither of us realized that Banks had in fact become a landed immigrant on 8 May 1952, when I was not yet an MP, and that the order of 6 July 1954 merely confirmed his immigrant status after the deportation order had been quashed.)

Diefenbaker read from an article which stated I had approved the decision Harris had made. I agreed I had done so, and added I was sure Harris made that decision 'in the full knowledge of his duty to this country and no man did so more conscientiously.' Diefenbaker accused me of embracing Banks and added that the degree to which Banks was embraced indicated he had 'friends in government circles.'

Diefenbaker asserted that Banks had been accepted as an immigrant because of support he had given to Liberal candidates in elections. Despite the fact that during his six years as prime minister, Diefenbaker had done nothing about Banks or the SIU except appoint the Norris inquiry in 1962, the insinuations about Banks being a 'pet' of the Liberal party continued throughout the numerous debates and exchanges on the subject.

MacEachen opened the debate on the public trusteeship over the SIU and the other maritime unions on 9 October. Good progress was made that day. On 10 October, the question period was prolonged. After an hour, I rose to remind members the House was considering an extraordinary and urgent piece of legislation. I was interrupted repeatedly by Donald MacInnis, the MP for Cape Breton South, who objected that I had spoken without being recognized by the Speaker. He argued that order should be applied to the government side of the House. When I replied that I believed the Speaker had recognized me, Macnaughton made the strange remark that he was inclined to admit that on occasion he had difficulties with the secretary of state. The Speaker's observation did not help me as House leader. This incident encouraged MacInnis, during the rest of my years in Parliament, to follow this tactic of rising frequently to claim I had not been recognized by the chair.

When the House finally reached the trusteeship legislation that day, Diefenbaker spoke. He accused the government and MacEachen of procrastination and delaying tactics. Of MacEachen he said, 'I think he has tried, but somebody has tied his hands from action. The secretary of state was one of those who had solicitude for Banks only a few years ago, and it is surprising the solicitude has continued.'

I rose at once on a question of privilege, to say that Diefenbaker had made a statement about me which was a downright falsehood. 'I had never had the faintest solicitude for Mr. Banks at any time whatever. I have never had any association with him, and have never seen him and never spoken to him in my life.'

Diefenbaker retorted that solicitude did not demand personal acquaintanceship. He claimed the order-in-council admitting Banks as a landed immigrant had given him the halo of government approval. The admission of Banks as a landed immigrant, he declared, had prevented his government from deporting Banks. As a lawyer, Diefenbaker, I replied, surely knew that statement was untrue. Any person who was not a citizen could be deported if there were legal grounds for deportation, but in six years in office Diefenbaker had never taken the trouble to find grounds to deport Banks. He replied that Judge Norris had said that, once the order-in-council landing Banks as an immigrant was passed, deportation procedures were prevented. I interjected: 'Read the law.' The exchange continued for some time. Twice I accused Diefenbaker of making statements which were not true. Despite these exchanges and other speeches, the first stage of the trusteeship legislation was completed and the bill introduced at the end of that day.

The debate on the trusteeship bill was the first item of business on Friday 11 October. When the House met there was a discussion about the business of the House and the importance of getting the trusteeship bill passed in the current week, even if it meant sitting on Saturday. We had a harmonious discussion in which the Speaker permitted Gregoire to participate. The House agreed that a motion for Saturday sitting could be moved at five o'clock, if it was needed.

Meanwhile a meeting of party spokesmen had been held behind the curtains. When the bill received second reading before 5 o'clock, I reported that the meeting had agreed the House should sit from seven to eleven in the expectation of completing the trusteeship bill. During the evening I was drawn into the debate by a question about whether a landed immigrant could be deported. I gave a brief outline of the law. When asked about Banks' criminal record at the time he was landed, which Diefenbaker had said the previous day was 'as long as your arm,' I called this a characteristic exaggeration. The offences were committed more than thirty years before by a man who had no subsequent convictions for more than twenty years except in connection with the smuggled cigarettes. Since the Immigration Act was amended in 1952, I reminded the House that a criminal record was no longer an absolute bar to landing as an immigrant. In 1952 Diefenbaker was an MP who had shared in changing the law, before I became a member of Parliament. The 1952 change in the Immigration Act had made it legally possible, despite his record, to give Banks immigrant status.

I admitted that, if one had had the advantage of hindsight, considering what had happened since 1954, Banks would not have been given landed status. That decision might have been an error of judgement, but I said again that anyone who suggested that Walter Harris had made his decision on any grounds other than a desire to carry out the law made by Parliament did not know Harris very well.

The trusteeship bill was passed before the House adjourned for the day. I expressed my gratitude for the excellent co-operation. It was an achievement to have completed this contentious legislation while the dispute over the status of the Social Credit groups still hung over our heads.

Our labour problems did not end with the passage of the trusteeship bill. On 21 October, Diefenbaker delivered a well-prepared and unusually coherent speech about the trouble on the Lakes and a strike of longshoremen in the St Lawrence ports which had begun on 4 October and was still going on. I had rather expected he would attack me and the government again over Banks' immigrant status, but he stuck instead to the longshoremen's strike. Diefenbaker so worded his motion of want of confidence that the spokesmen of the other three Opposition groups were highly critical and refused to support it.

MacEachen announced on 23 October that the trusteeship had been established. Shortly afterwards, the longshoremen's strike was settled. Once the public trustees were appointed and Banks removed as head of the union, it was expected he would be arrested to face criminal charges. Criticism developed over the delay, until Chevrier was able to report, on 5 November, that Banks had been arrested. The court, of course, granted him bail. Banks skipped bail and went off to the United States. Though the government was in no way to blame for the decision of the law court to allow bail or for Banks's escape, we were embarrassed. He was never extradited, despite a prolonged effort. In recent years, Banks lived in San Francisco where he died in 1985.

A recent sensational film on CBC television grossly exaggerated the role of the government in encouraging the SIU to replace the communist-led seamen's union; in condoning the intimidation and violence employed by Banks; in letting Banks skip bail; and in failing to have him extradited. The black picture of the role of governments of both parties was enhanced by the total omission of any reference to the action taken on the Norris report. There was not even a hint in the film that, on Allan MacEachen's initiative, Parliament had placed the SIU under the control of public trustees and removed Banks from his office as head of the SIU in Canada.

The SIU crisis had been dealt with resolutely while another parliamentary emergency was being resolved. In the end neither of these unforeseen problems disrupted the government's program for the session.

The Social Credit dispute settled

Another problem resulting from the dispute between the groups led by Thompson and Caouette arose on 9 October when Pearson made a statement about the storage of nuclear weapons at a United States base in Newfoundland. After the usual comments by Diefenbaker, Douglas, and Thompson, as party leaders, Caouette rose to comment on Pearson's statement. He was interrupted by the Speaker to say that, until the House decided otherwise, he was bound by the rules to permit only the spokesmen of recognized parties to comment on government statements. Caouette, on a question of privilege, demanded the right to be heard and, when it was again denied by the Speaker, Gregoire appealed the ruling. On the vote, the Créditistes were supported by the New Democratic party. Gregoire then raised another question of privilege and moved that the House adjourn its business until such time as all the rights and privileges of all its members had been acknowledged. The motion was ruled out of order and Gregoire appealed the Speaker's ruling. This time only the Créditistes voted against supporting the ruling. Notwithstanding the ruling of the Speaker, Gregoire had already been permitted to speak in one of the discussions on the business of the House and he had attended at least one meeting of party spokesmen behind the curtains. This was a partial recognition that Caouette was leader of a party.

The report of the Committee on Privileges and Elections was finally ready for debate on 17 October. Alexis Caron, the committee chairman, moved concurrence that day. The report recommended that the New Democratic party be seated next to the official Opposition because their membership was larger than that of either of the other groups. Instead of ranking the other two by their numerical strength, the report recommended that the Social Credit party of eleven members led by Robert Thompson should have precedence in seating over the group of thirteen led by Caouette. The report did not refer to this group by name, questioned whether it should be recognized as a separate party, since its members had not been elected as such, and recommended their legal status should be studied by an officer of the House of Commons who should report to the Speaker.

Knowles began the debate in a well-reasoned speech in which he argued that the House had no right to determine what the party designation of any group of members or any individual member should be. He argued that a group of members had a right to establish itself in Parliament at any time and to call the group a party by any name it chose. If that right was questioned by the House, it meant that the group concerned was being treated as second-class MPs. The principle of seating parties according to their numerical strength had been accepted after the elections of 1962 and 1963 and these should be regarded as precedents. He moved that the report be sent back to the committee with instructions to recommend that groups in opposition, apart from the official Opposition, should be seated according to the numerical strength of the groups. The speech by Knowles was a thorough and scholarly exposition of the problem, going back to 1921 when third parties had first appeared in the House.

Gérard Chapdelaine of the Thompson group opposed the Knowles amendment and argued that Caouette and his followers were a group of independents who had no right to be recognized as a party. When Caouette spoke later, he claimed that all the Social Credit MPs from Quebec had described themselves before the election as candidates of the Ralliement des Créditistes and that his group were, in fact, the real party from which the other Social Crediters who supported Thompson had seceded. During the debate many changes were rung on this theme.

Diefenbaker made a rather impressive speech supporting the Knowles amendment. He charged that the Social Credit schism had developed because a salary had been provided for the leader of any recognized party with twelve members or more.

Larry Pennell, one of the ablest of the new Liberal members, also made a very impressive speech in which he refuted many of the arguments Knowles had put forward and argued for the historical as opposed to the numerical principle in determining the precedence of parties other than the official Opposition.

When Caouette spoke it was apparent that members of the cabinet were not going to participate in the debate. Caouette said the whole matter should have been setttled by the government. He added that, if the government had given orders to its supporters on the committee, the result would have been different. I ignored this observation, as the whole cabinet had agreed that ministers should keep out of the controversy. The debate continued all day. There were one or two good speeches, but it was beginning to degenerate into a slanging match between members of Caouette's group and Thompson's. Gregoire charged that two parties, the Liberals and the Thompson group, were conspiring to deprive another party of its rights.

The Knowles amendment was defeated just before the adjournment for lunch on 18 June. Pearson and I hoped the final vote would be taken without further debate. But Gregoire said their group had several members who wanted to speak on the main motion. When the debate resumed later in the afternoon, it became more acrimonious and seemed likely to go on for the rest of the day. Pearson agreed that I should intervene, make a brief speech, and move the adjournment of the debate until Monday.

I had thought out carefully what I wanted to say. I knew it was of the utmost importance to say nothing that would offend any group and, if possible, any individual and to suggest a solution which would seem reasonable to most members and to the public. To achieve that objective what I said must be simple.

I began by asking members to realize what we were being asked to decide. If the House accepted the report of the committee, we would decide that the New Democratic party would be moved forward to the benches occupied at the beginning of the Parliament by the Social Credit party, that next to the NDP would be members led by the man recognized as leader of the Social Credit party when the new Parliament opened in May. At the far end of the chamber would be the group led by Caouette which would thereby be recognized as a party. I would not attempt to describe Caouette's group by name, because two different versions of the name were, I understood, given to the committee by two of its members. The only point I was seeking to make was that there was a group in the House under the leadership of Réal Caouette and that this group, which the report described as a group having a leader, would, if the Knowles motion had been adopted, have been given seating in the House ahead of Thompson's group.

With reference to the principle to be applied to the order of seating, Knowles had said the numerical principle should be applied, though he had admitted he had argued after the 1962 election for the historical principle. Any member, I said, could conscientiously take either view, but I happened to favour the historical principle. I thought it should have been followed in 1962 and 1963, as it was in the parliaments of 1935 and 1940, when the CCF had fewer members than Social Credit but was given priority because it had been in Parliament longer. I did not deny the right of any member to take the opposite view. The good faith of anyone who favoured the historical principle should not be questioned any more than the good faith of those who thought the numbers principle should be applied. I reviewed the experience of the more than forty years when the seniority principle had been followed, and regretted it had been abandoned in 1962. The report had recommended that we go back to the historical principle, since the numerical principle had not worked and was responsible for the present problem.

The hour was then twenty minutes past four; under the rules we had to go to private members' business at five o'clock; and there was a commitment to consider estimates that Friday evening. It was evident, I said, the House was not ready to make a decision in the forty minutes still available that day. It would, I believed, be to the benefit of all of us to reflect, and to reflect seriously, on the question over the weekend, and on the appearance of Parliament we were giving the public by the prolonged debate. For that reason, I was moving adjournment of the debate until Monday. My motion was adopted by a vote of 96 to 74.

On Monday 21 October, the debate was the first item of business for the third day. I continued my speech of Friday. I undertook to be very brief, because I hoped there was a general disposition to settle the question. In the debate three points, I said, had arisen. One point was irrelevant to the report of the committee: that was the question of the allowance for a party leader. Diefenbaker, I thought, had been right when he said the law had been made by Parliament and that the law courts, not Parliament, had the responsibility to interpret the law, if any interpretation was needed. The committee had

"IT WAS THE EGG !"

not discussed the question and there was no reason why anyone else should. I accepted without qualification Caouette's statement that the allowance was not a consideration at all in the matter, and I did not intend to say anything more about it.

The other two questions were, first, the order of seating in the House which had been dealt with in the report, and second, the recognition of certain members of the House as a group or a party. I said I was not subtle enough to understand the difference between a group or a party. It was no business of the House whether, when any number of members joined together, they called themselves a group or a party or something else, so long as they did not try to use the name of an existing party in the House.

The seating could be settled either on the historical principle or the numerical principle which I had somewhat disrespectfully referred to, on Friday, as 'the numbers game.' By rejecting the Knowles amendment, the House had decided by a majority not to follow the numerical principle. That problem would not have arisen if the House had stuck to the historical principle in 1962. Knowles interrupted to ask me what position our party had taken at the beginning of the parliaments of 1962 and 1963. I said 'None.' I added that neither the prime minister nor I had taken any position and I did not think anyone else was authorized to speak for the Liberal party on this matter. On the present occasion, and throughout, we had taken the view that the organization of the House was the business of the House, and it was not for the government to tell the House how it should be organized.

On the question of the recognition of groups or parties, I repeated that I could not see the difference between a group and a party. The report of the committee had referred to 'the members of the Group under the leadership of Mr. Caouette.' I was then asked to read paragraph 4 of the report which read: 'That the question of the privileges to be enjoyed by the *Group* under the leadership of Mr. Real Caouette be referred to the parliamentary counsel of the House of Commons for study and report to the Speaker.'

This fourth paragraph of the report, I suggested, had been superseded by action the Speaker had already taken on one or two occasions, as a courtesy, in recognizing Caouette. Two members interrupted me to say that these incidents were not to be regarded as precedents. I replied that it was only as a courtesy that members of the Opposition, except the leader of the Opposition, who was an officer of the House, were permitted to comment on statements by the government at the opening of the day's sitting. Such recognition had been the practice since 1921 and I thought it too late to change the practice now. Whether the Speaker sought the advice of the parliamentary counsel was a matter the Speaker would have to decide himself in his own good time.

The committee had given advice on two points, namely, the recognition that, in addition to the official Opposition, there were three groups in opposition, and the order in which the groups should sit. That was all the motion for concurrence was about. There might still be a great deal of argument about the order of seating, but I maintained that question had been settled when the amendment proposed by Knowles had been defeated.

I noted that when the new Parliament was constituted in May 1963, there was no doubt whatever that a group or party was recognized under Thompson's leadership. There was still a discernible group under Thompson's leadership. Caouette and Gregoire had said it was not for the Liberal party or the Conservative party or the New Democratic party to decide a question affecting the internal divisions of the Social Credit party; that was their business. How they described themselves was their business; and the only thing to decide was the order in which the three groups, other than the official Opposition, should be seated. Of the principles discussed, one had been rejected by the House. I concluded by suggesting it would be a wonderful idea now to have a vote, accept the committee's report, and get on with the business of the country.

My hope was not realized immediately. As the debate continued, Pearson became very impatient that it might never end and even I was discouraged. But there was a ray of hope when Caouette asked me whether I could assure his group that they would receive the same consideration as any political party in the House of Commons. That was not my business, I answered, and it would be improper for me or any other member, except the Speaker, to give such an assurance. One of the members of the Caouette group then spoke at some length and moved an amendment that it was not up to any other party to decide which of the two Social Credit groups was the Social Credit party and that that point should be decided by a majority vote among the Social Credit members. Though this was not a proper amendment at all, the Speaker did not question it and put the so-called amendment to a vote.

When the bells began to ring for the division on this amendment, one of our back-benchers told me Caouette wanted to see me. I told him to tell Caouette that, while the bells were ringing, I would be walking up and down the corridor in front of the Speaker's office. Caouette could find me there. Shortly after I began pacing up and down, Caouette emerged from the chamber, almost breathless. He said he was as sick of the debate as I was, and it could be settled in a few minutes once the vote on the amendment was taken if I could solve a problem he had, as leader of the new group. He was overwhelmed with mail and visitors and needed an extra secretary and an additional room. I replied that I had no authority to provide either, to which he retorted that everybody knew I ran the place. I said he was wrong, but that I would be glad to have a word with the Speaker about his problem.

He asked if I would really do that. I said 'yes.' He then assured me that, after the vote on the amendment was completed, the debate would be ended within ten minutes.

I was elated by Caouette's assurance which I reported at once to Pearson and told him never to ask me how it had been secured. The amendment was defeated. Caouette then made a brief speech, and the report of the committee was adopted without a recorded vote. The result was that Thompson and his group got the place nearer the Speaker; Caouette got his extra room and secretary and recognition of his group as a party. I had wanted Thompson to get the pride of place because his group had been more dependable in supporting the government in close votes than the Créditistes. As it turned out, I had managed to retain the good will of both leaders.

The resolution of the dispute between the two Social Credit groups ended the most difficult problem in managing the business of the House in that first session. That it had been resolved without my losing the good will of either Thompson or Caouette considerably reduced the risk of a defeat of the government in a close vote. However, as House leader, I had a continuing anxiety about making sure that the government's supporters were in the chamber when a vote was likely and that absentees were paired. Thanks, on several votes, to the support of the members of the Thompson group, the government was never defeated, though on one occasion on 28 October 1963 a Speaker's decision was overruled by a vote of 85 to 83. On that division Liberals alone voted to sustain the Speaker's ruling and all members of the four opposition parties then in the chamber voted against the ruling. No one suggested that the vote was a defeat for the government, but I felt humiliated. The press next day reported that I was very angry.

There was always trouble keeping government business moving smoothly and quickly through the House. Gregoire, who was the House leader for the Créditistes, was a spasmodic and unpredictable trouble-maker. He had quickly become a skilful parliamentarian, extremely adept at obstruction. On one occasion, when the government was anxious to conclude a particular measure, he threatened to hold up business indefinitely. I asked one of our back-benchers to find out what he really wanted. It was a Friday and the report was that Gregoire wanted two tickets to the hockey game in Montreal. I had never been to a professional hockey game in my life and had no idea how to go about getting tickets, but I told my friend to get the tickets for him, whatever they cost. The tickets were got and given to Gregoire who dropped his filibuster at once and went off to Montreal.

Further tribulations
of a House leader

Patronage raised its ugly head to delay business further. A member of the Opposition moved for the production of 'a list of consultants prepared in the office of the Postmaster General [Azellus Denis] for the guidance of Cabinet Ministers and copies of all correspondence between Ministers of the Crown and the consultants in each riding.'

Commenting on this motion, I said I had consulted the postmaster general who told me that no document of any description was prepared in his office for the guidance of other cabinet ministers. I had never received such a document for my own guidance. I objected that the language of the motion was so obscure no one reading it could discern what the mover was driving at.

After protracted discussion I agreed, on behalf of the government, to let the motion pass, instead of transferring it for debate. That proved to be an error of judgement. If the motion had been transferred for debate it could have come up for debate only once in the private members' hour. By letting it pass, a recurrent controversy arose which lasted until the end of the session.

The controversy began on 17 October when the chief opposition whip, on a question of privilege, claimed he had such a document and charged the postmaster general and me with misleading the House. The document in question was clearly not one for the guidance of cabinet ministers, but one prepared in the minister's office for his own guidance in consulting various persons, usually defeated candidates, about appointments and other matters affecting the post office. I was concerned only with clearing my name and Denis's of the charge of misleading the House and that was easily done.

Most of the steam was taken out of the controversy when Denis found and produced a similar list used by his Tory predecessor at the post office for the same purpose. The debates did, however, consume a good deal of time I had hoped to use for government business. Towards the end of the session a rumour began to circulate that Denis was going to the Senate. As a result, his estimates passed without difficulty. He was appointed to the Senate before the opening of the next session.

At the beginning of November I became increasingly uneasy about the possibility of completing the session before Christmas. Pearson, at my request, made a careful and conciliatory statement, listing the legislation we hoped to have passed and stressing the paramount importance of dealing with all the estimates. This statement had a good effect on the House since almost no one wanted to come back again after Christmas to complete the session. On 6 December, Pearson made a revised statement of the business the government still wanted to get done. This helped even more to encourage the House to end the session.

Another irritating problem remained which had plagued the government all through the session. The cabinet, in May, had made a quixotic decision to give a high priority to a measure to divide the Northwest Territories into two territories. This proposal had not even been in our election program, but Arthur Laing, the minister of northern affairs who had other good qualities but was a persistent and 'ornery' colleague, persuaded Pearson that the measure to divide the Northwest Territories was of exceptional urgency and would be quite uncontroversial. Unfortunately the debate took up precious time early in the session and provided Gilles Gregoire with his first chance to display his talents in obstruction and manipulation. Gregoire insisted that the bill should not be proceeded with unless it also provided for the transfer of the Belcher Islands in Hudson Bay from the Northwest Territories to the province of Quebec. He managed something like a one-man filibuster and we did not dare to bring the bill to a vote in case the combined opposition joined together to defeat us. When the session resumed in September, Laing no longer insisted on the same urgency, but he still pressed me to bring on the legislation, which I did finally on 8 November. Gregoire once more raised the question of the Belcher Islands. After some debate and some help from Baldwin of the Conservatives, I proposed a compromise which was acceptable to Gregoire. I said I felt sure my colleague would be happy to agree, but perhaps he should say so for himself.

Laing's reply was: 'My honourable friend's colleague, the Minister of Northern Affairs, is *not* happy.' I had never before seen a House leader on either side repudiated by one of his colleagues – and I was not happy either.

During an interruption of the debate, I was able to persuade Laing to agree to the compromise. When the debate resumed, the House gave me unanimous consent to have the subject matter of the bill considered by a committee. Normally this procedure kills a bill for that session, but the House agreed to keep it on the order paper so it could be considered after the committee had made its report.

That did not end the trouble. On 4 December, Gregoire complained about the proceedings in the committee. I objected that, under the rules, there could be no discussion in the House of proceedings in a committee until the committee presented its report. The Speaker ruled that Gregoire was out of order. Gregoire appealed; the vote was tied 106 to 106, and the Speaker gave a casting vote which upheld his ruling.

After the vote, a charge was made that a commitment I had given in the House about what would be done in the committee on the Northwest Territories bill was not being honoured by the committee. In reply to this charge, I offered to appear before the committee to give any information I could which would assist the committee. Churchill argued that the prime minister should instruct the chairman of the committee. At that point the Speaker intervened and stopped the discussion which had all been out of order. I was never invited to the committee. That was the last the House heard of this troublesome legislation. More than twenty years later, the division of the Territories into two is an acrimonious question still being debated.

On 12 November 1963, the Tory Opposition moved a vote of want of confidence which, if adopted, would have condemned the government for its alleged failure to carry out the spirit of co-operative federalism and for its neglecting to consult with the provinces before announcing or undertaking programs which fell wholly or partly within provincial jurisdiction. I was worried that there might be a close vote on this motion and was relieved when Tommy Douglas moved a sub-amendment to the Tory motion. Douglas's motion struck out the condemnation and read that: 'This House urges the government to carry out more fully the spirit of co-operative federalism and to consult with the provinces before announcing or undertaking programs which fall to any extent within provincial jurisdiction.' In doing so, Douglas said it was hardly fitting to criticize, much less condemn, a government for its failure to carry out co-operative federalism when the government had been less than seven months in office. Thompson and Gregoire supported the Douglas amendment.

When he replied, Pearson praised the constructive speeches made by Douglas, Thompson, and Gregoire. He concluded by saying Douglas's sub-amendment was clearly not a vote of want of confidence but an affirmation of a principle acceptable to the government. The government would be happy to support the Douglas amendment. If the Tory motion as amended by Douglas was accepted, Pearson said it would nullify the motion to go into supply and he would ask one of his colleagues to move a new motion that the House go into committee of supply. This was a very rare procedure, used only twice before in the history of our Parliament. But the procedure was clearly set out in the rules. While Thompson and Gregoire were speaking, I had suggested it to Pearson, who consulted one or two of our colleagues and then decided to support the Douglas amendment.

Diefenbaker was taken by surprise and tried to argue that, since acceptance of the original Tory motion would have defeated the government and voted it out of office, the House by voting for the vote of want of confidence even as amended would be voting the government out of office. He declared that I had advised Pearson badly in January 1958 and had now made another suggestion which put the prime minister in the most difficult position any prime minister had ever been put in, in the history of our country.

I interjected: 'Read standing order 56.' Diefenbaker went on to argue that any amendment to a motion to go into supply was a vote of want of confidence, regardless of its wording, and would be so regarded by the Opposition. When the vote was taken the Tories alone voted against the Douglas amendment. When it was adopted, every member in the House voted for the Tory motion as amended. Some Tories then exclaimed, 'Resign.'

The Speaker recognized me and, in order to get the House into committee of supply, I moved that the Speaker do now leave the chair. There was considerable debate on whether my motion was in order. The Speaker terminated the debate by accepting the motion. The whole affair had taken up considerable time, but had the good effect of widening the gap between the Tories and the smaller groups and isolating the Tories once more. It also served to strengthen our hold on the support of the House and to vindicate my judgement.

Redistribution under way

When the government was formed in April 1963, the procedure necessary to accomplish redistribution was my most immediate preoccupation. Even a superficial examination of the election results for 1963 made it obvious that, if a fair redistribution had taken place after the 1961 census, the Liberal party would have won a clear majority. I was under great pressure from our more electorally sophisticated colleagues, particularly Walter Gordon, to act swiftly. My own inclination was to lose no time, but to make sure we established non-partisan machinery which would result in a workable organization and fair results. I had not personally been an enthusiast for the idea of taking redistribution out of Parliament. The redistributions of 1947 and 1952, I felt, had been free of partisan bias. But there was no question of the effective political capital Diefenbaker had made of the amalgamation of his constituency with another in Saskatchewan in 1952. The main advantage of transferring redistribution to an independent, non-partisan agency would not be in greater fairness but in saving the greater part of one session of Parliament every ten years.

Since the government was committed to this fundamental reform, I was determined it would be done well. Having no knowledge of how to go about creating the new machinery, I lost no time in consulting Nelson Castonguay, the chief electoral officer. The integrity and independence of his father, Jules Castonguay, his immediate predecessor, had impressed me greatly. In principle, I had not approved of the appointment of the son as his successor. It seemed even worse than nepotism and bordering on making the office hereditary.

I saw Castonguay the day the government was sworn in. One conversation dispelled my prejudice. He seemed to me just as independent as, and even more knowledgeable than, his father. He soon convinced me that I had taken on no easy task. He pointed out the tremendous difficulty, if not the impossibility, of redistribution being undertaken for the whole country by one single commission. Up till that time all politicians had assumed that would be the procedure.

Castonguay persuaded me that the experience of redistribution by an independent agency in Australia seemed to have been the best in any country comparable to Canada. He suggested someone should go there and study it at first hand. Since it was obvious I could not go, I agreed he should. It was a wise decision. Castonguay also went to New Zealand, since that country also had a long experience of redistributing seats in its Parliament by independent commission. We felt that an examination on the spot with the officials who had performed these functions would be of great value, particularly in Australia which was, like Canada, a federal state. And so it proved to be.

Castonguay came home from Australia convinced that the task could not be performed effectively or in a reasonable time by a single commission for the whole country. He convinced me. I suggested four commissions, one each for Ontario and Quebec, one for the Atlantic provinces and one for the western provinces. But we soon concluded that plan would have no advantages and several disadvantages over having a separate commission for each province and that was what, after convincing the cabinet, I proposed to Parliament.

The more I discussed with Castonguay the problems involved in setting up machinery for a non-partisan and objective redistribution, the more complicated and time-consuming I realized it would be. I was resolved not to rush into hasty action and to know thoroughly what I wanted to recommend to the cabinet and to Parliament before introducing any legislation.

This study was not completed until November. Shortly afterwards, I introduced a resolution which provided for two bills. One bill was to establish the office of a representation commissioner with a small staff to administer the plan. The commissioner was to be an *ex officio* member of all ten commissions to co-ordinate their procedures and to provide technical advice. The second bill was to authorize the establishment of the ten commissions and to lay down the rules for their operations. This bill was intended to provide machinery for all succeeding decennial redistributions. To save duplication of debate, the one resolution recommended all expenditures to be made under both statutes.

When I rose on 26 November to move the resolution, Diefenbaker suggested that we agree to have a general debate at the resolution stage on the whole subject of redistribution. This was precisely what I had hoped would happen, mainly because I wanted to explain the whole plan at once.

I started my presentation by stating the attitude in which the government was approaching redistribution, and read a statement which elicited applause on both sides of the House. After it was read, I confessed the statement was almost word for word the statement Diefenbaker had made on the same subject a year earlier when he was prime minister. Except for the one word 'commission' which, under the plan I was proposing, would be plural, there had not been one word in his statement with which I could quarrel. Every member, I believed, would agree with the statement.

The government had to take responsibility for the financial requirements, but beyond that the government had no intention of trying to impose its will and no desire to do so. The bills were not government measures, except in a technical sense. We felt the collective wisdom of the House should be brought to bear on the problems, and that any good suggestions, from any quarter, should be incorporated into the legislaton without any thought of partisan considerations.

I explained why the government was suggesting a separate commission for each province. Castonguay, I reported, estimated that if both bills were adopted in the 1963 session, an election after redistribution should be possible as early as the fall of 1965, but if the legislation was delayed into the spring of 1964 the earliest date for an election under the new redistribution would be the spring of 1966. If there was only one commission for the whole country, Castonguay estimated the redistribution could not be completed in time for an election before 1968. That was one reason why we were recommending a commission for each province.

We felt the representation commissioner should be appointed by Parliament to co-ordinate the work of the ten commissions and to make sure they operated on a relatively uniform basis. I did not want to hide from the House that my own preference for this new official was the chief electoral officer. It was evident this suggestion met with general approval and we agreed that he should be named in the statute setting up the Office.

Knowles interrupted to ask me about the work of the provincial commission in Manitoba. This was the only province in which redistribution was performed by an independent body. I replied that I had gone to Winnipeg in September and conferred with the two surviving members of the Manitoba commission (the chairman having died), and had been greatly impressed by what they had told me of their operation. The Manitoba commission, I hoped, could serve as a model for the commissions Parliament would establish.

The basic principle of the proposed redistribution was to be representation by population, but we felt there should be sufficient tolerance to permit a slight bias in favour of rural as opposed to urban constituencies. Some consideration should also be given to historic or geographical factors. The representation of the two territories, despite their small population, would be preserved. The senatorial floor which provided that there must be as many members of the House as there were senators from a province would also be preserved.

I stressed the importance of fair representation in Parliament as a safeguard of peaceful change of government in Canada, instead of our having to shoot the head of the government to get a change, as happened in so many countries. I was convinced that no member in his heart, no matter what his party, thought we should try to win elections by rigging the machinery. I believed we all felt it our duty to make sure the people had a chance to register their opinions, fairly and honestly, by their votes.

In conclusion, I repeated words spoken on the same subject by Diefenbaker on 9 April 1962: 'We want to follow the lead which has been taken by almost every nation – certainly by the Commonwealth nations as well as by the Mother of Parliaments – that membership shall be determined fairly by the people.'

Diefenbaker was obviously flattered by being quoted. All members present appeared to approve the tone and substance of my speech, though subsequent Opposition speakers expressed some suspicion of the sincerity of my high-minded approach. Diefenbaker said he had never heard me spreading the charm as I had done that day. He added that it aroused his fears, in direct proportion, as to the probable contents of the bill. However, his tone was very friendly, though he expressed scepticism about the need for ten commissions and made a plea that wide-spread rural constituencies should have smaller populations than urban constituencies. Diefenbaker was also very concerned about how the commissioners would be appointed. I gave a categorical assurance that the cabinet would have no part in their appointment and that the method of appointment would be prescribed by Parliament. Knowles, Patterson, and Gregoire spoke for the three smaller parties.

The debate continued on 27 November mostly in the same harmonious vein. Douglas Fisher, who had been absent the previous day, made an impressive speech about constituencies like his own, with huge areas and small populations. Earlier in the session (12 October) I had spoken on a private member's bill on redistribution and had said then that I regarded Fisher as a grassroots egg-head. This time we got into a minor dispute about the lack of broadcast coverage in sparsely populated areas. At one point I said Fisher had done what no other member had done; he had got under my skin. Fisher retorted that when he returned to the House, he had been talking to a gentleman who had observed the proceedings the previous day and who asked him: 'Did you smell the incense burning, the perfume, and as you came to your seat did you hear the sweet tinkling of bells?' He said this gentleman had added that the day before 'was one of the sweetest, stickiest and stinkiest days he had ever seen in the House of Commons.' Fisher said this observer had gathered that partisanship had just disappeared and pleasantries reigned.

I did my best to retain the pleasantries and, on the whole, succeeded. But the resolution did not pass that day. The debate had to be deferred until 3 December when it took up the evening. There was no partisanship, but several members wanted to say their pieces. At the end of that day, I suggested we defer the debate on the subject for a few days while I had consultations with the party spokesmen.

Before redistribution came up again for debate, I had decided, if the session was to end before Christmas, there was no chance of getting the bill to set up the ten commissions passed. Pearson accordingly said, on 6 December, that the government would like to have the bill to appoint the representation commissioner adopted, but was willing to hold the other redistribution bill over until the session of 1964. Agreement was reached with the Opposition to have the resolution passed on 9 December without further debate, and the one bill introduced. Knowles asked me if I would also introduce the bill to establish the commissions so its terms would be public, but Diefenbaker objected.

There was no time to debate the bill to establish the office of representation commissioner until 16 December and then there was almost no debate. A few amendments were made by general agreement, including one to name Castonguay the first representation commissioner. The bill got third reading without debate the next day.

After inter-party discussion, I was able to get agreement to the introduction of the bill to establish the ten electoral boundaries commissions on 20 December. The provisions of the bill were then available for public study and criticism. I was encouraged that so much progress had been made in achieving this long-discussed reform.

Ministerial duties

Though the leadership of the House took most of my time and thought, I tried not to neglect my duties as minister for a department of government and several agencies. In the three weeks between the formation of the Pearson government and the meeting of Parliament on 16 May, there was an opportunity to become acquainted or reacquainted with the senior officers of the department and the other agencies for which I had to answer in Parliament. My deputy, the under secretary of state, Jean Miquelon, had been appointed by Diefenbaker. He belonged to a prominent family in the Union Nationale, but I never had any evidence that he was not completely loyal to me. As I planned no changes in the structure of the department and no legislation within its scope, our relations were largely formal and our contacts infrequent.

Guy Roberge, the head of the National Film Board, was a friend of long standing who had been appointed by Prime Minister St Laurent. We had worked together during my years in government until 1957. I had complete confidence in his administration and had no plans for changes in film board policy.

My association with Kaye Lamb, the head of the Public Archives and the National Library, had been as a close friend from the time of his appointment to the archives by Mackenzie King. Again I had no thought of any changes in policy, though I hoped to further his efforts to get new and more suitable quarters.

The National Gallery was another matter. During the years in Opposition, I had maintained a close relationship with Mrs H.A. Dyde, a friend of long standing, and with the distinguished painter, Lawren Harris, both of whom had been appointed to the Board of Trustees on my recommendation. The trustees, I knew, were almost in revolt and the morale was very low in the staff of the gallery. While we were in Opposition, I had been distressed by the resignations of Percy Fell as chairman of the board and of Alan Jarvis as director. I was resolved to find a replacement for Thomas Maher who had succeeded Fell as chairman of the board, not because he was a Tory worker in Quebec City, but because he had never shown any interest in art or in the activities of the gallery. According to reports which reached me, Maher took no initiative in promoting the interests of the gallery or even in understanding what those interests were. I wanted to replace him as chairman, but, first, a suitable replacement had to be found. Politically it was desirable that the new chairman be a French Canadian.

My friend, Donald Buchanan, recommended Jean Raymond, who had been associated with Buchanan on the Council on Industrial Design. I knew Raymond slightly and felt he was in every way suitable. He was reluctant to take on the post but, once he was convinced his appointment would be welcomed by most of the other trustees and by the artistic community, he was persuaded to accept. I then went to Quebec to see Maher, and told him the government wished to replace him as chairman but would be quite happy to have him remain a member of the board. He was naturally resentful and finally decided to resign both as chairman and as trustee. I had no thought of trying to replace Charles Comfort who had succeeded Alan Jarvis as director. I respected Comfort as an artist and I was sure he would co-operate willingly with Raymond. In the reorganization I had the encouragement and full support of Pearson. The effect on morale was gratifying.

Broadcasting took up very little time in Parliament in 1963, but it occupied a good deal of my own time and thought. The first time I had to deal with broadcasting in the House was on 31 May, when Robert Thompson, the Social Credit leader, objected to programs by Max Ferguson and others on the CBC. He asked what action I was taking or contemplating to ensure that the CBC did not carry programs obviously harmful to the security and well-being of the nation. I replied that I was sure Thompson and every other member would agree that, in any free society, nothing would be more undesirable than to have the government, or any member of the government, seek to direct broadcasting, the press, or any other medium of public opinion. No member of the government intended to attempt such direction. The CBC was responsible, not to the government, but to the whole Parliament. The method of assuring that responsibility to Parliament would always present a serious problem. The best way it could be done, in my view, was to appoint the ablest possible people to the board of directors and the ablest possible people to manage the CBC, to leave the direction of broadcasting to them while holding them accountable in a parliamentary committee for the way they administered the corporation.

The CBC, I was sure, would take proper account of criticism by any member of the House, even a member of the government. Members of the government, I felt, should not be deprived of their rights as citizens to express their opinions, but the CBC should pay no greater attention to views expressed by ministers than they would to the views of any other citizen. I was glad to have this early opportunity to state my total opposition to any attempt by government to direct or control broadcasting.

In Opposition, I had raised a question about the legality of the appointment of Dunsmore as chairman of the board of the CBC in place of Alphonse Ouimet who remained president. The Broadcasting Act specified that the president should also be chairman of the board. When the government was formed, I lost no time in getting from the Department of Justice a legal opinion on the point and tabling the opinion in the House. Once convinced Dunsmore was holding office illegally, Pearson willingly restored Ouimet's position as chairman, though Dunsmore was not removed from the board. I was resolved to restore Ouimet's authority which had been deliberately degraded by Diefenbaker, who had failed to increase Ouimet's salary when the salaries of others in comparable positions had been increased. It gave me particular satisfaction that Pearson agreed so readily to right this wrong.

One decision made by the CBC early in my term as secretary of state had political repercussions. The CBC had two radio stations in Toronto, both broadcasting in English. Ouimet informed me unofficially that the CBC board had decided to convert one outlet into a French station. I offered no objection. There was a loud outcry in letters to the press and, what was worse, from Liberal members from Toronto. There were bitter complaints in the Liberal caucus where several members accused me of assuring their defeat in the next election.

The station which was being converted to French had a very small audience and I was reasonably sure that at least 90 per cent of the complaints were inspired by CBC employees, their families, and friends. I predicted that, as soon as the employees were provided for, the agitation would cease. It did. I reminded my fellow Liberals on this, as on other occasions, that the test of a durable politician was a capacity to distinguish between a stiff breeze and a hurricane. I disclaimed any responsibility for the decision of the CBC, but said I agreed with it.

In Parliament, Fisher asked me whether I had any explanation for the action of the CBC. I replied that I had received no communication from the CBC on the subject and could provide no enlightenment not already provided by the press. Another NDP member asked me whether there had been any pressure from the government to have the change made. I denied categorically that there had been any pressure from the government to have the change made. It was, I understood, CBC policy, which I believed all members approved of, to see that there was radio broadcasting, either private or public, for any significant minority, either English- or French-speaking, in any part of the country. I would be very sorry to see English-language broadcasting jeopardized in the city of Quebec and felt, as a Canadian, that the very considerable French-speaking minority in southern Ontario was deserving of similar consideration.

The most innovative step I took about broadcasting was to establish a group consisting of the chairman of the Board of Broadcasting Governors, the president of the CBC, and the president of the Canadian Association of

Broadcasters to advise the government on broadcasting policy. In all areas where these three could reach a consensus, the government, I felt, would be spared thought and action, and in areas where they differed, if the differences were sharply defined, it would be much easier for the government to make decisions. This group was at once christened 'The Troika' by the media. It did not report until after I had ceased to be the minister concerned with broadcasting. Its work was helpful to the government and the public.

All three members of the Troika were well known to me. Ouimet had been a friend for several years. Many years earlier, at the University of Manitoba, I had known Andrew Stewart, the chairman of the BBG. We speedily developed a good personal and official relationship. Don Jamieson, the president of the Canadian Association of Broadcasters, was a Newfoundlander, a good friend and a discreet supporter during our years in Opposition. As we worked out our plans for the reforms in broadcasting in our Liberal program, all three of them would be helpful advisers. The president of the Association of French Broadcasters, David Gourd, was an old friend of mine who was knowledgeable and wise in his advice to me.

One broadcasting question I had to deal with in 1963 was whether there should be a CBC television station in St John's. On 5 April, only three days before the election, the BBG had approved in principle an application from the CBC for a licence. A number of conditions had been attached to the BBG approval which had to be met before a formal recommendation was to be made to the government. It was no secret that I had felt that an alternative TV station should not be established in any place until nation-wide TV service was achieved with single stations. The Diefenbaker government had abandoned this policy. Private stations had already been established in Toronto and one or two other places where the CBC had its own stations. In Edmonton, the CBC had been licensed to serve a city already served by a private station. I was convinced reluctantly that the pressure for a CBC station in St John's to provide alternative service to the privately owned station could no longer be resisted.

I felt the primary broadcasting need in Newfoundland was the extension of TV coverage to the rest of the island beyond the St John's region and the provision of CBC radio service in Labrador. But before the new Parliament met in May 1963, I assured Ouimet that I would support the financing of CBC-TV in Newfoundland, but that I hoped he would insist on extending service throughout the whole island of Newfoundland from existing premises in St John's before the CBC embarked on the construction of new and expensive facilities of its own. I had also told Andrew Stewart of the BBG that I would neither oppose nor delay the carrying out of their decision to approve a CBC licence in St John's.

After Parliament met, Douglas Fisher, no doubt suspecting I might try to frustrate the establishment of the St John's station, had sought to embarrass me. On 29 July, he referred to a petition bearing 22,000 signatures from a citizens committee in St John's supporting the establishment of a second TV station. He asked the prime minister about the delay in proceeding with a project already approved by the BBG. Pearson replied that he would look into the matter and take it up with the secretary of state. Fisher then asked whether Pearson realized that he had put the question to the prime minister because it was felt the secretary of state had a conflict of interest in this matter. Pearson ignored this observation.

The next day (30 July) I arranged to have Joseph O'Keefe, the MP for St John's East, ask me what was holding up approval of the CBC TV station in St John's. In view of the uncalled-for reflection on me by Fisher, I said I welcomed the opportunity to put the record straight. The BBG, I explained, had attached conditions to its approval. The conditions had not yet been met and therefore no recommendation was before the government. Until the BBG made a recommendation, the government had no legal authority to issue a licence.

I wanted to get the matter dealt with as soon as possible, because I knew there was suspicion in St John's that I was dragging my heels. Before I left Newfoundland at the end of August, Andrew Stewart advised me that the board proposed shortly to inform the Department of Transport that the clarification of the conditions on which the board recommended the issue of a licence for a CBC television station in St John's had reached the point where a licence could now be issued. The minister of transport, I was confident, would have the licence issued as soon as the BBG recommendation was received, so CBC TV broadcating could begin as early as possible. I was relieved when the licence was issued on 30 September, just before Parliament resumed its sittings after the summer recess.

In my statement at the end of August I had said that, if alternate service was desirable in St John's, I was convinced it was just as important to give television service to the rest of Newfoundland. I intended to do whatever I could to see that that happened as soon as possible. It was no less important, I felt, to give radio broadcasting service to the important and growing communities of Labrador City and Wabush and to tie that service in with broadcasting service in Newfoundland, so that the people of western Labrador would have a constant reminder that they were a part of Newfoundland.

If I had remained the minister dealing with broadcasting, the extension of service to the whole province would, I believe, have preceded the erection of new broadcast facilities in St John's. However, soon after I ceased to be directly involved, the building in St John's was started and several years passed before coverage was extended to the whole island.

The establishment of alternate television in Newfoundland made it impossible to resist it elsewhere, once the Board of Broadcast Governors decided the market in any place was great enough to sustain two stations and a second licence was applied for. It followed logically that a private network would be necessary to provide programs for the private stations that had previously depended on CBC programs while they were the only stations in the place. There was a real danger that a private network would be totally dominated by the Toronto station. That I did not want, and I made the suggestion that the principle of equalization be applied by giving one vote, and one only, to each station belonging to the network. This formula was, I believe, adopted, but how effective it was in reducing domination of the private network by Toronto, I do not know.

There was no debate in the 1963 session about broadcasting policy generally or alternate TV service in particular. But one aspect of broadcasting generated substantial public discussion. The BBG expressed concern about the possible effect on the national system of broadcasting in Canada of distribution on a commercial basis by cable systems and community antennas. The subject came up in Parliament on 29 November in the debate on a private member's bill Douglas Fisher had introduced. The object of the bill was to ensure control and regulation of cable distribution of TV through community antennas. The bill had no chance to pass in the hour allotted for debate, but when Fisher invited me, as spokesman for the government, to respond to his speech, I did so.

I recalled that, from the 1920s when radio broadcasting began, successive governments had been concerned to ensure that radio broadcasting would be Canadian. Because Canada had only one tenth of the population of the United States, Parliament had repeatedly legislated to this end. I did not believe any party in the House wanted to see any development which would indirectly undermine our national system of broadcasting, if Parliament could prevent it. We agreed national control of broadcasting was needed to preserve our existence as a separate country. The influence of television, I believed, would be far more pervasive than radio. Community antenna systems might provide television service in areas, like parts of Fisher's constituency and mine, which were so remote and sparsely populated that broadcasting from established stations could not reach them. That would be all to the good. But the establishment in large urban centres of community antenna systems linked by cable to broadcasting stations in the United States might circumvent the national broadcasting policy established by Parliament. This threat was under consideration by the minister of transport and by me, but we had so far reached no conclusion that we could recommend to cabinet about the way to deal with it by legislation or otherwise. If there was to be any effective control of these systems, some amendment of the law would be needed. But we had not yet worked out the kind of amendment we felt would be effective.

The policy of the government was to do everything we could to have broadcasting remain, to the greatest degree Parliament could make it, Canadian. (The main difficulty, I feared, was that wired services, unlike wireless, were probably within provincial jurisdiction, but I took care not to hint at that difficulty in my speech.)

I was satisfied when the 1963 session ended that the leadership of the House had not prevented me from discharging fully my duties as a minister. This was possible, in large part, because the portfolio of the secretary of state was at that time almost a sinecure.

Winding up
the session of 1963

The session proceeded with more than usual harmony and despatch in December. We were resolved to devote whatever time was necessary to securing the passage of the estimates of expenditure and the supply bills. We did not want to run the risk of a repetition of the embarrassment encountered repeatedly by the Diefenbaker government of having to spend money which Parliament had not voted. We had accomplished this objective by the time the session was ended on 21 December.

When the session was prorogued, every priority item on Pearson's list of the business the government hoped to have completed had been disposed of by the House, except for two or three measures the government had postponed because the cabinet was not ready to proceed with them. None of the priority items had failed to pass because of lack of parliamentary management. In addition, all but one or two of the less urgent measures before Parliament had been adopted. I was gratified.

On the last day of the session, the House adopted, without debate, a measure to increase the membership of the Exchequer Court by one judge, who was to serve as the commissioner to preside over hearings in the Senate committee on petitions for divorces. Arnold Peters who, with Frank Howard, had been obstructing these bills for years as a means to get a new, more judicial system adopted, expressed pleasure that the new method of dealing with divorce petitions had reached a satisfactory state and congratulated the government on its effort to assist in solving the problem. I expressed my appreciation for the help Gordon Churchill, as spokesman for the Opposition, had given in reaching this desirable goal which had worried the House for a long time. Tommy Douglas described it as an important and red-letter day in the history of the Canadian Parliament.

When all the other business had been concluded, I took the unprecedented step of having the item for written questions called so that all available answers could be given. At the beginning of the session, I had stressed to my colleagues the importance of answering written questions promptly. Ministers generally had co-operated. A record number of questions was answered and, in most cases, very speedily.

I had found the House leadership very strenuous and exacting. During the whole of the session, I rarely left the chamber except to go to the washroom. I learned a great deal about the virtues of patience and conciliation. I was able to ensure the passage of most of the government's business without too much obstruction and generally avoided long debates on procedure.

I took a great deal of satisfaction from the fact that a motion to extend the hours of sitting had been made only once during the whole session. Many extensions were achieved by inter-party conferences held outside the House or by unanimous concessions actually made in the House to extend the time to complete specific measures. Extensions of time were almost always necessary to complete the work of a parliamentary session. Securing these extensions was often time-consuming and contentious.

Going through *Hansard* twenty years later, I found only one occasion in the session of 1963 when I lost my composure. On 13 December I got into a slanging match with Tommy Douglas over a trivial dispute about a CBC news broadcast. The exchange quickly concluded when Gordon Churchill said, quite correctly, that the secretary of state was wasting the time of the House. I never complained about the length of debates or accused the Opposition of wasting the time of the House. I tried at all times to thank the Opposition, and particularly their party spokesmen, for co-operation whenever it was forthcoming, which it often was, especially late in the session.

On the whole I think the Opposition was better satisfied with my House leadership than our Liberal back-benchers were. Many of them were in Parliament for the first time and naturally anxious to build a reputation for taking part in debates. In order to get business completed, I restrained our back-benchers as much as possible. Some of them, I am sure, found the discipline frustrating.

But we had been successful in getting much more government business through the House than I had dared to count on, in spite of difficulties and delays resulting from our lack of a majority. The attitude of Opposition spokesmen on the last day of the session was gratifying, particularly the tribute from Tommy Douglas. He said it had been a remarkable session, which began in uncertain circumstances and could easily have been quite unproductive. He thought history might show it had been a remarkably productive session, although no party had a clear majority. He felt 'this has been due to the fine co-operation which has existed in all parts of the House and to the diplomacy and patience of the Secretary of State who has been the leader of the House for the government, and to our patience in putting up with him.'

George Nowlan for the official Opposition was a little more restrained about the co-operation. He said we started in a rough Parliament in the spring, but, following the series of disasters the government faced, he doubted whether any Parliament had worked better than this one since we returned from the summer recess.

I was deeply gratified to have the session end so harmoniously.

Reflections

After the Opposition spokesmen had so praised my leadership of the House, I assumed that Pearson was also satisfied. At the beginning of 1964, he asked me to become minister of transport and added that I could not administer that heavy department and continue as House leader. I was taken by surprise. He agreed that I should continue to be responsible for the thankless task of redistribution which I was anxious to see through to the end.

I was never able to decide whether Pearson felt I was really needed in transport or whether he had yielded to pressure from our caucus to have the House leadership changed. We discussed who should succeed me as leader, and I recommended Favreau strongly. I pointed out that he had been assiduous in his attendance, had developed a feel for procedure, and had very good relations with the party spokesmen on the Opposition side. I offered to act as his substitute and assistant whenever required. Pearson agreed, as did Favreau. Favreau and I had been seat mates, and we exchanged seats so Favreau would be seated next to Pearson.

It was widely asserted later that the additional burden of House leadership was too great for Favreau and contributed to his difficulties in the 1964 session. I do not agree with this opinion. Favreau's problems did not arise because of any difficulty relating to his leadership of the House, nor do I believe that the burden of leading the House left him too little time to perform his duties as minister of justice. He had succeeded Lionel Chevrier in that office when Chevrier was appointed high commissioner for Canada in London on 1

January 1964. In my opinion Favreau was the victim of his failure to appreciate the seamy side of political controversy, and the capacity of a man like Erik Nielsen to turn a trivial matter into an apparent scandal.

I was sorry to see Lionel Chevrier go. Friends for many years, we had been close comrades-in-arms in Opposition. His long experience, practical judgement, and conciliatory manner were precious assets in cabinet and parliament. Chevrier's departure weakened the government, especially in the House where he was a star performer.

Before I became minister of transport, Margaret and I had a short holiday in Italy and Spain. The holiday gave me time to reflect on the course of events since the Liberal party had given up office on 21 June 1957. I never changed my view that St Laurent did the right thing in resigning instead of meeting Parliament. It could be, and was argued, that we had not technically been beaten, but we had certainly suffered a moral defeat. I never doubted that St Laurent had adopted the right strategy when Parliament met in October 1957, in assuring the new government that the Liberal Opposition would do nothing to obstruct them in carrying out the program and the promises they had made to the voters.

I felt, at the time, that a substantial majority of the country had had enough of Liberal government and wanted the new administration to be given a chance. If we gave Diefenbaker any excuse to call an election, I was sure the Tories would win the majority they had failed to get in June 1957.

I never had the slightest doubt the Liberal convention of January 1958 had made the right decision by choosing Pearson as the party leader, though I continued to feel he had made a mistake in his speech accepting the leadership by promising to challenge the government as soon as an opportunity offered. I regretted the advice I had given him about the wording of his motion of want of confidence on 20 January 1958, which had enabled Diefenbaker to make Pearson and me look ridiculous. By 1963, I had concluded that Pearson would have been better advised to move the traditional vote of want of confidence which could not have been ridiculed. But at the time, I had feared the CCF would feel consistency required them to vote with us because they had already voted lack of confidence in October 1957. My fear was strengthened when their leader, M.J. Coldwell, told me before Christmas that he supposed the CCF was largely responsible, because of the pipeline debate, for the Tory government being in office. He said he was so unhappy about Diefenbaker's conduct as prime minister that his main aim was to assure his defeat. If the CCF voted with us, the Diefenbaker government would probably have been narrowly defeated. If Social Credit, which had also moved a vote of want of confidence in October, had also voted with us, the government would certainly have been defeated and Diefenbaker would have had the election he wanted. I had watched the way, in 1962 and 1963, the smaller parties, fearing extinction in an election, had repeatedly saved the government in office from defeat in critical votes. With hindsight, I believe that would have happened in 1958 if we had moved the usual want of confidence.

I rightly shared the blame for Pearson's disastrous motion in January 1958. I was not in good favour with the Liberal organization or much wanted in the national campaign. I had sense enough to realize my political career would be over unless I secured my own base in Newfoundland. I faced a real challenge in my own constituency in 1958 and put on a strenuous campaign. Not only did I win an overwhelming victory in Bonavista-Twillingate, but Newfoundland was the only province in which the Liberal party elected a majority of the members. The result in Newfoundland gave me a strong position in our 49-member Opposition.

I had resolved to make the greatest effort possible in Parliament. I had two main incentives. One was to help Pearson restore his damaged prestige and the other was to contribute to the defeat of a prime minister I considered inadequate and unworthy to hold that office. After the election of 1958, seasoned observers and most of our own members felt we could not hope to defeat the government in less than ten years; many felt it would take at least three parliaments; and some doubted if the Liberal party could ever recover. Optimist though I am by nature, I had no expectation of defeating the Diefenbaker government five years after their huge victory of 31 March 1958.

Historians will never agree on how much the Liberals under Pearson contributed to the defeat of Diefenbaker in 1963 and how much it was the work of Diefenbaker himself. I would give about 70 per cent of the credit to him and about 30 per cent to us. Diefenbaker alienated metropolitan Toronto by cancelling the Avro Arrow; he destroyed what little support he had in Newfoundland over the RCMP and term 29; he lost his astonishing support in Quebec by his ill-concealed contempt for French Canadians; he surrendered any hope of support among the armed forces by repudiating the undertaking his government had made to arm our defence forces in the North and in Europe with nuclear weapons; and he shook the public confidence in the financial management of our national affairs over the Coyne affair and the dollar crisis during the election of 1962. In spite of all these set-backs and, most serious of all, the growing discontent over persistent unemployment, it required two elections and a defeat in Parliament to end his government.

The reason I give 30 per cent of the credit to the Liberal Opposition was our maintenance of a united and articulate presence in Parliament; our steadily improving party organization in most parts of the country though, unhappily, not in the prairies; and a public perception that we were a credible alternative government.

Even so, we failed narrowly, in April 1963, to win a majority in Parliament. Throughout 1963 we had frequently come close to losing control of Parliament and the survival of the government was always in question. By the end of that first session of Parliament, while I was still leader of the House, we had demonstrated that, with vigilance and management, the government was no longer in danger of an early defeat. The years in Opposition had been strenuous, the road back had not been easy. Until December 1963, we were not sure we had a firm grip on office. No one could have predicted on 22 April 1963, when Pearson became prime minister, that the Liberal party had embarked, with a brief interval in 1979–80, on more than twenty years in government.

Index